Wine HERITAGE
The Story of Italian American Vintners

Wine HERITAGE

The Story of Italian American Vintners

Dick Rosano

∴

Forward by Robert Mondavi

THE WINE APPRECIATION GUILD

SAN FRANCISCO

The Wine Appreciation Guild Ltd.
360 Swift Avenue,
South San Francisco CA 94080
1-800-231-9463
www.wineappreciation.com

Library of Congress Cataloging-in-publication Data

Rosano, Richard P., 1950
Wine Heritage: The Story of Italian-American Vintners
1st ed., 20.4 x 25.5 cm
Includes bibliographic references and index.
ISBN 1-891267-13-2
Wine and wine making- California I. Title: Wine Heritage. II. Title: The Story of Italian-American Vinters.

TP. 548 xxx 2000   LC# 00-xxxxx

The author and publishers will be grateful for any information that will assist them in keeping further editions up to date. Although all reasonable care has been taken in the preparation of this book, neither publishers nor the author can accept any liability for any consequences arising from the uses thereof, or from the information contained herein.

Editor: Anna Boothe
Copy Editor: Carrie Pickett
Book Design: Ronna Nelson, Mirage Digital Media
Photo Editor: Elizabeth Mackey
Index: Therese Shere

Printed and bound in the United States

To the millions of Italians who came to America and learned the ways of the New World while teaching the ways of the Old.

To my wife, Linda, whose love gave me the strength and whose patience gave me the time to write this book.

But especially to my daughter, Kristen, so that she will never forget her heritage.

Contents

FOREWORD

Dick Rosano's book is already a favorite of mine. Since my family lived a story similar to those recounted in the book, it helps me to revisit their experiences with my mind and my heart.

I was born to a family of Italian immigrants living in a small mining town in Minnesota. The values that my mother and father brought from Italy helped us and other Italian-Americans become successful in America.

Italians value the family and the family table. It is here that we communicate our goals and dreams. Here is where we recognize the value of hard work, of togetherness, of openness, and of truth. These are the values that helped us in the early American wine business because wine is close to our 'Italian-ness.' Wine is looked upon as liquid food.

Think about this. Prior to 1900, we already had these names in the California wine industry: Seghesio, Rossi, Foppiano, Martini, Sebastiani, Simi, Gallo, Sattui, Petri, Bisceglia, and Bianchi. These names have survived a century. What a tribute to the wine business and Italians affection for the grape!

But the past is prologue. The Robert Mondavi family has put a special turn on the story by going back to Italy to form a joint venture with the Marchesi de Frescobaldi family, which is producing many new wines this year. While the world of wine is becoming international, I know that Italians and Italian-Americans will always play a predominant role in producing this wonderful product.

~ Robert Mondavi

PART I

A History

The Early Years

"The best wines in the world
will be made there."

— FILIPPO MAZZEI
Eighteenth Century Italian
philosopher, politician,
and winemaker,
commenting on America

The Ancient World

Like all great empires, the ancient Greek rulers traveled the seas in search of new lands to bring under their control. Crossing the Adriatic, they landed on a narrow peninsula that appeared to be a paradise of flora and fauna. The Greek civilization had already enjoyed wine for many centuries, and when they discovered that this new land had a plentiful supply of grapevines, they named it Enotria, "Land of Wine." Later, the land would be called Italy, and it would forever enjoy worldwide fame for the wines it produced—for which the Greeks had given it so apt a name.

Far to the west, another explorer took to the seas to discover new lands. Landing on the eastern shore of North America in about A.D. 1001, Leif Ericsson confronted a landscape abundant in natural grapevines, which grew wild in the forests. He was so impressed with the plentiful supply of grapes that he called this new land Vinland.

Unknown to the ancient Italians and to the Native Americans at the turn of the millennium, these two discoveries would represent an almost fateful connection. In the centuries to come, Italy's influence on American winemaking would be instrumental in first establishing, and then advancing, the American position in the world wine market.

The American East

No one can be precisely certain about the tales told of Ericsson's landing in America. He surely found vines, and there appear to have been an abundance of them, but there is no description of the types of grapes or their uses. Stories generated hundreds of years later by other sources describe a wild and fecund land, at no loss for wildlife of any kind. Based on these later accounts, it would not be difficult to believe the description of the land Ericsson chronicled. There were many species of wild animals and untold thousands of species of plants and trees. The vegetation was so thick in some places that the floor of the forest was said to be as crowded as the tree-blackened canopy above.

And there were vines. Vines that grew across the surface of the soil and vines that climbed the trees, using the spreading branches as a natural trellis. And they carried grapes—red grapes, white grapes, and blue-black grapes. It doesn't appear that American grapes had been used for wine before the time of Ericsson's landing, though grapes had been used to make wine since about 5000 B.C. in western Europe and Asia, where the fermented juice of the vine was heralded as the divinely inspired companion for culture, religion, and good food.

Many years later, an obscure (though now world-famous) Italian, Cristoforo Colombo (Christopher Columbus), brought America into the political orbit of western Europe. The stories of North America's natural wonders and fertile lands grew as readily as the seeds planted in its soil. In the coming centuries, America welcomed to its shores many people who explored the land's natural resources and established new colonies for their homelands. Some sought spices and precious gems, some religious tolerance, and some a refuge from political persecution. For centuries, these adventurers sent back to their native lands stories about the boundless riches of the New World.

Ericsson's description of North America as a land of vines appears not to have been repeated in these travellers' journals. While Colombo's New World landing introduced the culture of Europe and its wine history into America, the earliest references to wine date only to the 1560s. Certainly, the landing parties were a hardy bunch, and rum and other spirits were not unfamiliar to them. Perhaps the delay in launching an American viticulture was due to the need to establish settlements with permanent social organizations to tend a perennial crop that would reach its potential only after several years of development.

Another Italian explorer found not only Colombo's North America but the grapevines Ericsson had described. In 1524, Giovanni da Verrazzano landed in the area now known as Kitty Hawk, North Carolina, and found excellent vines for winemaking. It appears, from other accounts, that these were wild vines since the Native Americans were not known to have tended them for the production of wine. Verrazzano's history is rich in exploration and discovery, but, unfortunately, little is said about the grapevines he found on the east coast of America and why he thought they would be so good for wine.[1]

It is said that wine was first made in America farther south, in the area that is now Florida. In 1565, Huguenots cultivated and grew grapes there, though Captain John Hawkins, who journeyed there in that year, criticized the settlers for specializing in wine rather than agriculture, since their decision to do so brought them near to starvation.[2] The tropical climate with its rich growth of wild plants may have enticed some to cultivate vines but, as the world has since discovered, tropical climates are hard on fine wine grapes.

Those who explored America did not give up: grape growing and attempts to make wine moved north in the next century. Spanish colonists were active in settling a section of the East Coast north of Florida. In 1568 they planted vines on the island they called Santa Elena, off the coast of modern-day South Carolina, and they appear to have experimented with the vinification of the grapes they produced. These vines may have been Vitis vinifera, the classic European wine grape species, but it appears that the plantings failed. As interested as they were in wine production, the Spaniards no doubt turned to the wild grapes for their winemaking, possibly with the same success.[3]

In 1584 the English landed in North Carolina and reported finding a carpet of grapes crowding the shore. These observations are rather effusive in their description of the grapevines in the area, while it is unclear whether the English planted any vines themselves.[4]

Viticultural efforts continued to move north as Virginia became the focus of most of the winemakers' efforts in colonial America. As early as 1609 there were concerted efforts to make wine from grapes grown in Virginia. The Virginia colonists acknowledged the preeminence of Italians in the world of wine and encouraged them to emigrate to Virginia to assist in the emerging viticulture.[5] To prove its confidence in the venture, the Virginia Company openly and proudly predicted that it could make wine in America.[6] Many settlers cut into soil to plant grapes and some achieved a modicum of success. There must have been more than a little interest in the final product since, in 1611, the Virginia criminal code made stealing from a vineyard a capital offense.

In 1619 the Virginia Company upped the ante and authored a law that required all Virginia householders to plant at least ten grapevines. Then, in 1624, the law required every male family member to plant twenty vines by the following February.[7] Soon thereafter, King James I criticized the Virginia Company for its lack of viticultural success. Though the Company listed winemaking in its list of accomplishments, it didn't convince the king, who decided to dissolve the company and turn Virginia into a crown colony. Continued failures in viticulture were blamed on the French, who were penalized by being denied the right to plant tobacco.[8]

By 1622 Virginia settlers were showing some pride in the wines they produced, shipping some to England. Although the wines from this area would much later achieve international notice, the records from 1622 show many instances of this wine arriving spoiled at its destination, leaving some doubt as to the shipping methods if not also the quality of the product.[9]

During the next hundred years, laws were passed to entice people to grow grapes. Among them was a 1623 decision by the governor of Virginia to exempt wine from the price controls he had placed on alcoholic beverages.[10] In 1658 a Virginia Act of Assembly offered a reward to anyone who could produce wine from local grapes. The offer was dropped in 1685, apparently without ever having been awarded.[11]

The idea of a reward for wine production was revived in 1759 by a group in Virginia who called themselves the Society for the Promotion of Manufactures. They offered a reward to the person who could, in eight years' time, produce the best ten hogsheads of wine. Although the Virginia assembly apparently endorsed the competition, the record is unclear about whether this reward, either, was ever claimed.[12]

Amid all these attempts and—too often—failures, the Virginians and their fellow colonists were discovering that their climate and soil did not appear to allow them to produce sound wine from native grapes, nor to cultivate European wine grapes with any success. Wine must have been crucial to these settlements, however, because such attempts continued. By the middle of the eighteenth century, the people who were now calling themselves Americans were realizing that the native grapes had little to offer in terms of quality wine and that they should try to cultivate the Vitis vinifera species of grape from Europe, from which the world's most famous wines are made.

In the 1720s a dedicated and inventive grape grower, William Byrd, suggested turning over his estate to the cultivation of grapes and planting as many types of vines as he could find. He wanted to prove that grapevines could be grown successfully in spite of the criticism he had too often heard of regarding such experiments. He even proposed grafting European varieties onto American rootstock, an innovation that would be copied many years later by Americans and Europeans

A workman transplants young, rooted vines through a five-step process of staking, digging, filling, and dipping the vine roots into a special mud mixture.

alike to stave off the ravages of the phylloxera plant louse.[13]

In 1769 the Virginia assembly passed an act calling for a purchase of land for the purpose of cultivating grapevines.[14] The act was rescinded in 1776 for an assortment of reasons, including, no doubt, the occupation of funds to support the impending war with Britain.

As America entered its revolutionary period, eastern grape growing took a decided turn toward the Italian. Andrew Turnbull decided to import Italians to help him establish a wine industry in Florida. It appears that viticultural failure was only one of the maladies they suffered: scurvy, malaria, and other epidemics destroyed the project and ended the settlement.[15]

In the 1770s Robert Bolling championed the cause of importing European grapevines to America, with a special interest in those from Italy.[16] He criticized earlier failed attempts at growing *Vitis vinifera* grapes in Virginia, saying the experiments were too limited and careless, and he decided to import Italian grape varieties. Bolling died in 1775, before he could read the accounts of the success of his vineyard, and before his successors would allow it to perish.[17]

While Americans were attempting to get their viticulture going, Italians were independently seeking adventure and new beginnings in a land that had assumed nearly mythic proportion in the notions popular in Europe at the time.[18] Before the revolution of 1776 separated the United States from England, Italians were boarding ships bound for the promised land, their hopes high that the impressive reports of America's bounty were not unfounded.

One of the prominent Italians to make landfall in eighteenth-century America was Filippo Mazzei. He led an eventful life in Tuscany, marked by diverse experiences that enriched his life and his abilities. He studied medicine in his native Lucca on the west coast of Italy, then traveled to Turkey, where he plied his trade. A philosopher, politician, and merchant, Mazzei is known to have managed a firm in England that handled wine, olives, and cheese. And it was in London that he met Benjamin Franklin and Thomas Adams, Americans whose tales of their homeland would seduce the adventurous and always curious Mazzei to travel there.[19]

Mazzei also made the acquaintance of Thomas Jefferson, whose love of wine, during his years in France representing the newborn United States, had increased as he sampled from the many varieties of grapes grown successfully on the Continent. Once home, Jefferson

had dedicated himself to growing grapes that would yield fine wines, convinced that America could produce wine as good as that in Europe. He wanted to be the one to prove it, and all he needed was someone like Mazzei.

Mazzei and Thomas Jefferson corresponded before Mazzei's departure for the New World. Upon Mazzei's arrival in America, Thomas Adams introduced the two men, and Jefferson quickly recruited Mazzei to design and carry out a plan to cultivate European wine grapes in Virginia. One of the most telling stories about Jefferson's character and affability involves Mazzei. As the story goes, Adams, a friend of Jefferson's, brought Mazzei to meet the man from Monticello. When Jefferson and Mazzei returned from a walk around Monticello's gardens—a walk that undoubtedly included a discussion of Jefferson's grand agricultural plan—Adams noted the twinkle in Mazzei's eyes and said to Jefferson, "I see in your face that you have taken him from me."[20]

Jefferson offered Mazzei two thousand acres of land near Monticello in exchange for undertaking the project of starting a vineyard and proving that it could be done. Mazzei recruited Italian vignerons and stocked thousands of grapevines to be cultivated in Virginia.[21] As interested as he was in Jefferson's plans, Mazzei returned to America only to be distracted from viticulture by the American struggle for independence.[22] He joined in America's effort to free himself from England and served in many capacities throughout the struggle, save for the one that brought him here: winemaker.

Jefferson persevered in his attempts to grow grapes, filling his legendary Garden Book with many of his careful entries concerning the planting and cultivation of vines. His efforts suffered somewhat from his absence, since he was to spend the next thirty years occupied with the Continental Congress and, later, to serve as the secretary of state, vice president, and, finally, president of the United States. But he never wavered in the belief that viable vineyards could be brought to bear wine in Virginia. In Jefferson's declining years, a series of frustrations—bad weather, the destruction of his vineyards by Prussian horses, and Mazzei's sudden desertion—combined with agricultural hazards such as climatic conditions, pests, and diseases, caused him to conclude that perhaps European vines could not survive the vagaries of the American climate.

Edward Antill planted Italian grape varieties in New Jersey in 1764 and had some initial success, but his experiment ultimately failed. The soils and climate in that area likely posed a significant problem since even modern-day attempts to cultivate Italian grape varieties there have encountered difficulties.

During this early period, many other efforts to produce grapes and wine were underway on the east coast of the United States. John Adlum experimented with grapevines on a two-hundred-acre tract in what is now Rock Creek Park in Washington, D.C.; his wine was at least good enough to elicit favorable comments from Jefferson. Unfortunately, Adlum's most prolific grape was the Catawba, a grape with properties that could make sometimes palatable wine but never wine of great breeding. Adlum also wrote the first winemaking book to be published in America, *A Memoir on the Cultivation of the Vine in America and the Best Mode of Making Wine*.[23]

Meanwhile, the southern states had not abandoned their hopes of producing wine. In 1825 and 1827 serious attempts were made to get the South Carolina legislature to support a project to bring Italians over to work in that state's vineyards. Neither of the two attempts succeeded—nor did the vineyards the Italians would have been recruited to tend.

As wine writer Hugh Johnson has so mercilessly put it, "The seventeenth and eighteenth centuries [in the eastern U.S.] were a repetitive saga of wasted effort."[24] The environment eagerly supported a native species of grape, *Vitis labrusca*, but *V. labrusca* was not capable of producing wines of international quality. It would be many years before the knowledge of viticulture in the East would advance to the point that it could sustain *Vitis vinifera*.

Italy

The American revolutionary spirit caught on in Europe. France followed quickly in the footsteps of the rebellious Americans and overthrew its monarchical government, while the new United States was still deciding the organization of its own government. Other cultures throughout Europe were being transformed into democracies. Italy, while not gripped by the passion for independence as was America or France, suffered through tremendous social unrest and political upheaval in the early nineteenth century.

There were political and cultural revolutions in Italy in the three decades preceding the unification of the Italian provinces in 1870. These revolutions altered the Italians' perception of their society and ushered in a period of unrest and social disorganization; they also concentrated power in the hands of the middle class, who were unwilling to share the newfound power with the poor peasants of the south.[25]

Giuseppe Garibaldi used that unrest in his rise to national prominence during those years of change. He was often in a tussle with the law, but set his sights on liberating the Italian peasant from foreign control and unifying the peninsula into a single nation. His ideas were revolutionary enough that he was forced to leave Italy for a time, and he lived on Staten Island, plotting the day when he would return to complete his quest.

In the middle of the nineteenth century, the provinces in northern Italy enjoyed a higher standard of living than the southern provinces in the Mezzogiorno, the area south of Rome. The people in the north were generally better educated, the manufacturing sector was more advanced and closer to industrialization, and the economy was stronger than in the agricultural south.

In the Mezzogiorno, where the recent abolition of feudalism had once given hope, the typical peasant looked on as his family's economic stability slipped. First, he lost control of his land and was forced to work as a tenant farmer; then he watched helplessly as the rent exacted by the wealthy landowners increased almost beyond his ability to bear. The peasant farmers of southern Italy in the mid-nineteenth century often felt as though they worked night and day only to grow poorer.

The ownership of land continued to be concentrated in fewer and fewer hands, and many peasants were driven off their farms and forced to move their families long distances in a futile search for better jobs.[26] Many traveled to Italian cities in the north, forsaking the southern provinces, which were slowly being depopulated. Some people set their sights on other European countries, fearful of the prejudice northern Italians felt for them and hoping to escape the sun-baked, barren provinces of southern Italy for a new land.

During the period of 1840 to 1860, an active resettlement of the population took place in Italy. The numbers are not clear, but it became apparent to the remaining paesani of the Mezzogiorno that the villages and piazzas of their youth would soon be abandoned. Garibaldi, hero of the Italian revolution and father of Italian unification, promised land redistribution that the southerners had come to believe in as the last hope for redemption.[27] Unfortunately, that promise never came true, and the peasants' situation worsened in the years following the unification of Italy in 1870. The effects of this change for the worse will be described in the next chapter.

The American West

If Leif Ericsson had landed on the west coast of North America instead of the east, he would not have seen so many wild grapes growing throughout the trees. Few vines grew wild on the West Coast, but the weather and environment there dictated centuries ago that what has become California would also become one of the world's most fertile gardens for wine grapes.

The fecundity of the region was not lost on its earliest inhabitants. For hundreds of years, Native Americans had nearly unchallenged possession of the lush countryside and temperate climate of America's Pacific coast. Evidence shows that Native Americans did not take advantage of the environment to propagate grapes for wine.

Between the sixteenth and eighteenth centuries, the Mission program brought the Spanish culture to California. At that time, an Italian monk, Fra Marco da Nizza, was among the many foreigners working in the service of Spain in the American southwest. During the 1530s da Nizza traveled extensively throughout what would later be called California, establishing many missions for the Spanish government.[28] Missionaries were encouraged to settle the territory for Spanish occupation and ultimate control of the land along the Pacific coast of North

America. The project was called the Mission program because the religious orders that shepherded the influx of Spanish into the area were given the task of setting up missions to educate and baptize the Native Americans, considered the necessary first step toward civilization. The missionaries built in many locations along the coastline and interior lands and brought Spanish culture and social organization to the land of the Native Americans.

There were other Italian clerics active in the Mission program, mostly working in the service of Spain. Eusebio Francesco Chino (also spelled Kino), from Genoa, traveled through much of the same area and continued the Mission program by establishing missions during the 1680s and 1690s. He started raising cattle and made it a profitable business in the American southwest; he then brought grains and grapes to cultivate. Chino's work continued to move northward where he established more than twenty missions in what was then known as Greater Sonoma.

The fact that religious missionaries were in the vanguard of this Spanish expansion was significant to the development of grape growing in California. In addition to the crops and other plants that the Spanish brought north with them, the Franciscans brought grapevines to satisfy their need for sacramental wine; these imports included cuttings of the Criolla grape, a grape of little distinction[29] but of the

Father Narciso Durn of the San Jose Mission encounters a Native American child. Under his guidance, the Mission produced a number of notable wines and became a center of liturgical music.

species *Vitis vinifera*. The first grapes were likely planted in 1626 at the Socorro mission on the Rio Grande river, but it wasn't until the eighteenth century that the Criolla grape had a conspicuous presence.

Due to its proliferation and close association with the Mission movement, the Criolla came to be known as the Mission grape. Unfortunately, the Mission grape has never produced much better than simple wine and, as famed wine writer Hugh Johnson said, "[T]he Mission grape in California [was] a disincentive to experiment"[30] because its presence satisfied the need for sacramental wine and dulled the interest in experimentation.

The missions continued to serve as the centers of winemaking even after they were secularized by the Mexican government in 1833, a move that also secularized the vineyards and wineries. In the 1830s the mission at San Gabriel was the regions' largest winery. Given the large concentration of missions in southern California, it should come as no surprise that it was in the area around Los Angeles that the wine industry got started after being separated from its religious affiliate.[31] Among many others experimenting with grape growing around Los Angeles was Antonio Lugo, who planted his vineyards in 1809, though there is no record of a commercial winery in his name. Lugo very likely made wine for his own purposes and sold the remaining crop to other commercial operations.

The Mexican military commander in charge of the area around present-day Napa and Sonoma at the time of the secularization of the missions was Mariano Vallejo. He was interested in taking advantage of his position during the disestablishment of the missions, and he also was a lover of wine. It was his interest in wine that helped the California wine industry to make a transition from the Mission grape to better varietals. In 1833, when Mexico turned the missions over to the local populations that already owned them in fact, if not in law, Vallejo was already in Sonoma planting vineyards and planning how to make better wine from newer varieties of grapes.[32]

During the 1850s Italians became more prominent in the California wine market. The families that did travel to California were ahead of the great migration and were true adventurers in an area that was only recently liberated from Spanish influence. At the beginning of the decade, Andrea Sbarbaro arrived from Genoa. As an adult, his philanthropic efforts to help his fellow Italian immigrants would lead to the establishment of Italian Swiss Colony Winery in a town that he would name Asti, after the Piedmontese village of that name in northern Italy. Sbarboro was forthright in saying that he wanted his company to be composed of Italian immigrants in order to help them all build a financial base for themselves. That venture was so successful that it set the standard for Italian and Italian American efforts for the remainder of the nineteenth century and has continued to be a household name in American wine for more a hundred years.

Andrea Arata was probably the first Italian to plant a vineyard in Amador County, which he did in 1853. That same year, the Splivalo Vineyard and Winery was founded in San Jose.[33] But the surge was just beginning. Only 431 Italian immigrants entered the United States in 1850, the number rising slightly to 555 in 1853. By 1880, when the Great Migration began, the number reached 12,354 and, by 1903, the number of Italians entering the United States exceeded 230,000.[34] The Mezzogiorno was losing its population in great waves, and many of these wandering souls ended up in New York. A great portion of the unskilled and uneducated masses ended up in the squalid and over-crowded quarters of the New York City boroughs. Some, mostly Italians from the north who usually had more money and better education, escaped the East Coast and sought refuge in the beautiful regions to the west.

With the exception of Vallejo's vineyards around Sonoma, most of the grapes were still being planted in southern California; the climate might have killed the nascent industry had it not moved north under Vallejo's encouragement. Around this time of the wine industry's relocation, more Italians began to be seen in northern California.

The Gold Rush Years
and Beyond

"California's mild climate and
strong visual resemblance to
Italy helped make Italians
feel at home... Their wines
also resembled those of Italy."

— ANDREW F. ROLLE
The American Italians

The last half of the nineteenth century was the most significant period in
the history of the American wine industry. Many would argue that the
period from 1970 to the present day is more significant and has witnessed greater growth in American wine's stature in the international
community. Much of the recent progress, however, is built on the strides
made one hundred years ago, when the fledgling industry was struggling to find an even footing. This was a time of resettlement in
California, and the influx of Europeans to the area had a decided impact.

Although the birth of commercial winemaking in the West was clearly tied to the 1833 secularization of the missions, the wineries that opened soon after that date sputtered for a number of years and needed additional events to launch the industry into self-sustained growth. Starting in approximately 1850, the nascent industry would get a boost from two significant though unrelated events that would unfold and give life to the wines and vines of California over the next few decades: the Gold Rush in California and the Great Migration in the late 1800s that was spawned by the economic disasters and political turmoil in Europe.

In the early 1800s, viticulture and winemaking in California were concentrated in the area around Los Angeles,[35] the first region exploited by the missionaries. From 1800 to about 1830, the Mission program continued its northward march, bringing religion and grapes to areas as far north as present-day Sonoma county.[36] The secularization of the missions made a land grab possible, and Mariano Guadalupe Vallejo was right in the middle of it. He was the Mexican government's military commander in charge of the region surrounding Sonoma and Napa. But more importantly, he was a wine lover who was interested in promoting the emerging industry.

This land around Los Angeles was once part of William Wolfskill's agricultural estate where, at its height, four cellars held cooperage for a hundred thousand gallons of wine.

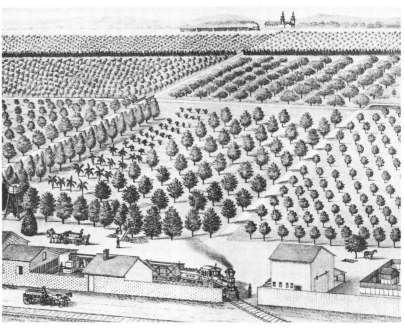

Vallejo planned to keep most of the best land around the Sonoma mission for himself. He gave large parcels of it to favored friends, however. George Yount benefited from his association with Vallejo when, in 1844, he was deeded 4,400 acres on Howell Mountain, one of today's most sought-after plots of vineyard land.[37] Pinney credits Yount with planting the first grapes in Napa Valley.[38] Yount went on to become one of California wine's most respected pioneers, and the town of Yountville is named after him.

During this time, arrivals of Italians on the eastern shore were on the increase, as many left their homeland to find opportunities in the New World they had heard about. In 1848 revolutions throughout Europe stripped the ruling class of some of its control, and pitted the middle class against the peasants in a struggle for the remaining power.[39] This struggle resulted in some demographic changes within Europe, including emigration from one country to another. But the Italians leaving home in the 1840s were as likely to drift to other European countries as find their way to America.

In 1848, the same year the European revolutions were at their peak, gold was discovered in Coloma, in the Sierra Foothills. Tens of thousands of prospectors, dreamers, and vagrants crossed the plains to try their hand at gold digging. Few would find enough to keep alive their dreams of fortune, but the shift in population from southern to northern California and the migration of untold thousands of easterners to the West changed the national demographics and established northern California as a popular destination, which it remains to this day.

One of the Italians to leave Italy in 1848 was Giuseppe Simi. Unlike many of his countrymen in those early years, he left Europe altogether and traveled to California in search of gold. When that didn't work out, he joined his brother in San Francisco selling vegetables. Giuseppe later moved to Sonoma and opened a winery with his brother (though Pietro continued working their vegetable business in San Francisco) that remains in business today. His experience will later be discussed in more detail.

Gold Rush fever accounted for another factor that would have a significant impact on the population in San Francisco and regions to the north: The get-rich-quick dreams of those migrating west were very attractive to those who were still struggling to make ends meet, including the recent immigrants from Europe and the long-term residents of the eastern cities that could never quite rise above the lower levels of America's melting pot. The idea that gold could be found on the streets of San Francisco—however preposterous it sounded—was all the poor immigrants in the east needed to hear. They had fled their countries in search of freedom and opportunity in the United States; why wouldn't they answer the clarion call of Gold Rush fever?

Italian emigration patterns hadn't changed much during the period leading up to 1848. From 1780 to 1850 the Italian American population in the United States grew slowly, reaching twelve thousand by the middle of the 1800s.[40] Most of these early immigrants came from the better educated classes of Italians, and the local American attitude toward Italian immigrants was positive; the Italians were regarded, in Mangione and Morreale's words, as "a civilizing influence on a society that was largely dependent on Europe for cultural guidance."[41] So, until 1850, the Italian immigrant population was very homogeneous, many of them arriving in this country intending to establish businesses and stay.

Starting in 1850, however, the eastern population of Italians that fed into the westward stream of California-bound immigrants began to change. The political, economic, and environmental troubles in Italy were mounting, affecting the southern Italians with disproportionate severity. Garibaldi's promises of land redistribution never materialized, and the support of the southerners that he sought in his quest to unify Italy began to fade. Added to these conditions was a severe crop failure that damaged many vineyards, a problem that fell hardest on the south with its historically meager economy. Subsequent disasters would include phylloxera, the root louse that was infecting then destroying vineyards in Europe at an alarming rate, then a tidal wave, a cholera epidemic, volcanic eruptions, severe drought, and soil erosion-all of which must have made southern Italy seem very close to Dante's seventh circle. These factors, and more, forced many southern Italian families to emigrate, along with many winemaking families from all over Italy. With the opportunities that beckoned in the New World, at least according to stories they had heard, many Italians were marking the United States as their preferred destination rather than the closer European countries they might have chosen earlier.

During the 1850s, then, the actual face of the Italian immigrant in America began to change. The sea of fair-skinned northerners was now intermingled with the ruddy complexions of their southern countrymen. Southern Italian immigrants were in worse financial shape

than the northerners, with less education and possessing considerably less in the way of marketable skills.[42] So many of these immigrants were quick to realize the advantage of moving west to seek their opportunities: They could see that staying in the east pitted them against the thousands of immigrants who had arrived earlier, a situation in which the new arrivals started at the bottom of the ladder. Those who went west arrived along with the great surge of settlers and entered on equal standing, no matter what their occupation.[43]

In 1851 Domenico Ghirardelli sensed the opportunities on the West Coast and settled there to later establish the Ghirardelli Chocolate Factory. The old factory has been converted to a shopping and restaurant center in San Francisco, although Ghirardelli chocolates are still made for millions of fans worldwide. As discussed earlier, the Splivalo Winery was founded in 1853 in San Jose.[44] This was the year Andrea Arata planted his vineyard in Amador County, establishing an Italian connection to an area that has since been prized as an ideal spot for the cultivation of Italian varietals.

By the late 1850s Andrea Sbarbaro had already arrived in California. Sbarbaro was only twelve years old when he first set foot in America, but his industriousness and his interest in helping his fellow Italians paid off, both for him and for them. In the coming years, Sbarbaro established several successful building and loan societies, reaping the profits from these, and in the 1880s he decided to turn his efforts to grape growing, planning to employ Italian immigrants and give them a chance to buy stock in the company. More of his history will be discussed later.

Anthony Caminetti was born in 1854 in Jackson Gate, California, to immigrant parents who arrived during the Gold Rush. He was responsible for transplanting thousands of vines from Napa County, among them many foreign varieties and a considerable number of Zinfandel vines.[45] He also became involved in politics, though his legislative contributions ranged far from the interests of the vineyard, as will be seen later in this work.

In 1856 a winery was built by Swiss immigrant, Adam Uhlinger, that would later become the D'Agostini Winery. Under the tutelage of the D'Agostini family, who bought it in the early 1900s, the winery flourished on the basis of honest, well-made varietal wines. The D'Agostini winery has since been purchased by the Sobon Estate Winery.

In 1857 Quirillo and Company was founded in South Fork, California; it would later be called the Italian Garden and Winery. In that year, Giuseppe Migliavacca came to America from Pavia, Italy. He opened a huge winery in the city of Napa and produced what Sullivan

has called the best wine of all such large operations in that area.[46]

In 1860 the future patriarch of the Seghesio wine empire, Edoardo, was born near Dogliani, Italy. He grew up in the wine business and was later invited to come to America to join Pietro Rossi at Italian Swiss Colony to make wine. His apprenticeship paid off because, while Italian Swiss Colony became a financial football and passed through many hands before disappearing from the scene, Edoardo started a family wine empire that has passed its hundredth birthday and is still going strong.

By 1860 there were more Italian immigrants in California than in any other state of the Union.[47] It is interesting to note that of the Italian immigrants who traveled west during this period, those from regions in northern Italy, such as Tuscany, Piedmont, and Lombardy, settled in northern California.[48] Of the many southern Italians making the trip west, a high percentage ended up in the area around Los Angeles.[49] The different climates of the California regions make an interesting analogy for the Italian settlers, that is, that the northern Italian regions that provide the most elegant and world-famous wines sent its immigrants to California's northern regions, which provide the state's most noble wines. The southern Italians settled mostly in southern California.

One of the secrets of the Gold Rush was that those selling goods and services to the prospectors often became richer than those digging gold out of the ground. Not surprisingly, the demand for wine increased with the population explosion in northern California and vineyards were planted to satisfy this demand.[50] But the price of grapes also went up, as did the price of every other commodity after gold was discovered.[51] The California legislature was helpful in this regard, however, and knew how much a thriving viticulture could do for the state. To encourage the new industry, the state legislature voted a tax exemption for the first four years of each new vineyard's life, giving aspiring winery owners a chance to turn a profit before embarking on an industry that promised only delayed capital gratification.

Many of the Italians arriving in California congregated in San Francisco, preferring at first to settle near the population centers where they were more likely to find collectives of other Italian immigrants and where opportunities for employment seemed greatest. The relative ease with which the Italians settled first in the urban environment was deceptive, though. It actually indicated a cultural bias: In Italy, those who farm the land live in towns and villages and travel out in the day to cultivate their crops and vines. In America, farmers live in the middle of their vast spread of land, beyond contact with their nearest neighbors. The American design did not appeal to the Italians, a gregarious race that puts family and community above just about everything. The Italian immigrants chose instead to live in the population centers, but there were no farms to travel to, so many of these immigrants sought jobs in the city. This made urban industrial workers out of many who had come from agricultural regions in Italy. In time, they gravitated to areas outside of San Francisco to resume the farming life they had known.[52]

By the 1860s nearly twelve million vines had been planted in California. The products from France, Germany, and Italy that flooded the American market were mostly cheap wines,[53] but they possessed the one essential ingredient for success in the New World that still lacked a heritage of wine: a European pedigree. The infatuation with European wine resulted in many local vinous products being given French and Italian names, a deceptive habit that continues today, seen in labels that tout California "Chianti," "Port," and "Burgundy."

During this time there was an extensive replanting of vines in

Grandfather Mario of V. Sattui Winery delivers wine by horse-drawn wagon.

California, mostly in Sonoma Valley.[54] This project diminished the acres previously given to the Mission grape, the vine that had given the California wine industry its start. The replanting signaled the beginning of the end for the Criolla in the United States; as well, it marked a turning point in California's grape-growing history.

The wine industry had gotten a foothold, better vines were being planted for better wines, and the Italians who had crossed the continent to take up farming were becoming part of the burgeoning American wine industry. In the 1860s, Angelo Marre came to America with his family to settle in Amador County. He started with a boarding house, a practice not uncommon among Italian families as a means of gaining a supplemental income. In 1877, he opened a winery in Amador County. According to Costa, his efforts were rewarded, and Marre became "one of the largest winegrowers in Amador."[55]

Around the same time, Giovanni Foppiano left Genoa in 1862 for America, traveling by ship to Panama, walking across the isthmus and boarding a ship bound for San Francisco. He ended up in Healdsburg in 1865. At the same time, Thomas Pettinelli was making Napa Valley's first sherry. The railroad link between the East and West coasts was completed, opening eastern markets to California wine. The railroad also made it more possible for more Americans and immigrants to cross the plains in search of a new life in California. During Prohibition, this link would prove vital for shipping grapes to eastern home winemakers. Unfortunately, the decade also witnessed the birth of the National Prohibition Party in California, formed to unify the efforts of the growing movement to ban the production and sale of alcoholic drinks.

The aftermath of the American Civil War, although it didn't appear to affect California much, brought new conflicts that had not been anticipated by politicians. Racial tensions were heightened due to the freeing of the slaves, and a general dislike for employing former slaves in paying positions resulted in many jobs going to Chinese labor. Later, mass unemployment caused the Chinese, paradoxically, to be blamed for taking jobs from whites. As a result, in the 1880s, Italians moved into the jobs the Chinese were forced to leave.

In 1870 a stone winery called Edge Hill was built for General Erasmus Delano Keyes in Napa. It later became the home of Louis P. Martini.[56] That same year, after spending four years building his business, Giuseppe Migliavacca decided he had enough capital to move his wine business to the city of Napa. His ambitious expansion would make his one of the most successful businesses of any sort in the Napa Valley during the 1870s.

Back in Italy, Giuseppe Garibaldi's unification of Italy had been ratified by the member provinces in 1870. A long period of adjustment then began for the citizens of this new country; many would be dissatisfied with the result and choose to leave for America. The unification put even more power in the hands of the northerners, who despised those from the Mezzogiorno so much that they diverted funds meant for education in the South to construction projects in the North. Government funds were so scarce for projects in the Mezzogiorno that the peasants there were stuck with an inferior water system whose poorly purified water caused trauchoma, an eye ailment later responsible for keeping many southern immigrants from entering the United States.[57]

There was an ironic twist to the Italian immigrants' increased productivity of fruit and vegetables in California. The northern Italian immigrants who settled there were so successful raising crops that local products soon replaced imported Italian fruit and vegetables as staples of the northern California meal.[58] Among those making a go of it was Marco Fontana's company called the California Fruit Packing Company, later known as Del Monte. This increased production in California reduced the American dependence on imports and resulted in a drastic reduction of an important southern Italian export item.[59] It appeared that even from another country, the northern Italians could still wreak havoc on the economy of the Mezzogiorno.

By 1880 Italians continued to plant vines and establish themselves in northern California as winemakers.[60] The effects of the Gold Rush were firmly established: the population had experienced a massive increase, and the businesses that had shot up to support the gold diggers were now well settled and supporting many large towns. There was a wine boom that evolved out of the first rush of gold diggers in the 1850s,[61] but the steady development of the industry through the 1860s and 1870s was essential to its establishment as an economic force.

From 1880 to 1900 thousands of Italians poured into the United States in the early stages of what would become known as the Great Migration. From the five thousand Italian immigrants in the United States in 1850 to ten thousand in 1860, the number would soar to 1,200,000 by 1903.[62] There were already several thousand in California,

involved in a variety of occupations, and the agriculturally minded were farming and selling produce in cities and towns while the grape growers were harvesting and crushing the grapes to serve to the thirsty masses.

In 1873 phylloxera was discovered in Sonoma Valley.[63] It was the beginning of the plague that would terrorize the wine industry for decades.

In 1874 Samuele Sebastiani was born in Lucca, Italy; Sutter Home Winery was built; and the beginnings of a worldwide economic depression were being felt in California. The financially hard times caused a wine market bust in 1876, and prices for grapes and wine plunged. To quote from Leon Adams:

"Barnyard animals were turned into the vineyards to dispose of the grapes. Many vineyardists uprooted their vines and planted fruit trees instead.[64]"

Into this gloomy market came the Italians, whose five-thousand-year affair with the grape gave them the determination to continue to plant and keep faith with the vine. From the ashes of that depression rose a better industry, one that had a chance to rethink its direction, and one that had a chance—through phylloxera damage and the uprooting caused by the poor economy—to plant better grapes and get set for the improvements that were destined to come.

Giuseppe Simi had given up on his dreams of finding gold in the hills, and he moved to San Francisco to join his brother, Pietro, who was farming vegetables and selling them in the city. By 1876 they had taken up winemaking, producing wine in their small downtown home from grapes shipped into the city from Sonoma County.[65] They were so successful with wine from their Montepulciano Winery that they bought land near Healdsburg and built a gravity-flow winery, a design that was popular at the time. Such wineries were built into the sides of hills so that the grapes could be delivered to the upper floors that backed up to the high side of the hill. The grapes were crushed there then fed by gravity through each of the successive steps in the process in the floors below. Pietro stayed in San Francisco to manage the vegetable business and handle the Simi wine sales in the city, and Giuseppe went to Healdsburg to become a full-time winemaker at what was called the Simi Winery.

The Ginocchio brothers borrowed an idea from the Italian *passito* method of drying grapes to concentrate the juice. In 1876, they built the Alden Fruit Dryer to dry their grapes and then they made their wine, no doubt a slightly sweet, concentrated potion. The Ginocchio brothers' wine was described as resembling port in both color and body. Apparently, it was a big success, though most of it never left Amador County.[66]

Giovanni Foppiano was now living near Healdsburg, farming vegetables and selling them to people in Sonoma County. He went back to Italy to find a bride, Rosa Rosasco, then returned to Healdsburg to start a family. In 1877 Louis A. Foppiano was born. The same year, Vincent Picchetti founded a winery near Cupertino.[67]

Angelo Marre had found his niche, making wine and brandy and selling most of it to the boarders at the house he owned in Amador County. By 1878, he was shipping wine to Chicago, Memphis, and New York, adding Philadelphia to the list in 1880.[68] By 1881, his interstate business was brisk enough that he opened wholesale warehouses in Chicago and New York to handle the volume of traffic in which he was engaged.

The Pelanconi Winery was operating near Los Angeles during this time, and it had one interesting feature. It employed Native Americans to trod the grapes barefoot,[69] a method by then abandoned by most of the wine world. The practice continued at Pelanconi until at least 1876. The Pelanconi Winery was later closed, and the foot-trodding method of crushing grapes in North America lost another supporter.

The year 1878 marked two very important events in American wine history. The vintage in California was especially good, taking advantage of the year's good weather and the preceding several years of replanting. As a result, 1878 produced wines that caught everyone's attention. The vintage represented an opportunity for northern California wine to get on the world map, and Napa benefited the most, using a great vintage as a springboard to establish its reputation and set the valley on a course to the worldwide fame it has enjoyed since.[70] Economic factors and good wine caused prices to begin rising again. To further stoke the fires, the phylloxera epidemic continued to reduce the European vineyards and threatened to kill their industry. So the conditions were right for California to step into that market.

Another significant event of 1878 was the arrival of Secondo Guasti in Los Angeles. He had spent some time in Sonora, Mexico, after leaving his hometown in Piedmont, Italy, and now came to California at just the right moment. In his early years there Guasti had to work hard to get established. He was employed in many kinds of jobs but slowly saved up enough money to open a business. Ultimately, and most significantly, he formed the Italian Vineyard Company in the Cucamonga desert. These accomplishments will be discussed later.

In 1880 Andrea Sbarbaro founded Italian Swiss Colony in a town he named Asti, in California.[71] He chose the name because the region resembled the town he remembered in Italy. He had organized banks for the business needs of Italian immigrants, and now he wanted to apply his talents to the wine industry. His plan was philanthropic, aiming to employ Italian and Swiss immigrants in a company that would pay its workers and provide room and board (and, of course, wine) but withhold a portion of their paychecks to purchase stock in the company. Sbarbaro hoped in this way to set the immigrants on a course for independence and financial security.

It was a good plan and one that deserves credit, but it met with opposition among those it was meant to serve. The workers didn't like having their paychecks reduced, even if the reduction went toward stock in the company, so they decided take the cash in hand and refused to allow the deduction from their paychecks.

The phylloxera epidemic was enough of a problem in California, too, that the state legislature formed the State Board of Viticultural Commissioners and a department of viticulture at the University of California in 1880. Although internal feuds on the Commission resulted in its early demise (1894), the legislature's efforts were effective, and the phylloxera-borne destruction was checked.[72]

By now Giuseppe Migliavacca was making two hundred thousand gallons of wine a year, and his product was very popular. In fact, his wine was so popular it was considered the best from among the large producers in Napa at that time.[73] Migliavacca had achieved fame and a certain standing in the community.

Augustus Quitzow built the Geyser Peak Winery in 1880. He built it to make both wine and brandy, since distilled spirits were very popular in the area in the late 1800s. The building and vineyards would later pass through many hands, including Bagnani's Italy Industries and the Ciocca Lombardi Winery Company; in 1982 it came to rest in the hands of Henry Trione, the Italian American who turned the winery into a very successful, fine-wine business.

By the 1880s, Anthony Caminetti had grown up and was in the wine business. He developed a reputation for applying scientific methods to winemaking and emphasizing quality and cleanliness.[74] These traits put in him the vanguard of a tradition that would later come to define California winemaking throughout the world.

In 1881 Twin Fir Winery was founded. Although Twin Fir did not last long under that name, it was later bought by Rafael Martini and renamed the R. Martini Winery, the first version of a winery that would belong to the Martini family, be sold, and then again be returned to the second generation of this family from Tuscany.

In 1881 Francesco Qualia left Castellanza, near Milan, and traveled to the United States, looking for work. In doing so, he abandoned the family farm, but he wanted to join the tide of immigrants that believed they would find a better life in America. He traveled through Louisiana and Texas, and spent some time in Mexico before settling near San Antonio. There, he formed a partnership with other Italian immigrants Franchi, Serafini, and Comolli and purchased a farm. Qualia and his partners added grapes to the crops on their newly purchased farm, but Qualia kept the winemaking as merely a sideline through 1919, when Prohibition made conversion to commercial production impossible. Francesco Qualia died during Prohibition, but his son, Louis, took over and, when Repeal legalized commercial winemaking again, he opened Val Verde Winery.

A most significant event occurred in 1882 that deliberately discriminated against one ethnic group while accidentally benefiting another

ethnic group. The decade saw increasing dislike and distrust of the Chinese who had come to the western shores of the United States, offering cheap labor and filling the ranks of workers in undesirable occupations. Many Americans were angry and suspicious that the Chinese were stealing their jobs. The passion of the times resulted in the Oriental Exclusion Act being passed, restricting Chinese access to jobs, setting quotas for their hiring, and in other ways making it diffi- cult—or impossible—for Chinese immigrants to find work in the West. The first irony of this situation was that Chinese people were forced out of work that many Caucasian Americans would have refused to do anyway, finding it too distasteful or too grueling. The second irony was that the Oriental Exclusion Act, in singling out a particular ethnic group, made it possible for another ethnic group—the Italians—to find employment in the jobs left open by the Chinese. This stimulated immigration from Italy and further fueled the Great Migration that was now underway.

In 1882 Giuseppe "Joe" Gallo, the father of Ernest and Julio Gallo was born in Fossano, Italy. He emigrated to the United States and laid the groundwork for one of America's greatest wine families and cer- tainly one of the largest producers of wine the world has yet seen. His story will be discussed later.

Also in 1882, Vittorio Sattui married Katerina Rossi in Carsi, Italy.

On their honeymoon, they moved to California, arriving virtually broke. Katerina ran a boarding house and Vittorio made bread at night and wine during the day, supplying most of both products to the boarders. By 1885, Vittorio's wine was selling well enough that he quit his job as a baker and devoted all his time to making wine. He purchased a property in San Francisco on what is now Columbus Avenue and called it the St. Helena Wine Cellars, named after the area from which he still bought his grapes. His business would grow, be interrupted, then flourish again in the hands of Daryl Sattui, his grandson.

In 1884 the B. Arata family came to America from Genoa and formed the Arata Winery. It was near Windsor, California, and only consisted of eighteen acres, but it was Zinfandel, a grape already popular among Italian immigrants due to its similarity to wines from their homeland.[75]

In 1886 Edoardo Seghesio left Dogliani, Italy, for America, to join his friend Pietro Rossi at Italian Swiss Colony. The same year, another wine market collapse occurred, reducing the price of grapes by 75 percent.[76] In its wake, Italian Swiss Colony could not survive solely as a vineyard company and, in 1887, built a winery and started making its own wine. In the right place at the right time, Edoardo Seghesio used his experience to become the head winemaker for Italian Swiss Colony.

In 1886 as well, Raffaello Petri, who had come from Tuscany, became tired of running a hotel in the North Beach section of San Francisco and decided to buy a vineyard in the Central Valley. He had made his money in the cigar business with Dante Forresti and he called his new enterprise the Petri Wine Company. It was a modest beginning for a business that would later buy Italian Swiss Colony, a winery in Lodi, and the Gambarelli & Davitto cellars in New York.[77] Under son Louis's stewardship, the Petri Wine Company by the late 1950s was selling nearly 25 percent of all the wine consumed in the United States. Petri later organized the Allied Grape Growers cooperative, which, in turn, ultimately bought the Petri Wine Company.[78]

In 1887 Louis M. Martini was born in Petra Ligure, Italy. The date was not marked in the annals wine history at that time, but Martini's contributions to the American wine industry are among its most significant, especially his founding of one of what many writers have called the four most important wineries in America following Repeal.

Also in 1887, the Rossini Winery was built in California. Souverain would later be born in the Rossini building, and the Rossini Winery itself would be turned into the Burgess Cellars, started by Ted Riboni and originally employing Samuele Sebastiani as winemaker.

In 1888 the Bisceglia brothers founded their winery. They began producing wine in San Jose and later managed wineries in St. Helena and Fresno.[79] The empire they began would later grow to produce eight million gallons of wine per year and be successful enough to afford to buy the historic Greystone Cellars in Napa.

In 1889 the Bernardo Winery opened near San Diego, based on a Spanish land grant. Originally, five Italian businessmen had a stake in it, but in 1918 it was purchased by Ferrari-Lanza. During Prohibition, it would be bought by the Rizzo family, survive Prohibition by making sacramental wine, and then return to the production of table wines after Repeal.

Also in 1889, Batiste Previtale left Lombardy for the United States to find a job with sufficient income to bring over his family. As soon as his family joined him, he bought land in Amador County, toiled with his sons to clear the land, planted a fruit ranch, and later opened the Previtali Winery.[80]

Amador County had become a magnet for Italian immigrants. John Bianchetti's family had settled there around 1850 and, upon his death in 1890, his widow and children turned the family farm into a vineyard to produce wine for their own use. Unfortunately, they chose the Mission grape, which was being overtaken by other varieties in the pursuit of fine wine. When Prohibition ended, they decided to enter the commercial wine market and they erected a winery building and planted new varietals. The business became the Bianchetti Brothers, which continued to produce wine for commercial sale into the 1960s.[81]

The Scatena brothers started the Santa Lucia Winery in 1890. It would later be called the Roma Winery and, after being sold several times (including to the wine-powerful Cella family), it would be bought by the Seghesios in 1949. It is still part of Seghesio vineyard holdings.

Victor Sioli opened his winery in 1892, but it was closed in 1919 due to Prohibition and was never reopened. And in 1893, Giuseppe Franzia came to the United States from Genoa. He worked in San Francisco to save money and established Franzia Winery in 1915. The family business later diversified and blossomed into an enterprise significant enough to be purchased by the Coca-Cola Company.

Also in 1893, Edoardo Seghesio married Angela Dionisia[82] Vasconi. Two years later, they bought their first grape ranch near Geyserville and named the area Chianti. It was in this vineyard that Edoardo planted a field blend of the grapes used to make Chianti in Tuscany. The vineyard was later ignored and fell into disrepair, but the vines stayed there and were rediscovered by Edoardo's descendants in the 1990s. The Seghesio family now makes a wine from the field blend called "Chianti Station."

The G. B. Vicini Winery was opened in Amador County in 1894. Antonio Forni bought the old Tychson property in 1895 and built the Lombarda Winery, after the Lombardy region from which he emigrated. Forni's winery went out of business during Prohibition and was sold to the Napa Cantina Winery in 1934. But Napa Cantina defaulted on the purchase and the property was returned to Forni's widow, who then sold it to the Ahern family. The Aherns reopened it in 1940 as Freemark Abbey Winery.[83]

In 1896 Giovanni Foppiano purchased Riverside Farm. Foppiano's business was originally designed to sell wine directly to the restaurants in San Francisco, especially the North Beach district that had become a favorite neighborhood for Italian Americans and Italian immigrants. In later years, the Foppiano family would achieve national success and switch their marketing to include retail outlets throughout the United States.

The Piccardo Winery was opened in 1895. Wine is no longer made there, but the building remains: now it is a restaurant on North Main Street in Jackson, California.

By this time, Samuele Sebastiani had emigrated to the United States, landing in New York, where he planned to stay only long enough to earn the money to move to California. When he did move west, he farmed vegetables before moving into the wine business. Around this time, in 1899, twelve-year-old Louis M. Martini was working with his father selling fish in the streets of San Francisco.

Vittorio Sattui was involved, in 1899, in a dispute with a landlord who wanted to raise the rent. Vittorio moved his business to a building in San Francisco's Mission District. It

Samuele Sebastiani, (1874-1944) founder of Sebastiani vineyards.

was formerly known as the Rottanzi Winery; Vittorio renamed it V. Sattui Wine Company. The building was renovated, allowing room for wine production in the cellar, retail space on the main floor, and apartments for the family and boarders on the upper floors.

Events on the international front were having an impact on the wine industry in California during this period. The Foran Act of 1885 had been passed by the United States Congress to make the *padrone* system illegal. This informal system had served for decades to bring Italian immigrants to America and give them jobs in exchange for a portion of their wages on arrival.[84]

Since the jobs were often in poor conditions paying sometimes less than subsistence wages, such arrangements were a tremendous burden on Italians whose only plan was to make money to send home to their families. The fact that the contracts were signed in Italy and could not be enforced in America further penalized the immigrants who wanted to hold the *padrone* responsible for the commitments they had made. While the Foran Act made this system illegal, an informal version of it persisted; the Italian government finally got involved by opening the Italian Bureau at Ellis Island in the 1890s to attempt to eradicate the *padrone* system.[85] The Foran Act was designed to protect the interests of the immigrants, but its passage evidenced a changing attitude toward the legions of foreigners entering America: it opened an era in which immigrant quotas and stiffer entry standards would be used to slow the tide of people seeking entry to the United States.

The scourge of phylloxera continued in Europe throughout the 1890s (though a solution appeared to be on the horizon). There was also a cholera epidemic in Italy that killed 55,000 people in the southern part of the country alone. This was followed by a severe economic depression in Italy.[86] Next, in 1891, a severe drought in Italy lasted for several years and reduced the fruit crop so much that wine production was cut in half. This crop failure led to riots in Sicily, Puglia, and Calabria[87] and fueled the desire of many to leave for America.

The original V. Sattui Winery, located in the Mission District of San Francisco.

During this period, America suffered troubles in the vineyard too. Pierce's Disease struck the area around southern California, wiping out many long-established vineyards there. The south was the birthplace of the California wine industry and the area where many Italians had settled to set up their business. The agricultural destruction

caused by Pierce's Disease ruined many of their vineyards and drove more winemakers north.

And so the Great Migration had begun. From the three thousand Italians who had entered the United States in 1870, the yearly arrivals were up to fifty-two thousand by 1890 and would rise to nearly three hundred thousand per year early in the next century.[88] The influx of immigrants to New York was so great at this point that Ellis Island was built to accommodate the thousands of daily arrivals. Ellis Island opened its gates January 1, 1892; one of its first interpreters was an Italian American who would later become famous in the fertile land of politics: Fiorello la Guardia.[89]

New Beginnings
for the Wine Industry

"Everybody works.
There's poverty...
Our people have to emigrate."

— PASCAL D'ANGELO
Abruzzi, Italia, 1910

"In America there was
the chance for change."

— A. BARTLETT GIAMATTI
President, Yale University

The mid-nineteenth century had its share of pioneers who explored the western United States, mapped its lands, and prospected for gold in the hills of California. These pioneers changed the frontier, sometimes at the expense of the Native Americans who had inhabited that area for hundreds of years, but their hard work and vision brought the western half of the continent into the European sphere of influence that now dominated the United States.

By 1880 the Gold Rush had nearly ended, and the settlements born in its wake had solidified into permanent towns and cities. New pioneers now took the stage: the owners of the businesses that had arisen to supply the multitudes brought west in the sudden population explosion. The time between 1880 and 1920 was one of industrial expansion, cultural definition, and economic development. It was also a time during which the American wine industry began an expansion of such self-sustaining force that it could only be halted by an act of Congress.

Also by 1880, the population of the American west had changed dramatically. For hundreds of years, Native American inhabitants had shared the stage with Mexicans who had continued to moved north, but both groups were subsequently overwhelmed by other cultures in the short thirty-year period following the discovery of gold in Coloma. From 1848 until 1880 hundreds of thousands of Germans, English, French, Irish, Italians, and a hodge-podge of mixed-heritage whites from the American melting pot surged across the country, squeezing out the Mexicans and Native Americans. The railroads and construction projects made work for the Chinese now arriving on the California shores, giving this new potpourri its first Far Eastern element.

The wine world had also changed. There were many vineyards planted to the Criolla, or Mission, grape by the Spanish missionaries and, at least in the beginning of the Gold Rush, these vineyards continued to satisfy the raw materials for wine for the new population. Slowly, the acres of rolling hills in northern California were being turned over to another, higher brand of viticulture. Throughout the late 1800s, scores of new varieties were planted, and the style of wine produced from these new grapes changed the image of American wine.

Another player stepped in about this time, whose presence would be felt with increasing intensity in the years to come: the Temperance Movement. Perhaps it was the vestiges of Puritanism inflamed by the apparently loose morals of America's new frontier towns, perhaps it was the beginning of an era in which Americans believed that social ills should be fought with public tools, but the end of the nineteenth century witnessed the dawning of the Prohibition Movement that would soon sweep onto the political stage.[90] The movement even spawned a political party: in 1869 the National Prohibition Party was founded in California, in the heart of America's vineyards. The movement would not succeed in its ultimate goal for another fifty years, but the seeds were planted for a weed that would nearly strangle the new American wine industry.

An interesting phenomenon was at work during this period. Many Italians who had fled dire conditions in Italy for the greener pastures of the New World were returning home. Some writers have attributed this to the Italians' particularly strong attachment to place and family, arguing that—try as they might—the Italians just couldn't shake the bonds that held them to their Mediterranean homeland. Others have said that economic woes in the United States in the late 1800s convinced Italian immigrants to change their minds and go home.[91]

In any case, nearly half of the Italian immigrants to reach America between 1870 and 1920 returned home.[92] This did not alter or reduce the impact Italian immigrants would have on American culture; in fact, the cycle of immigrants returning to Italy strengthened the ties between the two countries by establishing a conduit for tall tales about the New World[93] that would keep Italian interest in immigration strong through the 1920s.[94]

Starting in about 1880, the number of Italians arriving in the American west reached such a level that their economic and cultural impact could be felt, and wineries run by Italian Americans began to increase. In fact, the decade beginning in 1880 was a golden time for Italian Americans in the American wine business.

That year Andrea Sbarbaro formed the Italian Swiss Colony wine enterprise near Asti, California.[95] He had been in the United States since he was a young boy and he fashioned a dream of operating one of America's biggest wine businesses in one of America's biggest states. His Italian Swiss Colony included a plan to invest the Italian workers in the company. While the company was a huge success, the investment plan failed because of the workers' resistance to having an automatic deduction from a paycheck that was sorely needed for day-to-day survival. In spite of this setback, Italian Swiss Colony would go on to become a driving force in the national wine industry and continue operating into the late 1900s.

Also in 1880, Joseph Vezzetti brought Nebbiolo cuttings from northern Italy to Colorado. It was somewhat more unusual for Italians to bring grapevines with them than it was for French and German settlers. As much as they loved the fruit of the vine, most of the Italians coming to the United States were poor and they didn't anticipate having the capital to start a vineyard in the United States upon arrival. But some did, and it was the memory of Vezzetti tending his vines that inspired his grandson, John Balagna, to start the Balagna Winery in New Mexico in 1986.

The same year, the Frei brothers built a winery to produce wine from local Dry Creek Valley grapes. They started with a wooden winery, which was enlarged several times over the next twenty years. Their wines became quite well known and drew great respect for their quality. The property was later bought by Ernest and Julio Gallo in one of their early attempts to convert the Gallo operation and reputation from jugs to premium wines.

By 1880, Giuseppe and Pietro Simi were ready to move into the wine industry. For the previous two years, they had learned to make wine from Sonoma County grapes in their small house in San Francisco and were convinced by the popularity of their wines that they should invest themselves further in winemaking. In 1880, they bought property in Healdsburg, and Giuseppe moved there to manage the winemaking while Pietro stayed in San Francisco to continue the vegetable business, a good way to hedge their bet.

In the early 1880s, the Bay View Vineyard was planted in Napa County by Felix Borreo. Borreo planted many varieties of grapes, including some Italian varieties. The ethnic angle must have worked because the land would many years later be purchased by Walt Disney's family as the basis of the Silverado Vineyards, where they would cultivate Sangiovese, of undisputed Italian heritage, and

Isabelle Simi reins on her family's porch as the sixteen year old May Queen. For years she reigned over the Simi tasting room.

Zinfandel, said by some to hail from Puglia in southern Italy.

As discussed in the previous chapter, the aftermath of the Civil War, coupled with the labor-saving industrialization of America, created an imbalance in the workforce. There were more workers than there were jobs and unemployment became a problem across the country.[96] In areas like California, the Chinese filled many of the undesirable jobs, since they were willing to work difficult and sometimes dangerous jobs for low pay. But with the poor economy of the 1870s and 1880s, jobs were so scarce that whites competed with the Chinese for whatever work there was. While the Oriental Exclusion Act was passed in 1882 to deal with this, the name of the act made it obvious that the concern with foreigners didn't extend to Europeans.[97] This made it possible for more Italians to find jobs in California[98] and thereby establish themselves enough to later pursue dreams of owning their own farms.

Meanwhile, events in Italy were still conspiring to convince the people to leave and find safety and opportunity in the United States. The phylloxera root louse was endemic by this time in Italy. The pest had destroyed vineyards throughout France and other parts of northern Europe and, by the 1880s, it was attacking the vineyards in southern part of the continent.[99] It would eventually decimate the vineyards of Italy and practically sever the connection the Italian vignerons had to their soil. Many fled across the Atlantic, with most settling in the eastern United States in conditions totally unlike the pastoral settings they had left behind.[100] But some found their way to the Pacific Coast and were rewarded for their perseverance with a wine-friendly climate.

To make matters worse, in 1897 there was a severe crop failure in Italy that, combined with the oppressive policies of the north-led Italian national government, caused riots in Sicily, Puglia, and Calabria.[101] The riots were quelled, but the southerners were now certain that their life would be better in the United States.

The Italians who came to America were also discovering that the better-educated immigrants were getting ahead the fastest. Since so many of the recent arrivals were from the undereducated southern regions, this was a very important lesson. So they sent instructions home to those they left behind to have the children attend the church schools and get an education before the father came back to Italy to fetch them for the move to America.[102]

Back in America, it was obvious by the 1880s that California had become the most significant wine-producing region of the United

States. Despite the East Coast's attempts throughout the previous two hundred years, West Coast winemakers were able to produce fine wines with little or no effort, and so attention shifted away from experiments in the East and focused on California.

The California grape market went into a tailspin in 1886 due to the grape glut from too many farms, and the result was a market collapse.[103] For a couple years, grapes were hard to sell at a profit, and some vineyard companies went under. As noted above, the megagiant Italian Swiss Colony built its first winery to convert all those grapes into wine, and thereby "preserve" their fruit.[104] The great company that started with the goal of raising grapes and employing Italian immigrants had now switched from the grape business to the wine business.[105]

In 1887 Guiseppe and Louisa Martinelli came to America, and would later found the family winery that still operates under the Martinelli name.

By 1888 Anthony Caminetti was involved in politics. His first elected position was to the California state assembly, followed by election to the state senate, and his political career was capped by his election to the United States Congress in 1890. In spite of his affiliation with vineyards in California, he is known not for wine-related legislation but for the Caminetti Act, which dealt with re-opening of hydraulic placer mines. In 1888 he and State Senator Boggs founded a wine syndicate, with Boggs buying forty acres and planting fifty thousand cuttings there. Caminetti sent samples of his wines to the University of California for tasting and analysis, and they received positive comments. Unfortunately, Caminetti and Boggs's wine enterprise faded from view after that.[106]

The wine industry had begun to settle its roots in California. The next step was for small wineries to spawn big wineries, and for small vineyard owners to expand their holdings to satisfy the new demand of the growing western population. Italian immigrants led the way. In 1888, the Bisceglia brothers winery, discussed in the previous chapter, had expanded to a capacity of eight million gallons, Andrew Mattei was buying land near Fresno that gave him control of over twelve hundred acres of vineyards,[107] and Italian Swiss Colony continued to grow and employ more and more Italian immigrants in its plants.

Meanwhile, in the south, Giovanni Piuma followed the path so many Italians had taken and settled in southern California to start his winery near Los Angeles. Unfortunately, he undertook this in 1889, when Pierce's Disease was killing the vineyards in the south.

When the 1890s started, California already had its aristocracy of wine. Much of the best vineyard land was contained within about one hundred estates owned by wealthy families who were committed to producing fine wine.[108] They were successful in their enterprise, and the development of the California wine industry during that period owes much to the dedication of these wealthy families, but their access to great sums of money kept the wine-producing power concentrated in the hands of a few families.

Since approximately one-third of Italians in the United States were employed in unskilled work around the 1890s, there were few Italian immigrants with the financial clout to buy the preferred parcels of vineyard land. In one of the delicious ironies of history, though, the Italians were forced to buy "undesirable" land on the slopes, rather than the acres on the valley floor that were easier to farm.[109] In time, all would realize that truly extraordinary wines are produced from grapes grown on the hills.

In 1890 the Sutter family opened the new Sutter Home Winery on Howell Mountain. It was later moved to Napa and was taken over by the Trinchero family. In 1892 Pietro Biale was born in Santa Giustina, Italy. He would eventually emigrate and purchase a vineyard that would later be run by his son, Aldo, with a winery named after his grandson, Robert.

The decade of the 1890s had its share of problems for California vintners. Pierce's Disease was now at the height of its destructive power in southern California, while phylloxera was peaking in northern California.[110] Morale among winery owners was especially low, because no one knew how to deal with these menaces that were wiping out their vineyards.[111] Many vintners gave up. A great industrial depression was beginning to grip America, and it reduced the demand for the fine wines that were now coming out of the western states. And, as if things weren't already bad enough, the Anti-Saloon League was formed in Ohio in 1893, targeting what its members perceived as the moral corruption attributed to the establishments that served liquor.

In the midst of this growing anti-alcohol sentiment, it's interesting to note that the author of the Eighteenth Amendment, Senator Morris Sheppard, commented that he was fighting the monopoly enjoyed by the distillers and brewers, not individual consumption. He said, "I am fighting the liquor trade. I am not in any sense aiming to prevent the personal use of alcoholic beverages."[112] While he authored the Eighteenth Amendment to the U.S. Constitution, which led to the prohibition of production and sale of wine, the sentiment evident in the statment above lived on through the exception provided by the Volstead Act (which implemented Prohibition) that allowed home winemakers to continue their own, limited, production of wine.

In 1894 the California Wine Makers' Corporation was founded by Pietro Rossi and Andrea Sbarboro. The CWMC was run by the growers who were unhappy with the market power imposed on them by the California Wine Association, which was controlled by the merchants. After five years of close competition, the CWMC fizzled and dropped from the scene, yielding victory to the CWA.[113]

Secondo Guasti had such success with the winery he opened in 1894 that his dream was within reach: to form the Italian Vineyard Company on the scheme of a grand company town, which he named Guasti.[114] He sold shares to other Italians[115] and grew grapes for distribution throughout the country.

As the century was drawing to a close, the Italians were beginning to choose the locales that best suited them. Many went to Amador County, and it is no surprise today that Italian grape varieties enjoy

The gondolas of this locomotive, called the Italia, could be tipped sideways to slide the grapes directly into the crushers.

particular popularity there.[116] Many other Italians were moving to southern California and many went to Dry Creek Valley. The latter area appears to have been a particular favorite of the Italians, perhaps in part because the green hills and late fog that blankets the valley on many mornings reminds one of Tuscany.

In 1896 Giovanni "John" Foppiano bought the Riverside Winery and founded the Foppiano family business. With his son, Louis, John built a business providing wine to the restaurants in North Beach. As John was quoted as saying: "I see so many of my countrymen arrive in this beautiful community every year. They want good wine, like they had at home, in Italy. I want to make this wine for them."

The next year, James Frasinetti started making wine and delivering it in bulk to Sacramento by horse-drawn wagon. Like other Italian families, the Frasinetti family survived Prohibition by making sacramental wine and shipping grapes east to home winemakers.

Following continued incidents of violence against Italians in the southern United States, Father Pietro Bandini started, in 1898, to work to get Italians out of that region where they weren't welcome and to resettle them in the Midwest. The Italians who found themselves in Arkansas couldn't resist: they planted vines.[117] In fact, there are several wineries in the interior states that most likely stem from Father Bandini's efforts to find settlements for Italian immigrants in the American Midwest.

The Great Migration was in full swing now, with 550,000 Italians entering the United States between 1880 to 1900, just a warm-up for the two million who would come between 1900 and 1910.[118] It was about this time that the old habit of returning to Italy began to fade. Many of the couples that came to the United States built their families in America and the children quickly developed an attachment to the land of their birth. Upon repeated trips back to Italy, many children pressured their parents to bring them back to the United States to stay.[119] By the 1920s most of the Italian families arriving in the United States planned to make it their new home.[120]

In 1898 John Battista Cella and his brother Lorenzo arrived in the United States from Bardi in northern Italy. They worked in New York until they could build up their own grocery business, then turned that into a wine business using land they bought near Lodi, Manteca, and Healdsburg in California. Lorenzo stayed in New York to take care of sales in the east, and John Battista Cella ran the western operation.

In 1899 Louis M. Martini and his father, Agostino, came to America, and worked together selling fish to the people of San Francisco.[121] They started making wine in 1906 in their Bay View district home in San Francisco, but the vintage was spoiled. Louis returned to Italy, determined to learn to make wine, and came back later to salvage the winemaking process he and his father had started. Ultimately, Louis M. Martini would use this passion to build a wine business considered one of the best in the nation during the years following Prohibition.

Anthony Cappello and the Caparone family also came in 1899. Cappello would later change his name to Tony Hat (*cappello* is Italian for "hat") and found the Bella Napoli Winery, named after his beloved Naples. The Caparones stayed in Pennsylvania initially, where the father of the family worked in the coal mines. Dave Caparone, a third-generation Italian American, went to Paso Robles to start the Caparone Winery in 1979, basing it on Italian varietals, beginning with Nebbiolo in 1979, Sangiovese in 1982, then Aglianico in 1989.

There were so many Italian-run wineries by 1900 that, as a group, they could influence the style of wine being produced. Since the tastes of wine drinkers at the turn of the century were not as demanding nor as sophisticated as they are today, the preference was for hardy, drinkable wines, usually sold by the barrel, and vinified for the mass market. Italian viticulture had always given a priority to the down-to-earth, easy-to-drink style of wine, and the Italian immigrants who were settling into American vineyards continued the pattern. As a consequence, many of the Italian American wineries did a brisk business appealing to the tastes of the masses of commoners with simple tastes. Italian-style wines were, according to Novitski, "the foundation stones on which the mass market for California wines was eventually built."[122] It was better than the plonk produced from the Mission grape, though only a hint of the greatness to be produced in the late 1900s.

By 1900 Antonio Forni was ready to build on the land he bought in Napa. He erected the Lombarda Winery, a beautiful hand-hewn stone structure with a capacity of three hundred gallons, which was completed in 1906. It closed during Prohibition and, except for some occasional use, it remained so until investors bought it in 1940 and renamed it Freemark Abbey.

Antonio Nonini left northern Italy for America in 1900 and planted vines on his property in California. But it was his son, Reno, who showed enough interest in winemaking to start the A. Nonini Winery.

The vineyards planted by Reno reflect his Italian heritage and are rich in Barbera, Alicante Bouschet, and Palomino grapes.

Michele Teldeschi and his son, Lorenzo, left Casabasciana in 1900 in search of a better life in America. For the next two generations, the Teldeschi family farmed vineyard land for larger wineries, selling them grapes and bulk wine. During that time, they followed the old Italian habit of traveling back and forth to Italy, a habit that trapped Lorenzo there during World War I. It wasn't until Michele's great grandson, Dan, got involved that a winery was built with the Teldeschi name on it.

The century turned and the Great Migration was still picking up steam. There were nearly three hundred thousand Italians entering the United States every year. The Little Italys of New York, Philadelphia, and Baltimore were absorbing most of the new arrivals, and Italian language newspapers became common. Unfortunately, this was also a grim period in America's economy, and many of the immigrants were arriving without a job nor any hope of finding one. The situation was exacerbated by the high proportion of immigrants arriving without marketable skills.[123] Anti-Italian sentiment was born during this time, a change from the respect paid to the earlier, more educated and more skilled workers to the attitude that the low education and economic level of the immigrants now arriving were bringing down the economy. There would later be several congressional edicts designed to slow the tide of emigration, and they targeted certain countries, like Italy.

By now several Italian wineries had grown into huge operations, for example, Italian Swiss Colony and the Italian Vineyard Company. Wineries like Foppiano, Seghesio, Sebastiani, and Simi, which had been founded at the end of the nineteenth century, had now grown into substantial businesses, and there was a brisk trade in wine and grapes. The sudden prominence of Italian immigrants in the wine industry was evident. "With few exceptions," says Florence in *A Noble Heritage*, "the new wineries at the beginning of the twentieth century were built by Italian families."[124]

The buildup of wineries and vineyards with Italian roots had a hidden significance for the American wine industry. In too few years, the industry would be threatened with a virtual death sentence when Prohibition was adopted. Fortunately, a large share of the total California vineyard land was now in the hands of Italians. Many of the Italian families lacked the finances to switch careers, so they were bound to their vineyards. But they also kept faith with their heritage and every year insisted that repeal was around the corner. The faith of this group, and the fact that they controlled so many acres of vineyard land, combined to preserve the grape growing business in California during Prohibition.

During the first decade of the new century, a number of Italian wineries got their start. Antonio Perelli-Minetti came from Barletta, Italy, to start a vineyard in the New World. In 1902 Rafael Martini bought the 1881 Twin Fir Winery and renamed it the R. Martini Winery. Rafael Martini had come to America from Lucca, settling in Sonoma County to farm vegetables like brussel sprouts, artichokes, and broccoli, for which he opened a distribution center in San Francisco. The family winery was eventually sold, but Elmo Martini later teamed up with Enrico Prati and bought it back, naming the new business Martini & Prati Winery.

Also in 1902, the Seghesio family was ready to build its own winery. Production was primitive at first and the patriarch, Edoardo, crushed all the grapes with a hand-crank crusher. He made the wine in bulk and sold it to Italian Swiss Colony, as did many others at the time.

Samuele Sebastiani was working as the winemaker at Burgess Winery, hired by Ted Riboni. In 1903 Burgess Winery was gutted by a

Workers unloading grapes from horse-drawn wagon at Martini and Prati Winery, circa 1905.

great fire and Samuele found himself without a job. This nudged him closer to setting off on his own, and by 1904, he had bought the old Milani Winery near Sonoma. This was the first use of the name Sebastiani Winery.

In the midst of all this growth, tragedy struck a leading Italian family: In 1904 Giuseppe and Pietro Simi both died. They had built a wine empire in a very short time and were in the midst of the Italian wave that was sweeping California. Their business drifted for a while, but then Giuseppe's daughter, Isabelle, took over. She was only fourteen at the time, but her inspired leadership over the next few decades brought the business through and she steered the Simi Winery for nearly seventy years.

In the same year that the Simi brothers died, John Canata built the Canata Winery in Dry Creek Valley. He planted vineyards to mostly red grape varieties, particularly Zinfandel, and farmed the land and made wine for over twenty years. Later, this property would become the Pedroncelli family winery.

The Conradi Winery was also built in 1904. Many years later, the building would be reconditioned and renamed the Robert Keenan Winery.

The same year, Frank Giannini came from Elba and started making wine for himself and his friends. He was among the first to experiment with the Italian Aleatico grape in California, although there are now many vineyards planted to it, including a fine example made by the Trinchero family's Montevina Vineyards. Giannini named the winery Tulare and continued making wine for many years. Upon his death, Tulare passed through several owners until the Sierra Wine Corporation added it to its other winery holdings in 1963.[125]

In 1905 Julius Pagani built the Kenwood Winery and planted an eclectic mixture of grapes to make bulk wine.[126] This is the same property that was later replanted to premium grapes and established a reputation for fine wines in the 1970s. By 1905 Giuseppe Migliavacca's winery in Napa was making two hundred thousand gallons of wine a year, but his earlier reputation for good wine seemed to have slipped, and Sullivan reported that his winery made the process look industrial, that his wine was "fairly ordinary stuff."[127]

As noted above, Florence describes the early twentieth century as the Italian Period and names wineries such as Capelli, Lencione, Passalacqua, DelCarlo, Gaddini, Sarzotti, Stefani, and Pieroni, which were opened during this time.[128] Unfortunately, very little is known about these small operations, perhaps a fitting subject for more research into journals and local newspapers of the time.

1906 was a dramatic time for everyone in California, as the Great San Francisco Earthquake rattled homes and psyches. John Cadenasso had arrived just three days before the earthquake rumbled through the Bay Area, and he was in San Francisco at the time. The event didn't send him running from California, though. Cadenasso was broke when he arrived in America, like so many other Italian immigrants, but he was selling wine for another producer within one week of his arrival. He later started his own winery in Fairfield and it is still operated today by his grandchildren.

The Migliavacca Winery was badly damaged by the earthquake, but the Italian Swiss Colony warehouse fared better.[129] The Italians who populated Telegraph Hill in San Francisco had a unique solution for the fires that were raging through their neighborhood: they brought up the wine barrels from their cellars and soaked blankets in the wine to protect their houses.[130]

The year had its successes, too. Antonio Forni, who had taken over the Tychson property in 1895, was just finishing the construction of his Lombarda Winery in 1906. It had a capacity of three hundred thousand gallons (the winery would close during Prohibition). Agostino and Louis Martini were still selling fish in San Francisco, but now they were also making wine in a small shed behind their house.

Cesare Mondavi left Sassafarento and came to America. He would spend the next several years in Minnesota, working in the iron mines there, until he was enlisted by the Italian Club of Minnesota in 1918 to make an excursion to California to find grapes for them to make their own wine.[131] He liked California so much he moved his family there in 1923.

It was also in 1906 that the Sutter Home Winery was moved from Howell Mountain to St. Helena, its present location. In the same year, Frank and Rose Leonetti left Calabria to come to America. They settled in Washington and, initially, got California grapes shipped north for them to make wine for their own consumption. Eventually, they planted their own vineyards, and with grandson Gary Figgins's winemaking skills, they would make what is arguably the best Merlot in the country.

In 1907 more Italian immigrants came to America than in any other year. While that represented a fortunate circumstance for Italians, it was also the watershed year for American prejudice against Italian immigrants. The sheer numbers of the immigrants, many of which were uneducated, unskilled laborers, alarmed the already established American society and the former discrimination against Chinese people was now directed against Italians. In the next few years, legislation would be passed to limit the influx of Italians, setting overall quotas as well as new conditions related to health and job opportunities. By 1917 the United States would require a literacy test of all immigrants[132] and, in 1924, the Immigration Act was passed, setting quotas for admission and restricting Italian immigration more than immigration from other countries.[133]

In the same year, America experienced another severe economic depression, leaving many subsistence-level workers with no prospects for income. During this time, the steady rise of Italian immigrants was reversed and old habits were reborn as many recent arrivals from Italy went back home.[134]

In the next few years, however, Italians would continue to strengthen their hold on vineyards and winery properties throughout California. In 1908, Bruno Filice from Cosenza, Italy, built the San Martin Winery,[135] and Emilio Guglielmo came from Piedmont and opened his winery in Morgan Hill, California. Julius Nervo came from Venice and, in 1908, opened the Venezia Winery in Alexander Valley, changing the name to the Nervo Winery several years later. It would later be owned by the Trione family of Geyser Peak Vineyard and be renamed Venezia, for the line of premium wines being produced by the Triones.

In 1908 Samuele Sebastiani was ready to expand his vineyard holdings, so he leased a ranch originally owned by Mariano Vallejo near Sonoma. Franciscan missionaries had planted grapevines in this vineyard in 1825. By 1909 Samuele owned the Vallejo vineyard outright. This formed the basis for the Sebastiani wine empire that was to follow.

The Italian immigrants had now achieved enough success that they were becoming prominent members of society in California. Andrea Sbarbaro used his success and fame to establish the California Grape Protective Association to fight the continuing calls for Prohibition.[136] He used proceeds from Italian Swiss Colony to build a church shaped like a wine barrel, calling it the El Carmelo Chapel.

Just after 1900, Giuseppe "Joe" Gallo left Italy bound for Venezuela. After a while he left there and traveled to Philadelphia, then west to Oakland. He considered the benefits of getting into the wine business, and bought land in Modesto and planted his vineyards. Joe married

Assunta "Susie" Bianco in 1908 and their children Ernest and Julio were born in 1909 and 1910, respectively.[137]

In 1908 Guiseppe Migliavacca retired. His wine empire in Napa was still going strong, but he turned it over to others due to failing health. He died in 1911. But his success was emblematic of the new Italian presence in Napa: The area that had largely been settled by Germans now had an Italian population that, in number, rivaled that of the city's founders.[138]

Gustave Niebaum, founder of Inglenook, died in 1908. He played no part in the build-up of the Italian dynasty, but his winery did: Years later, Francis Ford Coppola would buy it and begin the lengthy process of rejoining the historic property that was Inglenook.

Also in 1908, twenty-eight years after it was built, the Augustus Quitzow winery was renamed Geyser Peak. Like the Niebaum operation, Geyser Peak had not yet seen its Italian connection, but it had also not yet seen the tremendous success it would enjoy while in the hands of the Trione family.

August Sebastiani— winemaker and ornithologist 1913 to 1980— Proprietor 1944/1980.

The year 1910 marked the first time that a refrigerated train car was used to ship grapes from California to Chicago. Grapes had already been shipped in great tonnage to cities in the Midwest and the East, but they suffered terrific spoilage. The demand had grown, and fears of a future prohibition were already inciting interest in home production of wine, so that now the amount of grapes shipped out of California was on the rise. Refrigerated cars were a logical and very beneficial solution.

By 1910 the Foppiano Winery was already fifteen years old, but John Foppiano was concerned that the business was too risky and a possible threat to his family's security. He considered selling the winery and might have gone through with it, but his son, Louis A. Foppiano, secretly borrowed money from his wife's family to buy the winery and keep it in the family. When he discovered what his son was doing, John was incensed, but the deed was done. The same year, Louis A. celebrated the birth of his first son, Louis J. Foppiano.

Vincenzo Graziano had arrived from Asti in the late 1800s, working first in the coal mines of Pennsylvania. Later, he moved to California and found work as a gardener, but in 1910, he bought land in Mendocino and started growing grapes. His grandson, Greg Graziano, started three wineries after 1970; they will be discussed later.

During the same year, the Ciocca Lombardi Winery Company bought Geyser Peak Winery to add to its other winery properties. The Crescini family arrived in 1910 from Asti and settled in Santa Cruz. They made two or three barrels of wine a year for their own consumption, but Rich Crescini, in the third generation, recalled learning winemaking from his grandparents when he started the Crescini Wine company. Also in 1910, Michele Teldeschi and his son, Lorenzo, planted another vineyard from which they could produce more bulk wines to sell to other wineries.

Edoardo Seghesio was enjoying the success of his long years of work. In 1910 he planted a vineyard that included Sangiovese cuttings from Italy and other grapes that appear in the standard Chianti. His planting was what is called a "field blend" by some, "promiscuous cultivation" by others; it essentially means that the vines were interplanted with no vineyard design to put each variety in specific blocks of land. This was the vineyard that Edoardo's descendants would later use to make a wine called "Chianti Station."

In 1911 the Uhlinger Vineyards and Winery in Amador County was bought by a partnership of Emelio D'Agostini, Giuseppe Gualtieri, and Antonio Pieroni.[139] Named the D'Agostini Winery, it continued to operate until 1989 when it was bought by the Sobon Estate.

Also in 1911, Alberto Rafanelli came to the United States from Tuscany. He and his wife were so proud to be in America that, when they found they were expecting a child, they were determined to name her America. As it turns out, the first child was a boy; so as not to waste a good idea, they named him Americo. Alberto started a small vineyard and winery in 1913 but, like many vintners, the squalls of Prohibition swept them out of business in 1919. Fortunately, Alberto's wife refused to believe that her beloved adopted country would tolerate the foolishness of Prohibition for long, so she insisted that the vineyards not be uprooted. Years later, their grandson used these vineyards to resume the family business.

The Prohibition forces were strong during these years, but split on their preferred approach to banning alcohol. While some worked to get Congress to pass a consitutional amendment making production illegal, other temperance groups concentrated on the local scene. In 1914, Virginia passed statewide prohibition but, more significantly, the Wylie Local Option law was adopted in 1912 in California, giving each community the right to decide for itself whether to allow the production and sale of alcohol. This law was repeated in many areas of the state and served as a spark to ignite the national prohibition referendum.

Demetrio Papagni was the third generation of winemakers in his family in Bari when he left in 1912 to settle in California. In the next few years, he planted vineyards and built a healthy business in selling grapes and juice to home winemakers in California and the East Coast.

By 1910, Batiste Previtali had managed to bring over his entire family from Lombardy and he could concentrate on starting a wine business. In 1912, the Previtale Winery was built in Amador County, but it is no longer in operation.

August Sebastiani was born in 1913, and Reno Nonini was born in 1914. The first would inherit the sizable Sebastiani wine empire while the second would become the driving force behind a smaller family winery in Fresno that concentrates on Italian grape varieties. Also during this period, in keeping with the wine world's emerging interest in Italian grapes, Camillo Colombano planted Barbera vines as the basis of his wine production. Later, his vineyard would be bought by the Pedrizzetti family from the Piedmont region of Italy and incorporated into their Pedrizzetti Winery.

The Italian emigration patterns continued, though slowing a bit from the first few years of the century. Giovanni Arciero came in 1914, from Santa Elia Fiumerapido near Rome. His family would arrive later and form the Arciero Winery in Paso Robles. Frank Pesenti left Bergamo in 1914 with his sister, Maria, to join Maria's husband, Pietro. Pietro had been working in Willow Creek, California, since 1910. Frank had no money and didn't understand English, but he knew how to work, so he joined Pietro in cutting trees and selling the lumber. Later, when he had earned enough money, he bought land and planted Zinfandel vines.

Costante Pastori had come from Lombardy around the turn of the century, bringing his family to America to start a better life. They settled in Geyserville, California, and opened the Pastori Winery in 1914, but closed it during Prohibition. Frank Pastori, Costante's son, reopened it in 1975.

Joe Cafaro's paternal and maternal grandparents left Adelfia-Canetto in southern Italy in 1914. The Cafaros made wine during Prohibition and, by Joe's reckoning, must have exceeded the limits allowed by the Volstead Act for household production of wine because Joe's grandfather kept barrels of the stuff hidden in the ground under the tomato plants. Although the Cafaros didn't continue the winemaking practice through the next few decades, Joe Cafaro revived it in the 1980s.

Giuseppe Franzia also started his winery during this period, but he enjoyed considerably greater success than did Pastori. The Franzia empire was built on cheap, bulk wines sold mostly in jugs. It was later sold to the Coca-Cola company, but the Franzia family kept on making wine, although they had sold the legal right to put their own name on the bottle. They now use the Bronco label.

In 1915 the Gabrielli family came from Capradosso, Italy, to America, settling in Pennsylvania. They made homemade wine from grapes shipped east from California, but it would be another two generations before a Gabrielli would own a commercial winery. In 1916, John Battista Cella bought Scatena Winery from Dante Forresti.[140]

In 1917 Lorenzo and Rena Nerelli purchased a vineyard on York Mountain and created Templeton Winery. Also in 1917, Santo Cambianica came to the United States and founded San Antonio Winery in Los Angeles.

With World War I threatening American freedom and lifestyle, Congress passed legislation, supportive of the war effort, that banned the use of foodstuffs in the production of alcohol. Wine and beer were exempt from this 1917 law. The war also cut off supplies of wine from Europe, which encouraged the domestic industry.[141] But the dark clouds of Prohibition were gathering. The movement was making political progress and swaying much of public opinion its way. The Sheppard Amendment was passed by Congress in 1917, approving national prohibition and sending it to the states for approval.

In the face of the impending disaster, Agostino and Angelica Martini, parents of Louis M. Martini, returned to Italy in 1918. The next year, Victor Sioli closed his winery, fearing the economic trouble that Prohibition would bring. Guiseppe Martinelli died at this time. The Seghesio family bought Italian Swiss Colony in 1919 for $127,500, though it is not clear whether it was bought on faith or sold in fear.

In 1919 the states ratified the Sheppard Amendment, approving Prohibition, and scheduling it to begin January 16, 1920.

Local maidens in Swiss peasant costumes celebrate the first rail shipment of wine from Asti at the end of Prohibition.

Prohibition, Repeal, and Recovery

"Perhaps it is true that the
Italians were more loyal
to the vine than any other
group during the trying times
of Prohibition, so that the
names that first came forth
on the morning of Repeal
were those of the faithful Italians."

— THOMAS PINNEY
A History of Wine in America

Prohibition started small, with each jurisdiction reaching the point of outlawing alcohol at its own pace. So-called "local option laws" allowing even small jurisdictions to outlaw liquor began in California but spread to other states like a brush fire. This approach overcame the inertia of some state legislatures and established dry pockets across the United States. Like watching the slow spread of an epidemic across a simulated map of the country, the pockets expanded and then began to reach each other's boundaries, until the spreading mania covered the nation. When the districts adopting local option showed their strength, it became obvious that the Temperance Movement had secured a political foothold that it would not lose—at least for the time being.

The Prohibitionists moved on to Congress and pushed through the Volstead Act. The act's author, Senator Morris Sheppard, has been quoted in the previous chapter as saying that he did not intend to prevent the personal use of alcoholic beverages.[142] But in the fervor to deny the saloonkeepers their "sinful" living of peddling intoxicating liquors, Prohibition also made it illegal for an average person to buy wine for his own consumption with meals around the family table.

Following passage, the Prohibition amendment was sent to the states for review. It was ratified in 1919 and the country began the countdown to dryness. Prohibition was due to go into effect one minute after midnight, January 16, 1920. The country was ringing in its impending dry state during the waning hours of January 15 in a not-entirely dry state, with massive parties throughout the country aiming to drink up as much of the legal liquor as they could before the stroke of midnight.

Few went down without a fight. Just before Prohibition took effect, H. L. Mencken, the famous editor and columnist, ordered a custom-built cellar to be designed, built, and stocked, and protected by a warning that read: "This vault is protected by a device releasing chlorine!"[143]

In 1926, during the height of Prohibition, federal agents forced Foppiano Vineyards to empty their tanks into a nearby creek.

Citizens across the country were in a panic to purchase all the liquor they could afford before it was beyond the reach of legal means.

The speakeasies and backroom bars were yet to come; in 1920, regardless, consumer demand for alcoholic beverages legally dried up. From the beginning, Prohibition encouraged enterprising, daring people to step slightly over the line to "procure" precious wines and spirits for paying customers,[144] but the traditional, neighborhood bar was a thing of the past. The Anti-Saloon League got what it wanted: It attacked the pocketbooks of the saloonkeepers and put them out of business. In the process, the league also denied the entire national population access to wine.

Soon after the bars closed, the distributors closed, and the producers were not far behind. Many wineries decided to pull up their vineyards and plant more legally acceptable crops. It was a purely practical choice to farm vegetables and fruit, as winemakers tried to enter a different market.

It should be remembered that the American wine industry was still in its infancy, with only about eighty years of serious commercial production, or less if one counts from 1850 when the population boom in western America gave the nascent industry a financial chance to succeed. The European vineyards had been farmed for a thousand years, while the upstart American industry was being killed by its own people in an act of infanticide before it had even emerged from its formative years.

But many of the vineyardists planted their feet as firmly in the ground as they planted their vines. They refused to give in to the foolishness that America called Prohibition—and many of these stalwarts were Italian. Perhaps it was due to their legacy of thousands of years of wine production, perhaps it was the incorporation of wine into the very fabric of their culture, including their religion, or perhaps it was simple economics: Many of the Italians came to America with too little money to jump from one enterprise to another. Having chosen wine production and invested their hard-earned money in the purchase of vineyard land, they had to stick it out because they had nowhere else to go.

David Rafanelli, the present-day owner/manager of A. Rafanelli Winery, described how his grandmother had insisted that the vineyards be nurtured and maintained, even though Prohibition had forced them to cease selling wine. She was certain that reason would defeat ignorance and that wine production would once again be legal. The Rafanelli family benefited from her advice and were well positioned at Repeal to jump back into the production of wine from grapes farmed from their own vineyards.

The Rafanelli family's story would be repeated many times over, but nearly always among Italian American families, and much less often among those of non-Italian roots. In fact, the American wine industry would have had to start all over again when Repeal rescued it in 1933, without any legacy or established vineyards, were it not for two significant pressures at work during Prohibition: the Italian Americans' insistence that the vineyards remain planted and the rise of a strong home winemaking cult that increased the demand for grapes beyond anything that California had ever known.

It happened this way: Vineyard land had increased in California throughout the fifty years leading up to 1920, so California appeared to have the most to lose from the idiocy of the Eighteenth Amendment. But there was a loophole in the Volstead Act that allowed individuals and families to continue to make wine, albeit only for home use and only in limited quantities. This loophole made it possible to continue producing wine in America during Prohibition, as long as it was made by and for individual households, and as long as no house produced more than two hundred gallons per year.[145]

The vineyardists could not make wine to sell, but there was no limit on the grapes they could sell. The Italian families turned from wine-makers to fruit dealers to get a foothold in a business cycle that was just beginning to take off. Nearly every vineyard that stayed in business between 1920 and 1933 sold grapes to home winemakers,[146] but the Italians developed a client base beyond any that could be imagined by the other vineyardists. It was not uncommon for a single family vineyard to have contacts as far away as Philadelphia, Baltimore, St. Louis, Chicago, and, of course, New York, with its immigrant population to buy the sometimes-bumper crop of grapes harvested during these years of Prohibition. In fact, private citizens soon discovered what the ancients knew, i.e., that production of at least palatable wine was not an impossible task. An interesting thing resulted: The acreage planted to grapes in California increased. It increased so much that there was more tonnage of grapes available during Prohibition than before and even more than would be available for several years after Prohibition had ended.[147]

Italian immigrants and Italian Americans moved quickly to exploit this new market. Some of the most prominent members in the current

American wine market got their start by selling grapes to the home winemakers during this period. Ellen Hawkes's list of the Italian families from the Central Valley alone who survived Prohibition by supplying grapes to home winemakers includes Franzia, Gallo, Turano, Panteleo, Ursini, DeLuca, and others.[148]

Buying grapes for his home-winemaking friends is what got Cesare Mondavi into the wine business during Prohibition. The Mondavi family decided to settle in the temperate climate of California to delve more deeply into the grape market. The move proved providential: They bought the Sunny St. Helena Winery, which had been built by Gioachino "Jack" Riorda in 1934, and later, the Charles Krug Winery, and started on the road to wine history. Their enterprise would later give birth to other wineries, including the now famous Robert Mondavi Winery.

The Foppiano Wine Company sold grapes to home winemakers in San Francisco and cities in the East. To supplement this income, Louis A. Foppiano returned to the farming occupation that his father had started before the Foppiano Vineyards were planted, while he continued growing grapes for sale to home winemakers. Upon the death of Louis A. Foppiano in 1924, the Foppiano grape business faltered, but it would come back later.

Ernest Gallo opened a market for his father's vineyards by developing good relations with regular customers in Chicago and cities to the east. He made many trips each autumn to these faraway places to sell the tons of grapes grown on his father's land and, in so doing, developed a keen sense of what the demand for wine was across the map of the United States. He would transfer that knowledge from the grape market to the wine market in building a family wine empire bigger than any other in the world.

Louis M. Martini founded the L. M. Martini Grape Products Company in 1922 on the notion of selling to home winemakers.[149] He also resorted to selling a concentrate for home winemakers, called "Forbidden Fruit."[150] Starting a business to provide the raw products to make wine during Prohibition was a daunting prospect, but Martini's hard work paid off in 1933 when his vineyard land put him far ahead of others in the race to return to legal wine production.

Like Martini, Giovanni Pedroncelli got into the grape business when wine was illegal. He bought the Canata Winery in 1927, trying to take advantage of the home-winemaking market that by then was a booming industry. The Canata vineyards were planted mostly to Zinfandel during those years, a hearty grape that was very popular among the amateur winemakers' set, since it produced a style of wine preferred by Italian Americans and it held up well during cross-country shipping. Pedroncelli therefore kept Zinfandel as the focus of his planting, a step that would later yield additional success when the Pedroncelli-labeled Zinfandel wine became a nation-wide bestseller.

The Pesenti family planted their vineyard in 1923 and sold their product the same way. Frank Pesenti had recently brought his bride, Caterina, from Italy, and he wanted to start farming. With Prohibition in effect, the Zinfandel the Pesentis grew was sold on the home-wine-making market. Their winery was bonded in 1934, and has remained a family business every since.

Angelo Petri, of the Petri Wine Company, used the financial clout gained in the wine industry to get involved in other businesses during Prohibition, but his partner, Dante Forresti, kept the vineyards going by selling to home winemakers. After Repeal, Angelo Petri returned to the family business, which grew to be one of the largest bulk wine producers in the nation under the leadership of Louis Petri, Angelo's son.

As soon as wine sales became illegal, more Italian families caught on to the amateur-winemaking market. Samuele Sebastiani resorted to shipping grapes in refrigerated cars to the East Coast to supply the home-winemaking boom, a step others would soon follow. In 1924 he got a permit to make fortified medicinal wines, which put to use the brandy distillery he had started before Prohibition. In 1926 Sebastiani

Concentrates, jelly, and medicinal wine were all products of the California wine industry during prohibition.

ATTENTION GRAPE GROWERS!

IF you do not care to gamble with weather and market conditions, we offer you an excellent opportunity to dispose of your grape crop locally.

During the vintage season, we intend to sell fresh grapes as well as fresh grape juice to householders. We will crush a large tonnage of white and black grapes at our new and modern plant, located on the corner of Front and Green streets, within a very short distance of all the team tracks of all the main railroad lines of San Francisco.

We are in the market to buy an unlimited tonnage of juice grapes of all varieties. COMMERCIAL CONDITION OF GRAPES, WITH ENOUGH SUGAR CONTENTS IS ALL WE EXPECT FROM YOU. NO OTHER RED TAPE. Advise us your tonnage and varieties. We have sufficient picking boxes to take care of 200 tons of grapes daily if necessary. Let us make you a proposition!

We have a large supply of No. 1 Oak barrels on sale which we can ship anywhere.

You are cordially invited to visit our plant at any time.

GOLDEN GATE GRAPE & JUICE Co.

We solicit grapes on consignment
Boxes furnished on request.

Office and Plant:
S. W. Corner Front and Green
San Francisco, Calif.
Garfield 5638

DISTRIBUTORS OF
GRAPE AND OTHER FRUIT JUICES

The New Product of FRUIT INDUSTRIES, Ltd.

Order here
VINE-GLO
THE PURE JUICE OF CALIFORNIA WINE GRAPES
FOR HOME USE ONLY

Tear Off and Mail to

FRUIT INDUSTRIES, LTD.
85 Second Street, San Francisco, California
I am interested in VINE-GLO. Please have your representative call on me.

purchased the Woodbridge Winery, partly because it had a great supply of port and sherry on hand that Samuele was permitted to sell. He also quickly switched his attention to shipping grapes eastward, convinced that the immigrant-rich population of cities in New York and New Jersey would be the wine industry's salvation during Prohibition.

The new market also spawned inventive promotional schemes. Some slyly provided the steps to make the taboo beverage. For example, Antonio Pirelli-Minetti made a grape syrup with a label that said: "When diluted, do not store in a warm place because it will ferment, which is against the law."[151] Some grape growers produced "bricks" of grape concentrate that carried the warning: "Do not add sugar or water, or the product might ferment into wine after sixty days."[152] A product called "Vine-Glo" was introduced by Fruit Industries; it was canned grape concentrate that could travel well, and it provided grape juice to home winemakers in remote parts of the country.[153]

Enrico D'Agostini sold grapes to home winemakers,[154] the beginning of the D'Agostini family wine business that lasted until 1989, when it was purchased by Sobon Estate.

In 1924 Gaspare Indelicato bought a dairy farm with his brother-in-law, Sebastiano Luppino, but the next year he planted vineyards and entered the home-winemaking market. Later, that vineyard served as the starting point for Delicato Vineyards, which is still run by the Indelicato family to this day.

The Frasinetti family sold their grapes to eastern home winemakers, but supplemented their income by making altar wine, an industry popular among the Catholic Italians. Repeal gave the Frasinetti family business a chance to expand, which it did, and is now run by the third generation of Frasinettis. In the 1990s, the Frasinetti family added oak cooperage and stainless steel tanks to update their process, but the winery still produces wines at friendly prices.

Demetrio Papagni planted a vineyard in Madera, California, in 1920, and had a healthy business selling grapes to home winemakers in California and the East Coast. This Prohibition-era business gave a jumpstart to Angelo Papagni, Demetrio's son, who decided after Repeal that fine table wines were the new wave.

Adolph Parducci bought a vineyard in Mendocino County in 1921, to make sacramental wine and sell grapes and grape juice to home winemakers throughout the country.[155] But he also took advantage of the insecurity among other commercial winemakers during the dark days of Prohibition and was able to procure significant winemaking equipment at fire-sale prices: all to build a base for the resumption of winemaking at the repeal he thought was inevitable.

In 1917, before Prohibition was ratified, four thousand train carloads of grapes were shipped east. In 1919, before commercial production was even made illegal, this figure had jumped to 9,300 carloads of grapes, and quantity quickly rose.[156] Shipping methods were more primitive in the 1920s than they are now and refrigerated cars were preferred, but by no means common. A great many shipments of grapes arrived "in red ink," a phrase that, according to some sources, was coined in reference to the grape-stained boxes, whose contents had begun to ferment in the inhospitable conditions of warm transport. Grapes arriving in that condition were often considered a loss, and the phrase survives in today's jargon to refer to any venture that loses money.

During all this, the Italian American families were looking for any business ideas that would help sustain them until Prohibition was repealed. In addition to selling grapes through various outlets, wineries switched to making medicinal and sacramental wine, categories of wine that stayed legal during Prohibition. Many sold the grapes for table consumption, though wine grapes are not well suited for this use.

While the grape business was booming, the political environment was a bust for incoming Italian immigrants. In 1921 a new American immigration policy reduced immigration of Italians by 80 percent,[157] and, in 1924, the U.S. National Origins Act was passed, which set up restrictive immigration quotas limiting Italian immigrants entering the U.S. to six thousand per year. The same law allowed more immigrants from England and northern European countries.[158] Medical barriers to entry also were used, included barring anyone with trauchoma and other diseases. Trauchoma was likely caused by the unsanitary water system that prevailed at the time in southern Italy (see Chapter 2).

This was a difficult time for Italy-bound Italians, too. In their homeland, the economy was going sour and many Italian peasants felt an urgent need to emigrate. They had spent the last fifty years traveling back and forth to the New World, hoping to make enough money in America to return to their beloved Italy and raise their families, but conditions continued to deteriorate, which made planning the future increasingly difficult.[159]

Many decided reluctantly to make one last journey to America—a one-way journey—hoping to squeeze in under the newly tightened quota system before the doors to the New World slammed shut. In doing so, they would have to abandon the land their ancestors had cherished since Roman days and journey to another country that, by all accounts, didn't seem happy to receive them. Older Italians knew that their offspring would have to adapt to the New World in order to assimilate. Many of the ideas engendered during this adaptation process would run counter to the religious and cultural principles their forefathers had embraced for centuries. But America still seemed to be the land of opportunity and the peasant population was willing to make this dramatic move during difficult times to ensure a brighter future for their children.

Meanwhile, Prohibition had become the law of the land in the United States. Although some vineyard owners prospered, as described above, some suffered from the restrictions, never making the jump to other markets, which was necessary for survival. In 1919 Victor Sioli closed the winery he had worked since 1892, either concluding that Prohibition would not relent, or simply possessing too little capital to survive the years of dryness.

In 1921 V. Sattui Winery also closed, facing the realities of Prohibition. Vittorio Sattui's grandson would rescue the family's dream and reopen V. Sattui Winery in 1975, while Victor Sioli's winery never restarted after Prohibition.

In 1926 grape cultivation ceased at Charles Krug Winery following the death of Bismark Bruck. The fine physical plant of this historic winery would be used by various groups during the coming years, but would remain largely without serious occupants until Cesare Mondavi bought it in 1943.

As if the death of wineries was not enough, Prohibition also witnessed the death in 1927 of Secondo Guasti. His Italian Vineyard Company had spawned a town named Guasti, and his plan to employ new Italian immigrants had worked, providing an occupation for many who enjoyed the relative familiarity of working for an Italian in an Italian vineyard, and living in a town modeled after an Italian community. The company was still going strong, though its future seemed considerably less certain with the onset of Prohibition.

Throughout this era, there was still a lot of wine being made. Some of it was made legally by families intent on supplying their own needs, and some was made to satisfy the legitimate needs for medicinal and sacramental wines. Since these two categories of wine were legal, the joke going around at the time was that Prohibition made a lot of people either sick or religious.

But a lot of the Prohibition-era wine was produced by those who dared to ignore the new law and make wine to sell under the table. There are many familiar stories of bootleg whiskey, and wine was not too pure to be swept up in the illegal trade. The stories include famous names like Al Capone and Lucky Luciano (many of them not so strangely Italian-sounding names), but infamous Italians were not the only ones involved in the illegal production of wine.

On the other hand, the sudden explosion in home winemaking far exceeded the potential of sacramental and medicinal wine production, and it created business opportunities that held the interest of those who wanted a legitimate outlet, luring more into the fold. Daring these difficult times were people like Mario and John Trinchero, who came from Asti, Italy, to the United States in 1923. They heralded from a family that had been in the wine business in Italy for six generations, and they wanted to do the same in the New World. The Trincheros moved to California and later bought the Sutter Home Winery in 1947.

In 1922 Giovanni Filippi and his son, Joseph, left Schio, Italy, for America. Giovanni had come to America once before, in 1904, when he emigrated here to work as a mason for Secondo Guasti's Italian Vineyard Company. But in 1922 Giovanni and Joseph settled in southern California, like many Italians, and started out growing grapes and citrus fruits. After Repeal, they turned their business to wine grapes. The company was originally called the G. Filippi Ranch, but the family changed the name to the J. Filippi Wine Company when it entered the commercial wine business. It continues to be a major producer of wine in southern California, with various labels and numerous types of wine being produced under the Filippi family auspices.

In 1923 Camillo Colombano founded a winery in Morgan Hill, California, planting the Italian varietal Barbera. Too little is known about the winery's operation to understand whether it produced legal or illegal wine, or sacramental or medicinal wine. The Camillo Colombano Winery was, however, sold to John Pedrizzetti in 1945.

Emilio Guglielmo had been in the United States since 1908, but it was in 1925, when the country was dry, that he started making wine in the basement. Planning for the end of Prohibition, Emilio and his wife, Emilia, started buying up vineyard land in the Santa Clara Valley near Morgan Hill. With Repeal, the business turned commercial but stayed in the family.

Greystone Cellars, the famous stone winery on what is now Route 29 in Napa, had been owned by several investment groups. In 1925, the Bisceglia family bought it, a good investment since, in 1931, during a time when the country was rethinking its stance on legal wine, they were able to sell it to Central California Wineries.

In 1926 Anselmo Conrotto built a gravity-flow winery in Santa Clara County, taking a lesson from the winemakers from the 1880s who popularized the design. That type of winery depended on the flow of gravity to feed the winemaking process, bringing grapes in to the crusher at the top of the winery built back into the hillside, and flowing downward through the several steps of vinification. Modern-day wineries continue to be designed with gravity as a major partner in the process.

Also in 1926, Domenico Galleano bought Estaban Cantu's ranch. He would work the property without selling any wine until 1933, when he established the Galleano Winery, which is still operated by the family.

In 1928 Vincent Rizzo bought the Bernardo Winery from Lanza-Ferrara. Since Prohibition was still in effect, he couldn't immediately launch into commercial production of wine, so he made a living selling sacramental wine and selling fresh grape juice to home winemakers. When the law allowed, the Bernardo Winery switched back to table-wine production.

All the wineries started during Prohibition were listed as such on official records, although they were not permitted to make wine other than for sacramental or medicinal purposes. Many still made wine for their own family, and did so legally, even if such a process was a terrific underuse of winery equipment and facilities. No doubt many of these wineries continued to make wine in very large quantities, storing it beyond government view or selling it so quickly that the government could not find it. A common story about the beginnings of the Gallo wine empire relates that Joe Gallo woke up the family many nights while digging huge trenches with his earthmoving equipment. He supposedly then lined these trenches with concrete walls to create gigantic underground wine-storage vaults.[160]

The Olivetto Winery in Healdsburg, California, had been owned by the Franceschini and Lorenzini families. One of the first gravity-fed wineries in the region, it fell on hard times during Prohibition. Rachele Passalacqua, whose husband Frank owned a winery that perished in a fire along with their home, bought the Olivetto Winery and, following

Repeal, turned it into a success. By then it was renamed the Sonoma County Cellars and provided sufficient economic power that Rachele passed it on to her children upon her death. Today, the winery is still in use, leased to the E. & J. Gallo Company.

Whatever the Prohibition-era enterprises of these vineyards and wineries, the Italian immigrant families dug in their heels and insisted on keeping their vines in the ground for the repeal that they always saw just on the horizon. In 1933 they were finally rewarded for their patience, and their family businesses were rewarded for the vineyards that had been nurtured during these troubling years.

The stranglehold the Temperance Movement had on Congress was beginning to loosen. Serious thought was now being given to repealing the Volstead Act, and the Federal Government was already lifting some of the restrictions and ignoring others. In August 1929, four years before Prohibition would officially end, the Commissioner of Prohibition in Washington, D.C., sent a letter to his field administrators instructing them to disregard the portion of the Volstead Act that related to production and storage of grape juice.[161] By 1928 there was a new push to redefine "intoxicating beverage" to permit the production of beer and wine. On April 7, 1933, Congress agreed and legalized wine and beer production.[162]

Ernest and Julio Gallo sample their wine in 1955.

On December 5, 1933, Utah became the final state to ratify the Twenty-first Amendment, ringing in Repeal. The Great Experiment was over less than fourteen years after it had begun. And the country celebrated in fine style. The joy over Repeal was so generally felt that Eleanor Roosevelt chose the opportunity to celebrate by serving American wines in the White House.[163] Italian immigrants, too, shared in the overall joy of the time, knowing then that their faith in the ultimate sanity of America had been well placed.

An interesting fact about Repeal is that many wine drinkers had been bitten by the winemaking bug during the years of Prohibition and continued to make their own wine after Repeal. The European immigrants were especially inclined to do so, not only to ensure their supply and have wine that mimicked that from their homeland, but sometimes also to avoid paying state taxes on the newly legal commercial wine.[164]

The building of wineries could now begin in earnest. In fact, several were bonded or became otherwise official on the very day Prohibition ended, like the Bargetto Winery, which wasted no time and proclaimed itself ready for winemaking on December 5, 1933. The Bargetto family produced a Cabernet Sauvignon that same year.

In 1933 Joe and Susie Gallo died of gunshot wounds in an event officially labeled a murder-suicide. As a result, Ernest and Julio Gallo inherited their parents' vineyards, a necessary possession to be granted a bond for a winery in those days. Ernest and Julio Gallo got the bond and used a converted warehouse in Modesto as their winery. They started making wine as soon as the new law allowed. In those days, they made bulk wine and sold much of it to East Coast distributors through contacts developed during the years of selling grapes. In the decades to follow, the Gallo wine empire would grow almost without limits, setting up successful markets in every corner of North America and selling wine throughout the world. In the 1990s, the Gallos were producing estate-bottled wines of distinction, using the massive fortunes from the bulk-wine business to finance a sudden, spectacular entry in the fine-wine market.

In the time right after Repeal, Charlie Barbera and Tony Paterno started the Pacific Wine Company. Their purpose was to buy and bottle bulk wine, then label it and sell it to retailers.[165] Luigi Banchero's winery, closed by Prohibition, was reopened by his son, Louis, in 1933. The winery stayed in family hands until closing again in 1942.

When Prohibition ended, Louis J. Foppiano set out to rebuild the family wine business. In 1937 he tore down the old winery and built a new one and started bottling wines under the Foppiano label. By 1946 the family business had rebounded sufficiently to allow for the purchase of more vineyard land.

When Repeal arrived in 1933, Louis M. Martini was also ready to resume winemaking operations. In 1934 he bought the Eccleston farm in St. Helena and moved his family there to stay.[166] There he built the Louis M. Martini Winery and devoted it to the production of dry table wines. In 1938 he added to his vineyard land by buying the Mt. Pisgah Vineyard in Sonoma County.[167] It had been planted in the 1880s by Samuel Goldstein. Martini renamed it the Monte Rosso vineyard. By 1940, when many wineries were still bottling generic wines in jugs, Martini was making and marketing varietally based wines. In a 1941 Treasury Department report, a reference was made to Martini's "W. Zinfandel,"[168] perhaps the earliest reference to the white wine made from the red grape, Zinfandel. It was a style of wine that would later be popularized by the Trincheros at Sutter Home and serve an important role in converting the huge soda-pop segment of American culture into a wine-drinking society; first, with a little sweetness and later, with dryer wine.

Louis M. Martini had also learned important lessons while studying winemaking in Italy. His professor stressed the necessity of using the best grapes and the best equipment, and employing new technologies whenever they were available. Martini employed that philosophy when he built his winemaking facilities following Prohibition, including refrigeration and insulation to control the temperatures of fermentation and of the storage vessels. In doing so, he led the way for Americans viniculturists looking for the "right" way to make wine. Lapsley reports that even Treasury Department inspectors were impressed. According to Lapsley, "Until the 1960s and the start of the 'wine boom,' the Martini Winery remained the most technically advanced winery in the [Napa] Valley."[169]

Martini was also busy in extracurricular activities. While he was restarting the family business, he also founded the Napa Valley Vintners Association[170] and cofounded the Wine Institute.[171] Throughout the 1940s, Martini used the base he had established with the L. M. Martini Grape Products Company to build his wine empire. And an empire it was. During the war years and for many years afterward, Louis M. Martini's winery continued to produce prodigious amounts of wine, and Martini was celebrated as a master winemaker (and businessman), receiving accolades for his award-winning wines. In 1940 he introduced a line of varietally labeled, vintage-dated wines and became an overnight sensation.[172] Martini's accomplishments presaged another, greater era for Italian Americans, an era in which families like Mondavi, Sebastiani, and Gallo would all but rule the American wine industry.

Louis Stralla arrived in Napa in 1933. He bought the Charles Krug Winery from Charles Moffitt, but only after convincing Moffitt to let Stralla move in without paying any money up front. The winery was not generating any income; Moffitt figured this was a way to get something out of it, so he agreed. Stralla called his new enterprise the Napa Wine Company, enlisted John Cella of the Roma Winery in the business, and produced four hundred thousand gallons of wine from various sources the first year. Later, Stralla would buy the Covick Winery in Oakville and, in 1940, move his operation from Krug to Oakville. He sold the bulk wine production to the Roma Wine Company in 1945, but held onto the Charles Krug Winery for the time being.[173]

John Garetto built a winery in Napa in 1933. Although the winery no longer carries his name, the building and operation he constructed are now part of Bouchaine Vineyards.[174] The same year, Domenico Galleano converted the Estaban ranch into the Galleano Winery.

The Bartolucci brothers had been grape growers throughout Prohibition, but switched to making wine soon after Repeal. They built a winery in Oakville, naming it the Oakville Winery, but then gave up the business in 1938.[175] Louis Bartolucci reopened the facility in 1942, installed modern equipment, and made a good business of selling bulk wine, mostly to Petri Wine Company. By 1943, his success came to the attention of Andrea Gusmano and other investors, who then formed a partnership with Bartolucci to produce and market their own wines from what was by then called the Oakville Winery. The Oakville Winery fell on hard times due to a convergence of factors: the collapse of the wine market in 1947, and the arrest and conviction of one of Bartolucci's partners. But a reorganization of the business, along with a short crop in 1949, increased the value of Oakville Winery's bulk wine product, and Bartolucci was back in the black.

Cesare Mondavi moved from the business of selling grapes to the business of selling wine. He did so at first by buying the Acampo

Winery soon after Repeal,[176] and then taking advantage of the seller's market in 1943[177] to sell it to the Gibson Wine Company for a handsome profit. He used the money earned to finance his purchase of the Charles Krug Winery[178] from James Moffitt.[179] Cesare's son, Robert, had pushed for the family to buy the abandoned Charles Krug Winery, recognizing it as a landmark in California wine, and saw it as a jumping-off point for a family dynasty. Robert was right, as will be seen later in this book, but not until great family troubles took their toll.

The Dry Creek Valley had developed into a haven for Italian immigrants. Many of them had started wineries before Prohibition and some had set up vineyard or winery operations during Prohibition. Since there were so many Italians in the Dry Creek area, though, it should come as no surprise that the area also had a large number of wineries prepared for instant startup at Repeal. Among them were Canata (called Pedroncelli by then), Pieroni, DelCarlo, and Oneto. Pieroni and DelCarlo survived Prohibition but couldn't make it through the Depression.[180]

In 1934 John Gemello wanted to make Italian-style wines, so he founded the Gemello Winery. He stuck to red wines, and passed on his methods to the following generations. In the same year, the Bella Napoli Winery was founded by Antonio Cappello. Cappello produced mostly jug wines, a path still chosen by his children, who now run the winery. The same year, Joseph Filippi used the vineyards he planted during Prohibition to start his family winery in Cucamonga in southern California, continuing a long tradition of Italians tilling vineyard land in southern California.

Also in 1934, Giovanni and Maria Cambiaso started the Cambiaso Winery near Healdsburg. The Cambiaso children took over in the 1940s, and replaced the Carignane that had been the favored grape with Cabernet Sauvignon, an up-and-coming European grape of distinction. The winery was later sold to a company from Thailand and the name was changed.

Gioachino "Jack" Riorda had emigrated from Bra, Italy, to the United States in 1911, but it wasn't until 1934 that he got seriously involved in the American wine industry. He moved to the Napa Valley in 1924 and, in 1934, built the Sunnyhill Winery, later the Sunny St. Helena Winery,[181] which would later be purchased by Cesare Mondavi. By 1939, the Sunny St. Helena Winery had proven to be a good investment and was so busy that Mondavi was forced to lease the Di Marco Winery in 1939 and the Gagetta Winery in 1941 to supplement the winery operation.[182] Joseph Gagetta had been the winemaker at Forni's Lombarda Winery, and took the Lombarda name when the Napa Cantina Winery bought the property. When he died soon afterward, his son, Dennis, restored the name to Joseph Gagetta Winery.[183]

After spending many years and most of his earnings to build the Seghesio family business into a position of prominence, Edoardo Seghesio died in 1934. He left the property and winery to his wife, Angela, who in turn gave it to their children in 1941.

In 1934, Miguel Carrari's son, Joe, was born. Miguelís father, Ferruccio Carrari, had moved the family to Argentina around the turn of the century, but he was killed in 1906, the same year Miguel was born, while working on the railroad. Subsequently raised in Italy, Miguel returned to Argentina in 1923, and then went on to California to work in the grape and wine business, including a stint from 1930 to 1933 with the Secondo Guasti wine empire. Miguel passed on his interest in wine to his son, Joe, who, by the time he was five years old, was already picking grapes for his father. After a short hitch in the military, Joe, too, tried farming in Argentina, and then returned to the United States to take up grape growing. Through the years, Joe Carrari worked for Winery Lake Vineyard and Paul Masson, but then planted his own vines near Los Alamos and called the land Carrari Vineyards. He does not make his own wine but has contracts with others to turn his grapes into wine, including one wine cheekily named "Dago Red."

Interest in commercial wine production was reawakening even in the east. In 1935 Joseph Della Monica founded Delmonico's in New York. His father had come from Italy during Prohibition, but the political climate at that time kept the family out of the wine business. But, after Repeal, Joseph made arrangements to buy grapes from other vineyards and start making and selling wine.

The vineyards Gaspare Indelicato and Sebastiano Luppino planted in the San Joaquin Valley were in trouble after Repeal because their business was one of selling grapes to home winemakers. To survive, they switched their production to winemaking, buying the basic equipment and settling into a hay barn. The Indelicato and Luppino families lived together in a small farmhouse while making their first vintage.

In 1936 Antonio Nonini founded the Nonini Winery at the urging of his son, Reno. The Nonini's vineyards were made up of Zinfandel,

Barbera, Alicante Bouschet, and Palomino grapes, typically Italian varieties making typically Italian-style wine.

In 1937 Italy Industries, the company owned by the Bagnani family, bought Geyser Peak Winery. They produced wines that were called the Redwood Empire Wines, but the Geyser Peak Winery was also sometimes referred to as the Bagnani Winery. Geyser Peak saw many owners through the years, and was later owned by the Henry Trione family.

Also in 1937, Emil Bandiera, who had come to the United States from Lucca around the turn of the century, founded the Bandiera Winery to produce jug wines. His goal was to make wine that was good, affordable, and able to be consumed by Americans with every meal. Although most of his wine was sold in barrels, it was made with the same philosophy.

Pietro and Christina Biale bought vineyard land in 1937 that their son, Aldo, and grandson, Robert, would use to later form the Robert Biale Vineyard. The Biale wines now include Zinfandel, Sangiovese, and Petite Sirah grapes.

As the 1930s were ending, the Italians were still buying up vineyard land and opening wineries. In 1938 Joe Rochioli, Sr., leased a vineyard in California that would later be farmed by his son and grandson. Originally, the Rochiolis built the business on selling the fruit, but later

The Golden Gate International Exposition, held in 1939 and 1940, showed the progress California wine growers had made since Prohibition.

they would turn their attention to winemaking.

Also that year, the Morello Cellar was built as a wine storage facility. In the 1970s the Bianchi family bought it to form the basis of the Villa Bianchi winery. The Bianchis modernized the winery and would later change the name of the operation to the Bianchi Vineyards and Winery. They also switched production from the generic wines sold in jugs to wines made from premium varietals.

The country had readjusted after Prohibition by the time 1940 rolled around. Many new wineries were being founded each year and the production of jug wines was beginning to show some signs of switching to premium varietals. Exiting Prohibition, Louis M. Martini Winery was considered one of the four best wineries in California, but during the 1940s, the list of top properties increased to eight, and all four wineries added to the prestigious club were Italian in origin: Ben Migliaccio's Napa Valley Grape Products (based on the purchase of the Fagiani Winery near Oakville), Mondavi's Charles Krug Winery, Bragno Wine Company (headed up by Frank Bragno), and Louis Bartolucci's bulk wine business in Oakville. Migliaccio had used several brand names, including B. Migliaccio Winery, Boncore Winery, Colombo, and Santarpia, but in 1944, he consolidated his brands under the Napa Valley Grape Products name.[184]

Bragno Wine Company was the Illinois distributor for Italian Swiss Colony wines, but when National Distributors' purchase of Italian Swiss Colony in 1943 stripped Bragno of its contract, it purchased of Larkmead Winery to enter the field as winemakers rather than distributors. Bragno tried to expand by buying the Riverbank Wine Company near Modesto, then the giant Alta Winery, but he decided against the deals, settling later for Larkmead. Unfortunately, Bragno did not pay back a loan from his partner: Larkmead fell into Harry Blum's hands, and Bragno resigned from the company.[185]

In 1949 the Seghesio family ended the mourning period following the death of family patriarch, Edoardo Seghesio, by buying the Alta Vineyard Company to build upon the base established by Edoardo.

Antonio Forni's Lombarda Winery had been used for a brief period by Walter Martini just after Repeal, but in 1940, it was sold and renamed the Freemark Abbey.[186] The Valley of the Moon Winery was purchased by Enrico Parducci (no relation to the Parducci family of Parducci Wine Cellars), and Angela Seghesio turned over the family winery and vineyards to her children.

In 1942 Louis M. Martini was pulling out all the stops on his purchases of vineyard land to add to his current holdings. He added the La Loma vineyard and Stanley Ranch to the Monte Rosso vineyard he had purchased earlier. These vineyards would become a significant part of the new Martini production, providing quality fruit over the decades. In 1943, he formed the Napa Vintners Association. The charter members included Martini, Fred Abruzzini (Beringer's winemaker), Louie Stralla, Charles Forni, and the Mondavis.[187]

National Distillers grew in prominence during this period and, in 1942, it bought the two Italian Swiss Colony wineries in Asti and Clovis as well as the Roma Wine Company. These properties would continue to change hands over the years, as will be shown below.

Also in 1942, Pietro Biale died in an explosion in a rock quarry, but his wife, Christina, and their son, Aldo, kept the vineyard in the family.

Narciso Martini, the son of Rafael Martini, sold the R. Martini Winery to Hiram Walker in 1943. The sale was conditioned on the continued employment of Narciso's son, Elmo, as the winemaker. The deal didn't last long, since the Martini family bought it back from Hiram Walker seven years later.

Like the passing of Edoardo Seghesio, Samuele Sebastiani's death in 1944 made a deep impression on California wine. The Sebastiani family had established itself as a cornerstone of the wine industry, starting early, surviving Prohibition, and then quickly jumping back into wine production upon Repeal. And Samuele had established a trend for the family with his many generous contributions to the welfare of Sonoma. He built and operated a cannery in the hopes of putting as many people to work as possible. He paid for lighting in the streets of Sonoma, and then later paid for the streets to be paved. His death would be keenly felt, but the family carried on his dreams.

Also in 1944, the Roma Winery changed hands again, this time from the Domitilli and Massoni families to the Alta Vineyards Company. The Alta Vineyards Company later was bought by the Seghesio family and used to produce bulk wine.

Louis Petri ascended the ladder in his family business in 1944 to become president of the Petri Wine Company. He used his acquired power to purchase the Italian Swiss Colony operation, the Shewan-Jones winery in Lodi, and the Gambarelli & Davitto cellars in New York. The Petri empire continued to grow through the 1960s, when it was eclipsed by the new mega-winery operation, E. & J. Gallo. But during those decades, Louis Petri founded the Allied Grape Growers Association and United Vintners, both to support the interests of the Petri wine family. During the 1950s, Petri Wines regularly sold nearly 25 percent of all wine consumed in the United States.[188] Louis Petri's last, and perhaps most significant, purchase occurred in the 1960s, when he bought Inglenook, which he later sold to Heublein and which later came back into the control of an Italian American when Francis Ford Coppola bought the property.

In 1944 as well, the Cella family bought the old Rusconi Vineyard and used it as the beginning of the huge Cella Wine empire. After expanding the operation to twelve million gallons, the property was later sold to the Petri family's United Vintners, and then again to Heublein.

In 1945, John Pedrizzetti bought the Camillo Colombano Winery, which had been making Italian-style Barbera wines from its own vineyards since approximately 1913. Pedrizzetti used the facility to make bulk wine, and later passed on the business to his son, Ed, who has kept it in the family, raising his children to make wine just as his father raised him to do.

In 1946 the Mondavis sold their remaining interest in the Sunny St. Helena Winery to Martin Stelling, Jr., and concentrated on production at Charles Krug. That year, they made the first of their illustrious Vintage Selection Cabernets, a line of premium wines that established a reputation for quality in the days when few people believed quality wine was possible in California. It was a tribute to Cesare's dream, Robert's desire and foresight, and Peter's winemaking that this wine took hold and developed such recognition. It was also the first chapter in prestige wines to be made by that family.

Also that year, Frank and Mike Teldeschi bought a farm in Dry Creek Valley, planted vines, and started making their own wine. It was a return to their father's occupation and would return the family to winemaking that would last to the present day.

Giuseppe Giumarra had come from Sicily, worked in Toronto for a while, and then settled in Bakersfield, California. In 1946 he built a winery designed to make bulk dessert wines and concentrate. His brother, John, however, later convinced him to get involved in table wines. Although the Giumarra family still makes wine it sells in bulk to other wineries, it has latched onto a much more ambitious, and potentially more lucrative, business: the Giumarras own Snapple, an Arizona brand of soft drinks that are sweeping the nation.

Also in 1946, Conrad Viano converted some 1880s-vintage vineyards his father had bought and started the Conrad Viano Winery. The Viano family had come to America from Piedmont in the early twentieth century, staying for a few years in Alaska before settling in California. Since founding the Viano Winery, four generations of Vianos have worked at the family winery, two of whom studied enology at the University of California at Davis.

The Foppiano family was also busy in 1946. Things were going well enough in their wine business that they needed more vineyard land, so they purchased the Sotoyome Vineyard. And, like so many other Italian immigrants before him, Louis J. Foppiano got involved with community needs, founding the Sonoma County Wine Growers Association and, later, cofounding the California Wine Institute.

By now, the Italian involvement in American vineyards had become a tradition. Many GIs returning from the war in Europe brought back memories of the good, down-to-earth wines of Italy at a time when the Italian presence in American vineyards was solidifying. Americans in general were developing an affection for Italian wines during the 1940s that is still in place.

In 1947 Ernest and Julio Gallo formed a partnership with the Frei brothers in Dry Creek Valley that would mark the beginning of a new era. Today, the original Frei brothers facility has been expanded many times and is the source of some of E. & J. Gallo's best wines. It was from this property in 1982 that the Gallo family introduced the Wine Cellars of Ernest and Julio Gallo Cabernet Sauvignon, the first of a series of wines that would transform the image of Gallo from jug giant to fine wine producer.[189] Based on this new line, called Gallo Sonoma, the family of Ernest and Julio Gallo have positioned themselves for a run at the premium wine market

Elmo Martini, a third generation, Italian American winemaker, displayed his product proudly, in 1945.

at the dawn of the twenty-first century.

Mario and John Trinchero had been in the hotel business in New York since emigrating to the United States in the early 1920s. In 1947, they sold the business and moved to California. Although it is not clear whether their plans included farming, they soon bought the Sutter Home Winery and immediately starting upgrading its equipment and style of wine.

In 1949, the Seghesio family joined the list of those who had owned the Roma Winery. They bought it for seventy-five thousand dollars from the Alta Vineyards Company which, by most accounts, hadn't done much significant with the property in the four years it had owned it. The Seghesio plan was to add it to their other properties and use it as the source of their bulk wines.

Elmo Martini had stayed on as winemaker of the family winery when his father sold it to Hiram Walker in 1943. In 1950, he teamed up with Enrico Prati and bought the R. Martini Winery back from Hiram Walker, this time naming it the Martini and Prati Winery. As a salute to the past, Martini and Prati preserved much of the original equipment, which is now exhibited in the winery's museum, something of a window into the past of American winemaking for Martini and Prati visitors. Today, the winery invites its visitors to fill their jugs straight from the tanks, an age-old practice common in Europe but which has not been in general use in this country since Prohibition.

Also in 1950, a stonemason named Andrew Colaruotolo arrived from Gaeta, Italy, and settled in New York. He had learned to make wine in Italy, and kept up the custom when he arrived in this country. He originally planned just to make wine for himself, but when by 1974 his vineyard was yielding more than the two hundred gallons permitted for home consumption, he applied for a license to start selling wine. He called the new venture Casa Larga Vineyard. His planting of classic European vines like Cabernet Sauvignon, Pinot Noir, Chardonnay, and others proved that these grapes could be brought to fruition on America's East Coast, a proof that had eluded centuries of winemakers before him.

In 1952 August and Sylvia Sebastiani bought the remaining interest in the Sebastiani Winery still held by Samuele Sebastiani's widow. August believed in the profitability of good, earthy, no-nonsense wines, a philosophy that was continued after his death. But this philosophy set the stage for an historic split many years later, when his sons Sam and

Don would argue over the future of the family business and their mother would step in to decide which son would be victorious.

In 1959 Joe Rochioli, Jr., planted Sauvignon Blanc and Cabernet Sauvignon on land his father had bought in 1938 to farm fruit. Pinot Noir, Chardonnay, and Zinfandel were added later. His selection of the super-premium grapes has served him well, as the wines of the Rochioli Vineyards continue to get very high marks from every wine reviewer.

Cesare Mondavi died in 1959. He had left most of the wine empire he worked so hard to create to his wife, but he left a fair portion of it to his sons, Peter and Robert. They were still each responsible for their separate duties: Robert for sales and marketing and Peter for winemaking. But the brothers did not get along and there are many stories about the arguments they had about the future of the Mondavi family wine operation. One common tale alleges a conversation between the brothers in which Robert said he could sell as much wine as Peter could make, and Peter responded that he could make as much wine as Robert could sell. The brothers' dislike for each other's practices would finally reach a boiling point and create an event that would split the family and lead to the founding of one of the most famous wineries in American history.

In 1959 Leo and Evelyn Trentadue got tired of the encroaching subdivisions in the Santa Clara Valley, and they moved to Geyserville. They bought some land, including one parcel that had belonged to another Italian American family. They ended up with forty-two acres of vines and started making wine right away. Initially, they sold wine to Italian Swiss Colony but they later converted an old barn into a winery and started to produce the Trentadue wines.

In the next few years new generations of Italian Americans took over the reins of wineries their families had started many years before. Adolph Parducci passed control of the Parducci Winery to his sons. Jim and John Pedroncelli, Jr., assumed management of Pedroncelli Winery from their father, and Ed and Phyllis Pedrizzetti took control of Pedrizzetti Winery. The Martini family was still buying more land, as Louis P. Martini purchased the Los Vinedos del Rio vineyard and the first half of Las Amigas vineyard. He would later acquire the second half.

Angelo Rapazzini had come to the United States in 1929 from Varese, Italy, setting up a bakery in San Jose, California, for business. In 1961 his sons founded the Rapazzini Winery in Gilroy, California, where they now produce wines from Cabernet Sauvignon, Zinfandel,

Merlot, Chardonnay, Gewürztraminer, and other grapes, but the most interesting product is called Chateau de Garlic, a white wine infused with garlic that has the intense aroma and taste of a cooking wine.

During the 1960s many changes were made in the American wine industry. The University of California at Davis turned out skilled, highly trained winemakers who found work at wineries all over the world, but principally in California. Refrigeration and temperature control of vinification processes were common, as was the use of steel tanks. Italian American families were in the forefront of such technological changes. By the mid-1960s, the Charles Krug Winery had installed glass-lined steel tanks to prevent oxidation of the delicate white wines being produced. The Mondavis also installed a nitrogen system for filling the partially filled tanks, again to ward off spoilage of the wine. And the Louis M. Martini Winery continued its focus on clean, technically perfect wine production by upgrading its bottling line to fill bottles with carbon dioxide before corking.[190]

In 1964 Frank Arciero started Arciero Ranches, an alfalfa business, veering off the course originally set when he and his brother Phil had founded the family cement contracting business. But the alfalfa spread was an extension of the farming the Arcieros had done in Italy, and it would provide the financial backing for a wine venture the brothers would begin in 1983.

In 1964 Louis Petri's United Vintners bought Inglenook,[191] a fabulous estate with a significant portion of California wine history etched into

The Arciero Winery, situated on the Paso Robles estate, began as an alfalfa business in 1964 when Frank Arciero started Arciero Ranches.

its cellars.[192] In the years during which he had controlled the Petri Wine Company and later, as president of United Vintners, Louis Petri proved that he was a businessman who could make things happen.

In 1965 Robert Mondavi was convinced that he knew better how to make and sell wine, and he didn't care for Peter's winemaking style. Peter was convinced that his brother knew only marketing, and resented the constant interference from Robert in the winery. Finally, the feud became cataclysmic. Robert was voted out of an active role in the family business, and he left Charles Krug Winery. At the time, this was probably considered a serious blow to the future of Charles Krug and to whatever Robert might try to accomplish outside of the family wine business. As it turned out, Robert's freedom from the restrictions of the Mondavi history would be the seminal event in the transformation of California wine.

The wine tanker S.S. Angelo Petri, carried two-and-a-half million gallons of wine from California to Newark and Chicago for bottling in the early 1960s.

The Modern Era

"The Italians now seem to be almost synonymous with winemaking in America, especially in California."

— THOMAS PINNEY
A History of Wine in America

It is ironic that the commercial wine industry was liberated from Prohibition in 1933, exactly one hundred years after its first liberation in 1833 from the Mission program. But the irony does little to heal the wounds made by Prohibition. Instead of enjoying the fruits of a mature industry that has had 160 years to develop, early-twenty-first century America must be satisfied with one that is only seventy years old, still an infant by the world standards against which American wines are judged.

Many vines stayed in the ground and many vineyards survived intact through the Dark Ages between 1919 and 1933, but to blossom, an industry needs time to grow; it needs a vitality that comes with mature confidence and a careful blend of old methods and new blood. Prohibition cut off this time for growth, robbed the wine industry of its vitality and, even though some groups kept the old methods alive, it minimized the next generation's interest in studying winemaking and in making technological improvements.

Fortunately, some continuity was provided by the vintners who hung on until Repeal. And GIs returning from Europe after World War II brought back an interest in wine and were eager to buy the product that the born-again American wine industry began producing in the 1940s. The American economy enjoyed boom years in the 1950s and 1960s in nearly every sector, allowing most industries to thrive. The wine industry merely survived during those years, however, with little increase in the level of interest carried over from the bright days after the Armistice. As the 1960s were nearing a close, things began to change.

From 1969 to 1974 wine consumption in America rose 12 percent.[193] This increase could be attributed to several factors, but the principle factor was the coming of age of the Baby Boomers born in the 1940s and 1950s. They represented a bump in the demographic curve that had carried the American economy through each of their adolescent buying stages, so it should be expected that commodities like wine would rise in stature during a time in which the Baby Boomers were reaching young adulthood.

Wine columns began to appear in local journals and nationally syndicated newspapers. Food magazines became more popular, and wine-advice columns appeared in them. There were even some special-interest publications dedicated to wine that began during this period. In the 1970s Americans not only began to appreciate wine more, but also became more able to debate the merits of certain wines, a preoccupation that is indicative of a growing interest in the various levels of quality in wine.

This interest coincided with an age of technological advances in winemaking in this country. The University of California at Davis had been turning out graduates in enology (i.e, the science of winemaking) for years, but the industry needed twenty or thirty years of these graduates tinkering with the process before their ideas and innovations could begin to ferment. Some of the finest winemakers to work in American wineries in this century were just beginning to make their mark in the 1960s and 1970s, and people were sitting up and taking note.

One such interested person was Steven Spurrier, who was convinced that American wines could compete favorably with French wines—if the bottles were tasted blind. So he set out to prove his point. In 1976, Spurrier matched a selection of famous French wines with a selection of similarly notable, though decidedly less famous, American wines. There were ten reds and ten whites and the tasting was conducted blind using French judges at the Hotel Inter-Continental in Paris. American wines won both the red and white categories, and three of the top four white wines were subsequently revealed to be American. The wine world was stunned and, despite some stammering by devoted Francophiles, no explanation would suffice except that the American wines had reached a new level of quality.

With increased consumption, advances in technology, and exulting news on comparisons with French wines, the 1960s and 1970s were an exciting time for Americans interested in wine. So it should come as no surprise that a man as inspired as Robert Mondavi would step forward to seize the moment.

As discussed in the previous chapter, Robert disagreed with his brother about the way wine should be made and disagreed with the Mondavi approach to the future of the family business at Charles Krug Winery. Robert Mondavi was passionate about quality and determined to apply all the modern know-how to produce the finest, most consistently excellent wines possible. But he was more passionate and determined than he was persuasive because, in 1965, the Mondavi family had heard enough, and Robert was voted out of active membership in the Charles Krug Winery and removed from his position of control. The split created a personal rift between Robert and Peter that would continue unrepaired for nearly twenty years and started a bitter legal battle over Robert's right to profits from Charles Krug Winery. He eventually won a settlement that rewarded him handsomely for his contributions to the family business.

In 1965 Robert Mondavi set about starting his own winery, one he swore would be an example of his principles of good management, careful application of technology, and awareness of consumer desires. He opened it in 1966 and even his earliest bottlings won praise. As personally difficult as the schism with the family must have been for

Robert Mondavi, it launched him on a career that made him a cornerstone of the American wine industry, enabling him to set standards that American wineries still see as their most ambitious goals.

By the mid-1960s, there were nearly one hundred Italian American wineries in the United States. Many of these were survivors from Prohibition, some with histories that stretched back into the last century. Most of the wineries were small, local concerns, selling their wine through the tasting room, at local restaurants, or to a band of faithful fans spread across the country. Some of them, like Mondavi, Sebastiani, Leonetti, Louis M. Martini, Simi, Sutter Home, and Seghesio stood out as shining examples of the way exceptional wineries ought to be run. And the efforts of the Italian Americans throughout the decades at last began to pay dividends.

Like many of their counterparts throughout the country, Italian Americans now experimented with other approaches either to making better wine or making their product more appealing to the ultimate judge: the consumer. In 1963, Jim and John Pedroncelli, Jr., changed the approach that John, Sr., had chosen and started producing varietally based wines. It was a logical step for a family that had a commitment to producing varietally based wines from the sixty-year-old Canata vineyards. In 1966, they began producing vintage-dated wines.

In 1968 the Trincheros of Sutter Home Winery looked for better sources of fruit to enrich their wines and enhance their reputation. They settled on buying Zinfandel from Deaver Ranch, a premium property known for its densely structured fruit.

John Poole planted vineyards in Temecula, California, in 1969. It would be six more years before the operation went commercial but, when it did in 1977, he called it Mount

Isabelle Simi, in 1975, displayed her love of wine and her winning personality with an assortment of wacky buttons.

Palomar Winery. The winery would later add a line of wines called Castelletto, John's wife's maiden name, and the Mediterranean-style wines would be so successful that Mount Palomar would later add another line called Le Mediterrane. The winery has a fervid interest in Italian varietals, like Sangiovese and Cortese, but also tends French vines such as Chardonnay, Rousanne, Marsanne, and Sauvignon Blanc.

Wherever profitable businesses take root in America, corporate interests are not far behind. During the 1960s and 1970s, corporations showed a heightened interest in buying wineries because of the profits they generated, not because they had suddenly become enamored of wine. So many of the previously family-run wineries that had been dedicated to top-end wines were now becoming corporate behemoths dedicated to bottom-line profits.[194] The corporate takeover of American vineyard land was so ambitious that Sullivan stated, "By the late 1970s, the idea of a farm family buying Napa vineyard land was virtually unheard of."[195]

Some Italian American wineries were recognized for their potential and targeted by investors interested in buying a winemaking property. The 1898 Rossi Winery was owned by Leon Brendel who, in 1964, sold it to Joe Heitz.[196] Heitz then took advantage of Grignolino, Barbera, and Zinfandel plantings to raise the market impact of the property.[197] Heitz's reputation for fine wines goes far beyond this early investment, but the Rossi property formed a basis for his vineyard land.

In 1970 Isabelle Simi wanted to retire from her nearly seventy-year control of the Simi Brothers Winery. Russell Green was interested and bought the property. Today, the Simi Winery stands as a monument to American success, blending corporate acumen with Old World grace.

The Bartolucci Brothers Winery was bought in 1971 by Oakville Vineyards when Wilfred E. Van Loben Sels decided to put together his wine empire. Made up of hundreds of small investors, the Oakville Vineyards business had grand plans, even purchasing Gustave Niebaum's mansion to add to its holdings, but it failed by 1976. The buyers of the various components of the Oakville Vineyards estate are a testament to the growing power of Italian American families in the American wine industry: the Bartoluccis bought back their winery, Robert Mondavi bought the Oakville label, and Francis Ford Coppola bought the Niebaum estate.[198]

In 1972 the Likitprakong family from Thailand bought the

Cambiaso Winery, which had started right after Repeal, and changed the name to Domaine St. George Winery. The same year, the Schlitz Brewing Company bought Geyser Peak from the Bagnani family, another chain in the history of this notable property that would later end up in the hands of the Trione family.

In 1973 Coca-Cola Company bought the Franzia wine label then, in 1981, sold it to The Wine Group, headed up by Arthur Ciocca. In spite of this sale the Franzia family couldn't resist the wine business. They later reentered the market when John, Fred, and Joseph Franzia started JFJ Bronco Winery, an amalgam of their initials that became necessary when Coca-Cola claimed title to the Franzia name as part of the purchase of the family's original wine business.

In 1980 the Bandiera Winery was bought by some investors and renamed the California Wine Company. Later, Stonegate Winery was added to the property and dedicated to the production of reserve-style wines.

But Italians were also buying up vineyards and wineries, purchases made possible by the great success that the earthy, honest wines made in the Italian style had earned. In 1967, the Filippi family bought the Thomas Winery to add to its holdings. Built in 1839, Thomas is considered California's oldest winery. The Filippis' business had grown so much since Giovanni Filippi had first planted crops and vines in the early part of the century, that his descendants needed to expand their production and storage facilities.

In 1968 the first vineyard in Temecula was planted by Vincenzo Cilurzo. Cilurzo had already had a career as a Hollywood lighting director, working with celebrities such as Merv Griffin, Frank Sinatra, and Debbie Reynolds. In 1968, he decided to return to the winemaking habits his father had taught him when making wine for the family in Syracuse, New York. But the younger Cilurzo went beyond the home-production plans of his father and planted Vitis vinifera grapes in Temecula. His son, Vinnie, took the idea one step further and started a microbrewery in California during the 1990s, when specialty beers were gaining a foothold in the premium beverage market.

The Ponzi family had come from Campotosto, Italy, and settled in Michigan, where Dick Ponzi grew up. His childhood was spent like many Italian American kids, smelling his father's homemade wine brewing in the basement. Dick Ponzi became an aerospace engineer for United Technologies and Lockheed, but he never lost interest in making wine. After much deliberation, he and his wife, Nancy, decided to move to Oregon and buy a vineyard. They were among the pioneers in Oregon wine, putting faith in the region's viticultural potential when others were still scratching their heads trying to decide whether to risk it. Dick's contributions to the local wine industry include not only world-class wines; he was also the founding member and first president of the Oregon Winegrowers Association. He has recently started planting Italian varietals in Oregon.

Ernest Fortino had been born in Calabria, Italy, into a family that had been in the wine business for four generations. Coming to America in the 1960s, his first job was working in the fields since he didn't speak any English. His prospects looked up, however, and he was later able to apply his knowledge of wine when he became winemaker for the Bargetto Winery. By 1970 he had saved enough money to set out on his own. He bought the Cassa Brothers Winery in Gilroy, California, and renamed it the Fortino Winery.

In 1970 the Montevina Winery was established in California's Shenandoah Valley. It was the first winery to open in the Amador foothills since Prohibition, and was planted to Zinfandel, Sauvignon Blanc, Sangiovese, and Barbera. Later, the property was bought by Sutter Home Winery, allowing the Trinchero family to take advantage of Montevina's extensive Italian varietal plantings to start its own Cal-Ital movement.

In 1973 Angelo Papagni added to the business that his father, Demetrio, had started, and built the Papagni Winery. Papagni wines, according to Adams, "astonished the wine world and contradicted the opinions of experts" about the quality of wine that could be made in Madera.[199]

Perhaps the most important development of the time in any American vineyard was the "discovery" in 1972 of White Zinfandel. Evolution stories abound, but the most likely one suggests that Bob Trinchero had a batch of Zinfandel that didn't ferment out to dryness, i.e., the fermentation stopped before all of the sugar had been converted to alcohol, leaving a slight but very pleasing note of sweetness in the wine and preserving the delicate fruit flavors. He thought it was a batch that went wrong, but tried it out on some friends and it engendered an immediate following. Subsequent forays into the market showed that such a wine would be popular, and Sutter Home began to increase its production. The wine's popularity grew until "White Zin" became the most commonly requested wine in the U.S., outselling all other varietals.

The innovation made the Trinchero family rich, but it also served two greater purposes: Its soda-pop freshness convinced a willing society of beer drinkers to switch to wine, and it ensured that the many acres of Zinfandel would stay in the ground. In the 1970s, while Americans were showboating their newly acquired wine savvy—some real and some feigned—wineries had to switch to the premium varieties like Cabernet Sauvignon, Chardonnay, and Merlot and would have replanted the Zinfandel vineyards had there not been a market for this hybrid wine. The Trincheros' discovery allowed the Zinfandel vines to be preserved for a later—and more mature—American wine public to return to red Zinfandel.

The 1970s also saw the first interest in Italian grape varieties being planted in the United States. While many French grapes had been transported to America during the nineteenth and early twentieth centuries, Italian varieties were not. The introduction of grapes such as Sangiovese, Nebbiolo, Dolcetto, Barbera, Aglianico, and Grignolino was a late occurrence.

And then there were the second- and third-generation Italian Americans who reminisced about the ways of their grandparents. Americo and David Rafanelli had grown grapes on their ranch in Dry Creek Valley for many years to supply the fruit for their own homemade

This Victorian house, once the Sutter Home Winery, is now a historic bed and breakfast guesthouse.

wine. In 1974, however, they fulfilled Alberto Rafanelli's dream and established the A. Rafanelli Winery in the basement of Americo's house.

Similarly, Daryl Sattui followed his grandfather's dream when, in 1974, he leased land in Napa with plans to reopen V. Sattui Winery, which his grandfather had closed in 1921. The dream was realized in 1976 when, after a long struggle with financial backers, Daryl Sattui christened the new V. Sattui Winery on Route 29 in Napa. Although all of the V. Sattui wines are sold at the winery, the family has a tremendous following and regularly attracts visitors to California who eagerly return to V. Sattui to get their stock of otherwise impossible-to-find Sattui wines.

In 1975 Frank Pastori reopened his father's Pastori Winery and joined other Italian Americans returning to their roots. The majority of wine produced at Pastori Winery is sold at the winery as generic red and white wine, but the family plans to switch to vintage-dated estate bottlings.

Dreams of past glories even captured the attention of Francis Ford Coppola. As a movie director, he had blockbuster hits like the *Godfather* series, *Apocalypse Now*, and *Bram Stoker's Dracula*. But in 1975, he decided to buy a vineyard and "make enough wine to drink and pretend I was my grandfather." He bought the historic Niebaum Estate and renamed it Niebaum-Coppola, where he produced a wine he called "Vinoforte." Fortunately, this first attempt was followed by others, and Coppola soon introduced a wine called Rubicon, a California rendition of the standard Bordeaux blend, and Edizione Pennino, a Zinfandel named after his maternal grandfather.

In 1974 Joe Carrari started the Vineyard Development Company to cultivate vines and serve as a consultant to other vineyardists. By 1984, he decided to heed his own advice and started the Carrari Vineyards Wine Company. He does not make his own wine, but has contracts with others to produce it from the grapes he grows.

In 1975 Fred Bucci planted French hybrid vines in Ohio and started making wine in his basement in 1978. When he went commercial, he added an *a* to his name, believing the change would made it easier to remember, and created Buccia Vineyard. As further proof that the Italian influence was not limited to California, Mike and Rose Fiore opened Fiore Winery and La Felicetta Vineyard in Maryland. Their small vineyard turned into a large vineyard and then their small wine production turned into a large winery, where fifteen thousand gallons of wine are now made annually.

The decade was not without significant losses in the Italian community. In 1974, Louis M. Martini died and, in 1976, Antonio Perelli-Minetti died at the age of ninety-five. At the time of his death, Perelli-Minetti was the oldest of the remaining pre-Prohibition winegrowers.[200]

In 1976 the Gallo brothers bought the remaining shares of the Frei Ranch. The grapes grown on that property are used in a number of Gallo's premium bottlings and the Frei estate is still a significant factor in the Gallo family's success in the fine-wine market.

Also in 1976, the Zonin family in Italy bought land in Virginia and formed Barboursville Vineyards and Winery. Zonin installed an Italian winemaker, a tradition that continues to this day with the current holder of that position, Luca Paschina. Barboursville now grows many types of Vitis vinifera on its many acres in rural Virginia, proving that such premium varietals will grow to fruition in the Mid-Atlantic states. Included in the eclectic mix of grapes are many Italian varietals such as Pinot Grigio, Barbera, and Malvasia, from which a delicious dessert wine is made.

In 1977 Ray Signorello fell in love with a plot of land in Napa Valley and bought it to create Signorello Vineyards. He planted it to Chardonnay at first, and later added Sauvignon Blanc and Semillon. By 1985 his crop had increased, and when the grape market collapsed

Cilurzo's Petite Sirah Vineyard in Temecula, California (1994).

that year, he did what Andrea Sbarbaro had done with Italian Swiss Colony ninety-nine years before: he switched from grape growing to winemaking to preserve the excess fruit. He now makes some of the finest Chardonnay in the country.

Also in 1977, Cliff Giacobine retired from his job in the space industry and formed the Estrella River Winery in Paso Robles. The Giacobine winery was later sold to Wine World Estates and renamed Meridian. Since that time, the JFJ Bronco company has revived the Estrella River name and is producing wines under that label.

The same year, Greg Graziano, whose family came from Asti, joined with Jim Milone, whose family came from Brindisi, to start the Milano Winery. The winery occupied an old hop kiln built by Jim's grandfather in the 1940s, a building that had remained unoccupied most of the years since the war. The partnership dissolved in 1980, with Greg Graziano selling his interest to Jim Milone to start the Domaine St. Gregory and Monte Volpe lines of wines.

In 1979 Robert Mondavi expanded his base by buying the Woodbridge Winery. But of greater significance that year was his partnership with the Rothschild family of France. Their goal was to produce a super-premium wine in California, which they called Opus One, and which has garnered significant attention and numerous awards since its inception. It would become one of California's greatest wines and a paradigm for age-worthy reds from the New World.

In two short years, 1978 and 1979, several new wineries opened under the guidance of Italian Americans. Vince Cilurzo used his ten-year-old vineyards to enter the commercial market in 1978, making Petite Syrah and Cabernet Sauvignon.

In 1979 the Caparone, Coturri, Baldinelli, Santino, and Donatoni wineries were founded. Dave Caparone was building on the dreams of his father and grandfather, the latter coming to the United States in 1899 and working in the coal mines of Pennsylvania for a while to make ends meet. Dave Caparone's first experiments with grape growing included Nebbiolo, Sangiovese, and Aglianico, some of the noblest grapes that Italy has to offer. In time he added Cabernet Sauvignon, Merlot, and Zinfandel.

Tony Coturri insisted on keeping the Coturri wines organic, including such traditional methods as organic fertilizers, natural yeasts, and the use of basket presses and open-top fermenters. Reconditioned French oak barrels are used, and the wines are neither fined nor filtered before bottling, retaining the rich flavors and layered complexity of wine in its natural state.

Edward Baldinelli teamed up with John Miller and bought a 1920s-vintage vineyard to form the Baldinelli Vineyards in Plymouth, California. Wine production ceased in 1994, and sole ownership now belongs to Miller.

The Santino family formed their winery in 1979, but they owned only the winery and purchased grapes from the 125-year old Grandpere Vineyard. In 1994 Renwood bought Santino Winery.

Hank Donatoni retired from his job as pilot for United Airlines after thirty-six years in the cockpit. After all that time, he was ready for more peaceful, tranquil work—like winemaking. However, the flight line is in his blood, so, for his winery, he selected a building right at the end of the Los Angeles Airport runway. His paternal grandfather was a winemaker near Verona, though by the time Hank's father was born, the Donatoni family had moved to the United States.

Also in 1979, Bob Frugoli bought a vineyard that would later become the source of the Armida Winery's grapes. He had been raised near San Francisco, but spent his summers with his Italian grandparents in Healdsburg. With an extended contact with the part of his family that had lived in Italy, Bob developed an intense interest in everything Italian, including an interest in making wine. He spent his career in the brokerage business, but retired from E. F. Hutton to start a vineyard.

August Sebastiani died in 1980, leaving his oldest son, Sam, in charge of the family operation at Sebastiani Vineyards. August was better at marketing and promotion than winemaking and, under his control, Sebastiani Vineyards focused on pleasant and error-free jug wines. When Sam took over, he quickly shifted the emphasis to premium varietals. It was a difficult change for the family to undergo, and residual feelings about the change brought about the Sebastiani family's schism some few years later.

In 1981 the Ferrari-Carano Winery was founded and would later grow to become one of Sonoma County's most significant players, with its production of premium varietals as well as an ambitious program of experimentation in cultivation of Italian grape varieties. Don and Rhonda Carano have poured a small fortune into the property, and have insisted that everything be first-class, from the consistent excellence of their wines to the beautiful Villa Fiore visitors center and the heavenly gardens that sweep across the land around the winery and main buildings.

The same year, the J. H. Gentili and Piconi wineries were founded, and Mitch Cosentino started the Crystal Valley Cellars. Cosentino later moved to Yountville and started the Cosentino Winery.

The Stroh's Brewing Company sold Geyser Peak Winery to Trione family in 1982. One of the first things Henry Trione did back then was drop the Summit line, a wine product packaged as wine-in-a-box. Summit was a moderate financial success but it prevented Trione from achieving the status of a fine-wine producer. Several years later, Trione would sell off half of the estate to the Penfolds Wine Company from Australia and, in the process, acquire the services of a master wine-maker from Penfolds, Daryl Groom. The restructured company didn't work to Henry Trione's satisfaction so he later bought back the 50 per-cent interest in Geyser Peak that he had sold to Penfolds, kept Daryl Groom around, and resumed operations as a family winery.

Also in 1982, the Seghesios started bottling their wine with their own label rather than selling it in bulk. It was a big step for a family that had been successful selling jug wine and wine in bulk, but the quality of the Seghesio product had improved significantly over the years and deserved to be labeled as such. The Seghesio Winery now produces wines from a wide variety of grapes and the family recently started a program of cultivating traditional Italian varieties. Almost as if it were destiny, the Seghesios discovered a vineyard Edoardo had planted to a field blend of the classic grapes in Chianti; and the fami-ly began making a wine from the blend and calling it Chianti Station. With all the recent interest in planting Italian varieties in the United States, this plot of land could be the oldest vineyard in the country planted to such varieties.

The same year brought Gustav Dalla Valle to Napa Valley to buy twenty-five acres of vineyard land. He hailed from a family with more than one hundred years of winemaking experience in Italy, and Gustav used the rich soils of Napa to plant traditional red European varieties like Cabernet Sauvignon, Sangiovese, Cabernet Franc, and Merlot, some of which go into to Dalla Valle's ultra-premium wines, Pietre Rosse and Maya.

Eugene and Nancy Pucci founded the Pucci Winery in Sandpoint, Idaho, originally basing their production on California grapes shipped to Idaho for their own use. In time, after the wine had developed some fans, they decided to go commercial. Unfortunately, the success didn't last and, in 1995, the winery went out of business.

The winery that Secondo Guasti founded in California ceased operation in 1982. It was the largest wine business in southern California and continued without interruption for nearly one hundred years. Guasti's vision of a company town that provided gainful employment, security, and a noble beverage gave strength to the enterprise and allowed it to thrive, but the concentration of interest in the northern vineyards had finally taken its toll.

In 1982 the old Gemello Winery was purchased by John Gemello's niece and absorbed into the Obester Winery she owned with her husband. The next year, the first vines were planted on Arciero Estate Vineyards, the foundation of what would later become Arciero Winery. Today, the winery has seventy-eight thousand square feet, with underground cellars and the capacity to produce five hundred thousand cases of wine. The Arcieros use stainless steel for fermentation of most of their wines, including some experimental lots of Sangiovese, and French and American oak barrels for aging. The six-thousand-square-foot visitors center is surrounded by gardens, a fountain, and picnic area. The vineyards have many grape varieties planted, including Merlot, Nebbiolo, Cabernet Sauvignon, Zinfandel, Chardonnay, Sauvignon Blanc, Semillon, and others.

Also in 1982, the Napa Vintners Association formally became the

Francis Ford Coppola stands beside his original Tucker automobile. In the background is the old Niebaum Mansion, which he now owns.

Napa Valley Vintners Association. It had been founded in 1943 by Louis M. Martini and included Martini, Fred Abruzzini, Louie Stralla, Charles Forni, and the Mondavis as charter members.

In 1984 Paul DiGrazia started selling wine from the vineyards he had planted in Connecticut six years earlier. The grapes are exclusively French hybrids, and the winery turns out a wide array of wines, including late harvest, dessert, ice wine, and port.

In 1985 Signorello Vineyards decided to stop selling so much of its product to other wineries and start making wine under its own label. Frank Teldeschi died that year, and his son John took over the vineyard operation. John now sells grapes to wineries like E. & J. Gallo, Ravenswood, Rafanelli and others, but Dan Teldeschi decided to buy some of the grapes and start making Teldeschi wines. By 1993, Dan had a license for his new winery in Dry Creek Valley, buying grapes from his mother, who still owns the family vineyards.

Other significant events occurred in the mid-1980s that would continue to affect Robert Mondavi's future. First, in 1985, he and his brother, Peter, repaired their relationship, but Robert also began devoting serious time to his "Mission." This represented a personal goal Robert set for himself to educate the American public about the cultural, social, and health benefits of moderate consumption of wine. By 1990, his interest in the Mission had grown to the point that he decided to pass control of the winery to his sons to allow him more time to concentrate on his educational project.

Another interesting event occurred in 1985. Roy Cecchetti decided he wanted to make wine. He knew Don Sebastiani from the famed Sebastiani family, and he knew that Don was not actively involved in the production or marketing at Sebastiani Vineyards. So he invited Don to consider joining him in a partnership that they would call the Cecchetti-Sebastiani Cellar. In 1986, Sam Sebastiani was fired by Sylvia, his mother, and replaced by Don, an event that sapped Don's time for the Cecchetti-Sebastiani Cellar. Since that time, Don has maintained control over the Sebastiani family business while Sam manages Viansa, which opened in 1990. Roy Cecchetti has stayed in the winery he and Don founded and which they still co-own. Today, the winery also produces wine under a label called Pepperwood Grove, making about seventy thousand cases under that name. The Cecchetti-Sebastiani company also produces extra virgin olive oil in Italy which it imports to the United States for sale.

In 1986 Piero Antinori of Tuscany finally decided to buy California land, a move he had been considering for some time. He chose a plot in what is now called the Atlas Peak appellation, naming the venture Atlas Peak Vineyards, and formed a partnership with Bollinger and Whitbread to buy it. In 1991, the winery's first bottling, a 1989 Sangiovese, was released. The Wine Alliance now owns Atlas Peak, and caves have been dug into the volcanic hillside to house and age the wines produced at Atlas Peak. The venture has been so successful, especially with respect to its production of Sangiovese-based wines, that in 1997, an international symposium of Sangiovese producers, including many Chianti houses from Tuscany, was held at Atlas Peak.

That same year, Lou Facelli moved from Idaho to Washington in search of better vineyard land. He had lived in Santa Cruz, California but, in 1973, he moved his family to Wilder, Idaho, looking to escape the busy life of the West Coast. He planted vines in Wilder and used the training he got from his grandfather to make wine from the grapes he harvested. In 1981 he opened the Lou Facelli Winery, but later decided that he wanted to move to where better grapes could be grown. He and his wife selected Washington State, and took the plunge into commercial wine. Lou worked for a while at Salmon Bay Winery, then Haviland Winery, but soon reopened the Facelli Winery in this new territory.

In 1986 Joe Cafaro opened his own winery. He had inherited a multigenerational interest in winemaking from his immigrant grandparents and spent time learning the business at Chappellet, Acacia, Robert Sinskey Vineyards, Oakville Ranch Vineyards, Dalla Valle, and Lewis Cellars before setting out on his own. Today he produces Cabernet Sauvignon and Merlot.

Events in 1986 proved that the Italian American interest in wine was not limited to California. That year, the Balagna Winery opened in New Mexico, based on John Balagna's loving memories of his grandfather tending the Nebbiolo cuttings he brought from Italy to the New World. In addition, Bert and Lynn Basignani started the Basignani Winery in Maryland, using a converted garage/winery for the basis of their production.

Americo Rafanelli died in 1987, and his son, David, became the winemaker for A. Rafanelli Winery.

In 1988 the Montevina Winery was bought by the Trinchero family, who had an interest in getting a foothold in Amador County. Bob

Trinchero had for years cherished the fruit from that county, buying many tons of it over the years to make the Sutter Home wines. The Trincheros added vineyard land to the Montevina holdings and planted additional Italian varietals such as Refosco and Aleatico. Grapes from the more than one-hundred-year-old vines on that property are still used to make the Sutter Home Reserve Zinfandel.

The same year, Greg Graziano sold his interest in the Milano Winery and opened the Domaine St. Gregory Winery to specialize in French varietals. Later, he sought out a property that would allow him to concentrate on noble Italian varietals, naming it Monte Volpe. The Estrella River Winery was sold to Wine World Estates in 1988.

Also in 1988, Bob Pellegrini bought a thirty-six-acre tract of land called Island Vineyards in New York. He tended the vines planted there and produced his first vintage in 1991. The property concentrates on table wines but also makes a line called Commonage, a line of light, fruity wines in both red and white for easy drinking.

In 1989 Sam Gabrielli started the Gabrielli Winery in Redwood Valley, California, after moving from Pennsylvania. Saverio Gabrielli had come from the Marches region of Italy in 1915, but had only made homemade wine from California grapes shipped east. Sam's memories of making wine as a youth are strong, and remind him of the life and times of Italian immigrants on the East Coast. Working as a carpenter, Sam was not close to the commercial end of winemaking until he found a book on the subject in the public library. A spark was lit and he soon followed his passion for wine to California, where he enrolled in the enology curriculum at the University of California at Davis.

In 1989 Robert Frugoli retired from E. F. Hutton and added to his vineyards by buying a nonoperating winery in Dry Creek Valley to make wine from the vineyard he bought in 1980. He named it Armida Winery, after his grandmother from Italy, at whose table he grew to love food and wine.

The same year, Mitch Cosentino decided to quit the Crystal Valley Cellars project he founded in Modesto in 1981 and move to Yountville to open the Cosentino Winery. His wines were so good that, on March 6, 1990, a date that also happens to be his grandmother's birthday, the Cosentino Cabernet Franc was served by President and Mrs. Bush to the Prime Minister of the Italian Republic.

In 1991 Elmo Martini (of Martini and Prati Winery) died. His dedication to wine had brought the Martini winery back into family hands through a partnership with Enrico Prati, after the original Martini Winery had been sold off to Hiram Walker. The maintenance of the vintage equipment at Martini & Prati makes an interesting tour through the past for visitors at the winery.

In 1993 Julio Gallo died when his sports car went out of control and careened over a mountainside embankment. For decades, Julio had been considered the softer side of the Gallo brothers duo, often bringing Ernest back in line. Now he was gone, and the wine world wondered what would be done with the Gallo empire in his absence. Fortunately, Ernest remained true to the dream he shared with his brother, moving the operation more in the direction of premium wines and producing vineyard-designated bottling that could compete on an international level.

In 1992 Silverado Vineyards bought the Bay View vineyard that had been planted by Felix Borreo in 1883. The new Pezzi-King Winery was founded in 1993, based on Zinfandel, Cabernet Sauvignon, and Chardonnay plantings. Pietro Pezzi had come to the United States in the late 1800s from northern Italy. He settled in northern California and became involved in the Italian American community there. His work included stints with the Bank of Italy (later Bank of America), with a primary interest in helping the Italian families get financing for their agricultural businesses.

In 1994 the Baldinelli Winery ceased making wine. In 1995 Francis Ford Coppola bought Inglenook Estate to reunite it with the Niebaum Estate, the two halves of the original property owned by Gustave Niebaum, property that has produced such magnificent wines over the years that it has set the standard for quality for age-worthy wines. And in 1996 the splendid Villa Fiore, Ferrari-Carano's hospitality center, opened its doors to the public. The grounds are adorned with seemingly endless flower gardens, the villa is a modern relic of Renaissance Italy, and the library cellar stocks multiple vintages of the fabulous wines that Ferrari-Carano has been producing for the fifteen years of its young existence.

We may well be entering the golden years of the Italian American experience in wine. Throughout this rich history, which includes the thousands of wines produced by the hundreds of wineries with an Italian accent since 1850, the American passion for all things Italian has continued to grow and has become even more intense at the beginning of the twenty-first century. This passion reflects some of the vagaries of culture and fashion, but it also reflects some of the glory of the wines that Italian methods can produce. With so many Italian American wineries still in production, there is little doubt that the wines they deliver to the American public will strike a resonant chord and continue the legacy begun by Italian immigrants when they first landed on the shores of America in the early seventeenth century.

Notes for Part I

1. Thomas Pinney, *A History of Wine in America: From the Beginnings to Prohibition* (Berkeley and Los Angeles: University of California Press, 1989), 11.

2. Ibid., 11.

3. Ibid., 11.

4. Ibid., 11-12.

5. Luciano J. Iorizzo and Salvatore Mondello, *The Italian Americans* (New York: Twayne Publishers, Inc., 1971), 10.

6. Pinney, op. cit., 13.

7. Pinney tells us that this law, "the last in a series of attempts to legislate an industry, was quietly repealed in 1641." op. cit., 21.

8. Hilde Gabriel Lee and Allan E. Lee, *Virginia Wine Country Revisited* (Charlottesville, Va.: Hildesigns Press, 1993), 10.

9. Pinney, op. cit., 19.

10. Ibid., 19.

11. Ibid., 24.

12. Ibid., 67.

13. Ibid., 67.

14. Lee, op. cit., 11.

15. Andrew F. Rolle, *The American Italians: Their History and Culture* (Belmont, Ca.: Wadsworth Publishing Co., 1972), 15.

16. Pinney, op cit., 75-76.

17. Pinney, op. cit., 77.

18. Jerre Mangione and Ben Morreale, *La Storia: Five Centuries of the Italian American Experience* (New York: Harper-Collins, 1992), 45.

19. Humbert S. Nelli, *From Immigrants to Ethnics: The Italian Americans* (Oxford: Oxford University Press, 1983), 12.

20. R. de Treville Lawrence, III, ed., *Jefferson and Wine: Model of Moderation* (Virginia: Vinifera Wine Growers Association, 1989), 21.

21. Leon D. Adams, *The Wines of America* (New York: McGraw-Hill Publishing Company, 1990), 60.

22. Jefferson gained more from Mazzei than just an understanding of viticulture. Mazzei vented his political fire in articles in the Virginia Gazette, writing under the name of Furioso. Jefferson later opened the Declaration of Independence with a paraphrase of a line from one of Mazzei's articles: "All men are by nature equally free and independent."

23. Adams, op. cit., 66.

24. Hugh Johnson, *Vintage: The Story of Wine* (New York: Simon and Schuster, 1989), 353.

25. Iorizzo and Mondello, op. cit., 3.

26. J. Philip di Franco, *The Italian Americans, The People of North America* (New York: Chelsea House Publishers, 1988), 31.

27. Rolle, op. cit., 2.

28. Ibid., 10.

29. This critique of the Mission grape may partly be blamed on the Franciscans' manufacturing methods. Apparently, they cared little for high-tech answers, preferring to use as their winery manual a treatise unrevised since 1513.

30. Johnson, op. cit., 360.

31. Ibid., 360.

32. Vallejo allowed the Indians to continue to make wine the Mission way. Among other things, this included an inventive glossary of terms. For example, the free-run wine, i.e., the wine that runs clear of the skins and stems without pressing, was called white wine, and the pressed wine was called red (see Johnson, op. cit., 361).

33. Pinney, op. cit., 330.

34. Iorizzo and Mondello, op. cit., 218.

35. Johnson, op. cit., 359.

36. Ibid., 359.

37. Charles L. Sullivan, *Napa Wine: A History* (San Francisco: The Wine Appreciation Guild, 1994), 18.

38. Pinney also comments that Yount's grapes were grown from cuttings taken from Vallejo's Sonoma Mission, making Napa viticulture the progeny of Sonoma viticulture (Pinney, op. cit., 259).

39. Iorizzo and Mondello, op. cit., 3.

40. Mangione and Morreale, op. cit., 14.

41. Ibid., 25.

42. Ibid., p. 37

43. Wayne Moquin, ed., *A Documentary History of the Italian Americans* (New York: Praeger Publishers, 1974), 65.

44. Pinney, op cit., 330.

45. Eric Costa, *Old Vines: A History of Winegrowing in Amador County* (California: Cenotto Publications, 1994), 59.

46. Sullivan, op. cit., 55.

47. Nelli, op. cit., 40.

48. Moquin, op. cit., 64.

49. Southern California reminds many of the flat, sometimes arid lands of southern Italy, from which many of the Italian immigrants hailed. Northern California is strongly reminiscent of Tuscany, one of Italy's noble wine regions. In fact, Sonoma County, the ultimate destination for most of the Italian winemakers, has green hills, a temperate climate, and warm nights that are almost identical to that of Tuscany.

50. Costa, op. cit., 1.

51. Johnson, op. cit., 362.

52. Mangione and Morreale, op. cit., 194.

53. Sullivan, op. cit., 135.

54. Johnson, op. cit., 366.

55. Costa, op. cit., 56.

56. Sullivan, op. cit., 43.

57. Mangione and Morreale, op. cit., 75.

58. Iorizzo and Mondello, op. cit., 41.

59. di Franco, op. cit., 34.

60. Whereas the French habit has been to label wines by the locales in which the wines were made (Bordeaux, Chablis, Burgundy, Champagne, etc.), the winemakers

in Piedmont, in northern Italy, according to Hugh Johnson (op. cit.), have been accustomed to naming their wines by the grapes contained within them. It is interesting to note that northern California, the region in which many northern Italians settled, established a pattern of naming wines after the grape varietals used in them, a habit now copied by other emerging wine regions in the world.

61. Adams, op. cit., 193.

62. Rolle, op. cit., 47, 63.

63. Johnson, op. cit., 369.

64. Adams, op. cit., 194.

65. Ibid., 233.

66. Costa, op. cit., 52.

67. Pinney, op. cit., 331.

68. Costa, op. cit., 56.

69. Pinney, op. cit., 481.

70. Sullivan, op. cit., 63.

71. Nelli, op. cit., 84.

72. Adams, op. cit., 194.

73. Sullivan, op. cit., 55.

74. Costa, op. cit., 58.

75. Pinney, op. cit., 337.

76. Ibid., 328.

77. Adams, op. cit., 382.

78. Adams, op. cit., 382.

79. Adams, op. cit., 396.

80. Costa, op. cit., 70.

81. Ibid., 73.

82. It is an interesting bit of trivia that Angela's middle name, Dionisia, is the feminine form of the Italian name for the Greek god of wine, Dionysus.

83. James T. Lapsley, Bottled Poetry: Napa Winemaking from Prohibition to the Modern Era, (Berkeley and Los Angeles: University of California Press, 1996), 34.

84. Michael A. Musmanno, *The Story of Italians in America* (New York: Doubleday & Co., 1965), 91.

85. Iorizzo and Mondello, op. cit., 133.

86. Mangione and Morreale, op. cit., 78.

87. di Franco, op. cit., 35.

88. Dick Rosano, "California's Italian Accent," *Wine News* (August-September 1995).

89. Mangione and Morreale, op. cit., 114.

90. Sullivan asserts that Prohibition was the product of "[t]he seemingly chance convergence of three historical factors": the Temperance Movement, the Progressive Movement, and the onset of World War I, the last of which challenged Americans to sacrifice for the common cause (Sullivan, op. cit., 181).

91. Nelli, op. cit., 44.

92. di Franco, op. cit., 41.

93. Mangione and Morreale, op. cit., 45.

94. Rolle, op. cit., 80.

95. Pinney, op. cit., 327.

96. Mangione and Morreale, op. cit., 129.

97. Pinney, op. cit., 329.

98. James Conaway, *Napa: The Story of an American Eden* (Boston: Houghton Mifflin Company, 1990), 15.

99. Mangione and Morreale, op. cit., 78.

100. Ibid., 131.

101. di Franco, op. cit., 35.

102. Iorizzo and Mondello, op. cit., 93.

103. Pinney, op. cit., 328.

104. This method of grape preservation was not lost on the Federal government as Prohibition was nearing an end: exceptions were granted to allow vineyards to preserve their fruit in the only way known, i.e., turning it into wine, pending the expected Repeal.

105. Adams, op. cit., 244.

106. Costa, op. cit., 60.

107. Pinney, op. cit., 331.

108. Adams, op. cit., 196.

109. Joseph Novitski, *A Vineyard Year* (San Francisco: Chronicle Books, 1983), 27.

110. Sullivan recounts how the St. Helena Star attempted to coordinate the efforts of scientists and winemakers to solve the problem of phylloxera, acting as a clearinghouse for all information known about the topic. Professor Arthur Hayne, who claimed to have discovered the cure for phylloxera by replanting onto St. George rootstock, first published his recommendations in the St. Helena Star (op. cit., 117).

111. Sullivan, op. cit., 102.

112. Ibid., 183.

113. Pinney, op. cit., 359.

114. Ibid., 362.

115. Guasti's efforts in this regard appear to differ from those of Sbarbaro. Guasti offered to sell stock to Italians to help his countrymen make money. While Sbarbaro's plan had the same goal, he originally planned to sell only to his employees and to require them to participate in the stock plan. As discussed above, this was not accepted by the employees of Sbarbaro's Italian Swiss Colony.

116. It is likely that Benidet Murphy, an Italian immigrant who changed his name, was the first commercial vintner in Amador County. Costa lists a sample of names from that area near the end of the nineteenth century: Arata, Bacigalupi, Belluomini, Carroli, Cuneo, Devoto, Fregulia, Garbarini, Lavesso, Molfino, Oneto, Raggio, and Ratta (Costa, op. cit., 10 and 54, respectively).

117. Iorizzo and Mondello, op. cit., 116.

118. Musmanno, op. cit., 88.

119. Gay Talese's insight into this problem is almost painful: "[T]he process toward Americanization for Italians began by learning to be ashamed of our parents" (Talese, Gay, Unto the Sons (New York: Alfred A. Knopf, 1992), 463).

120. The experience of the Guarino family from Apulia points this out: Domenico Guarino first came to the United States soon after the turn of the century, returned home, then came back again to America, where he and his wife, Maria Santa DeVito, started their family. When they returned once again to their rural area of Italy, the family was divided over which country to call home. The possibility that some children might choose America and leave the family settled it: the entire family moved back to New York for good.

121. Lapsley, op. cit., 120.

122. Novitski, op. cit., 28.

123. Mangione and Morreale state that of the 286,814 Italians entering the United States in 1906, 184,832 were listed as unskilled (Mangione and Morreale, op. cit., 272).

124. Jack W. Florence, Sr., *A Noble Heritage: The Wines and Vineyards of Dry Creek Valley* (California: Wine Growers of Dry Creek Valley, 1993), 52.

125. Adams, op. cit., 402.

126. Ibid., 221.

127. Sullivan, op. cit., 154.

128. Florence, op. cit., 52.

129. Sullivan, op. cit., 168.

130. Mangione and Morreale, op. cit., 194.

131. Lapsley, op. cit., 31.

132. Over President Wilson's veto (Mangione and Morreale, op. cit., 101).

133. Ibid., 316.

134. Mangione and Morreale claim that three times as many Italians left the United States as entered it during this period. The number is credible and it demonstrates the severe shift in fortunes for those entering the United States during these years (op. cit., 118).

135. Adams, op. cit., 331.

136. Pinney, op. cit., 502.

137. Ellen Hawkes, *Blood and Wine: The Unauthorized Story of the Gallo Wine Empire* (New York: Simon & Schuster, 1993), 28-29.

138. Sullivan, op. cit., 160.

139. Costa, op. cit., 27.

140. Adams, op. cit., 398.

141. Sullivan, op. cit., 189.

142. Sullivan, op. cit., 183.

143. Peter Meltzer, "Prohibition Pipeline: How Wine and Spirits Survived," *Wine Enthusiast* (May 1994).

144. Nelli, op. cit., 161.

145. This limit still exists today, more than sixty years after Repeal. In fact, there was a resurgence of interest in the late 1980s, extending into the 1990s, in home-wine production that may be traced to the merging of the 1960s "back-to-nature" philosophy of self-sustenance with the return to ethnic traditions by the second- and third-generations of immigrant families.

146. Other legal avenues were production of wine for medical or religious applications.

147. Although Repeal in 1933 made wine production legal again, the acreage planted to vines actually began to decline after that year as the new generation of hobbyist winemakers got over their crush on homebrew. The acreage planted to vines in California did not make a strong comeback until the 1970s (Sullivan, op. cit., 196).

148. Hawkes, op. cit., 62.

149. A family story says that Louis M. once sold one hundred thousand gallons of grape juice to home winemakers in one day.

150. Lapsley, op. cit., 20.

151. Adams, op. cit., 404.

152. Meltzer, op. cit. [n.pag.].

153. Adams, op. cit., 26.

154. Costa, op. cit., 68.

155. Many Italian families retain close ties to the home-winemaking industry that kept the vineyards alive during Prohibition. When Andrew Colaruotolo's crop at Casa Larga Vineyards exceeded the two hundred gallons he was allowed to make before turning pro in the 1970s, he sold off the excess to home winemakers. A. Conrotto Winery still supplies grapes to its home-winemaking customers, as does the Fiore Vineyard in Maryland. Rich Crescini of Crescini Vineyards started as a home winemaker. So did Dick Ponzi of Ponzi Vineyards in Oregon and David Rafanelli in Sonoma County.

156. Sullivan, op. cit., 191.

157. Talese, op. cit., 462.

158. Nelli, op. cit., 178.

159. As Talese reminds us, "The pessimism among peasants [in Italy in the early 1920s] was such that charity workers noted in their dialect a conspicuous absence of the future tense" (Talese, op. cit., 462).

160. Hawkes, op. cit., 82-83.

161. Ibid., 84.

162. Sullivan, op. cit., 207.

163. Adams, op. cit., 30.

164. Lapsley, op. cit., 3.

165. Hawkes, op. cit., 63.

166. Lapsley, op. cit., 22.

167. Adams, op. cit., 280.

168. Lapsley, op. cit., 23.

169. Ibid., 21.

170. Of the nine original members of the Napa Valley Vintners Association, five were Italian Americans (Sullivan, op. cit., 240).

171. Conaway, op. cit., 47.

172. Lapsley, op. cit., 131.

173. Ibid., p. 29.

174. Sullivan, op. cit., 324.

175. Lapsley, op. cit., 111.

176. Adams, op. cit., 289.

177. Lapsley, op. cit., 105.

178. Sullivan, op. cit., 118.

179. Adams, op. cit., 289.

180. Florence, op. cit., 63.

181. Lapsley, op. cit., 30.

182. Ibid., 32.

183. Ibid., 34.

184. Ibid., 120-121.

185. Ibid., 124.

186. Sullivan, op. cit., 158.

187. Ibid., 240.

188. Adams, op. cit., 382.

189. Ibid., 388.

190. Lapsley, op. cit., 167.

191. Conaway, op. cit., 80.

192. In 1995 Francis Ford Coppola bought Inglenook to reunite it with the Niebaum Estate.

193. Sullivan, op. cit., 289.

194. Ibid., 265.

195. Ibid., 322.

196. Ibid., 278.

197. Ibid., 279

198. Ibid., 294, 311.

199. Adams, op. cit., 394.

200. Ibid., 403.

PART II

The Wineries

Prologue

The intensity was always there in his eyes, but the energy level took on a softer glow when he looked out over the vineyards that had possessed his heart and mind for so many years. He was standing there now, in the clean and casual dress of a man who has reached the status of nobility in his society, resting his still-calloused hands on the smooth, cool marble balustrade that wrapped around the south and east sides of his Italian villa in California.

It was now many years since his father left Italy to settle in America. The family struggled to survive the economic disasters of the American Depression, then moved to California to make wine as they had done for generations in Italy.

His father knew that California's climate would one day make the region a dominant force in the world of wine. He also knew that Italians could master that industry, applying their genius for art and respect for science to prove that California wine could stand with the best in the world.

The son shared his father's dream, but stood on the shoulders of those who had come before. In a land that his Italian kin had developed into one of the world's premier wine regions, the son could now see a farther horizon.

ARCIERO WINERY
Paso Robles, California

Giovanni Arciero came to the United States without his family in 1914 from Santa Elia Fiumerapido near Rome. He arranged for his oldest son, Mike, to come to the U.S. in 1937, followed by sons Frank and Phil in 1939 and the youngest son, Anthony, and their mother, Cristina, in 1948.

Frank and Phil were fourteen and ten years old, respectively, when they came to the United States. Neither spoke any English. Approximately ten years later, in 1948, the two brothers moved to California and started a cement contracting business. In 1955 they founded Arciero Brothers, a construction company that was successful enough to later finance other ventures, such as their interests in motor racing (with drivers such as Al and Bobby Unser and Mario Andretti) and viticulture.

Frank Arciero had managed the family farm, which included olives, grapes, and tomatoes, before he emigrated to the United States. In 1964, he ventured into New World agriculture when he created Arciero Ranches, an alfalfa business. In 1983 Frank and Phil Arciero began planting vines on what would become the Arciero Estate Vineyards. The more than seven hundred acres of vines are maintained with drip-irrigation and without herbicides or pesticides. The winery was built in 1984 and is modeled after Monte Cassino, a former

The Arciero Estate Vineyard, founded in 1983, has the architectural style and ambiance of an Italian monastery.

monastery near the Arciero's ancestral home in Italy.

Arciero has its own rootstock nursery for clone selection. Chardonnay is the most planted grape, over 190 acres. They have now begun to experiment with the Nebbiolo (ten acres), and now Arciero is planting Sangiovese (five acres).

The winery comprises seventy-eight thousand square feet, with underground cellars and a production capacity of five hundred thousand cases of wine. Arciero uses temperature-controlled, stainless steel tanks for fermentation and French and American oak barrels for aging. The winery has a six-thousand-square-foot visitors center and landscaped gardens, including a rose garden, fountain, and picnic area.

Recently, Arciero started an ambitious program of trenching the rows of vines, a process whereby the topsoil is broken up and mixed into the lower strata as deep as six feet. Although expensive, this process can increase yields.

Grape varieties produced: Merlot, Sangiovese, Nebbiolo, Cabernet Sauvignon, Zinfandel, Petite Syrah, Cabernet Franc, Chardonnay, Sauvignon Blanc, Chenin Blanc, Muscat Canelli, Semillon

Proprietary blends and other labels: none

Arciero Winery, 5625 Highway 46 East, Paso Robles, California 93447-1287 phone: 805-239-2562, fax: 805-239-2317

ARMIDA WINERY
Healdsburg, California

Bob Frugoli grew up near San Francisco, but spent his summers with his Italian grandparents in Healdsburg. There he developed an intense interest in things Italian, an interest that was nurtured by his grandmother's Italian cooking and his grandfather's homemade wine. He decided that one day he would own his own winery.

He got involved in the brokerage business, where he worked for many years, but in 1979 he took the plunge and bought a vineyard in the Russian River Valley. He tended this vineyard while working at E. F. Hutton until his retirement in 1989. Then he bought a nonoperating winery on West Side Road near the southern border of the Dry Creek Valley, spent a year renovating it and, when it was ready, he knew just what to name his new enterprise: Armida, for the grandmother whose home and table inspired it.

Bob built the business into a small production (four thousand cases per year) of handmade wines, but by 1994 he realized that the winery business is anything but retirement. That year, he sold majority interest to two partners, Steve and Bruce Cousins. The three partners intend to stay with Bob's philosophy about making wine: small-lot wines, handmade, from the best grapes they can buy. Today, the Armida Winery farms from Russian River vineyard land and produces grapes at its Dry Creek Valley Winery, combining the two appellations in Bob's original dream.

Grape varieties produced: Chardonnay, Merlot, Pinot Noir

Proprietary blends and other labels: none

Armida Winery, 2201 Westside Road, Healdsburg, California 95448 phone: 707-433-2222, fax: 707-433-2202

ATLAS PEAK VINEYARDS
Napa, California

An unusual venture was jointly embarked on by Piero Antinori (of the six-hundred-year-old Antinori house of wines from Tuscany), Bollinger (of champagne repute from France), and Whitbread (of London). These parties founded Atlas Peak Vineyards in Napa in 1986, in a unique plot of land some 1450 to 1800 feet above the floor of the

Napa Valley. The group's goal was to produce premium wines from Sangiovese and Cabernet Sauvignon, some varietally specific and some blended.

One of the blends of the two red grapes, Consenso, was meant to tack onto the Italian trend toward super-Tuscan wines, i.e., wines made from the main grape in Chianti (Sangiovese) blended with Cabernet Sauvignon. The super-Tuscan wines in Italy were surprising the world with their elegance and Antinori, who invented the craze with his Antinori Tignanello in the 1970s, wanted to capitalize on it in America.

Caves have been dug deep into the volcanic hillside of Atlas Peak, forming an interlacing network of tunnels to house the wines they produce. The bare wires stringing dim and lonely lights cast a romantic light on row upon row of bottles, reaching back into the mountain as far as the eye can see. It is a scene out of the ancient vineyards of Europe.

In 1994 the business arrangements changed. Today, the wines and vineyards are handled through a partnership between The Wine Alliance and Antinori. But the goal has remained the same: produce ultra-premium wines with an international character and an Italian accent.

Grape varieties produced: Sangiovese, Cabernet Sauvignon, Merlot, Cabernet Franc, Petite Verdot, Chardonnay

Proprietary blends and other labels: Consenso (predominantly Cabernet, blended with Sangiovese)

Atlas Peak Vineyards, 3700 Soda Canyon Road, P.O. Box 5660, Napa, California 94581-0660 phone: 707-252-7971, fax: 707-252-7974

BAGNANI WINERY
Geyserville, California

In 1937 Italy Industries, the company owned by the Bagnani family, bought Geyser Peak Winery, which had been established by Augustus Quitzow in 1880. There they produced what were called the Redwood Empire Wines, but the Geyser Peak Winery was also sometimes referred to as the Bagnani Winery.

In 1945 Redwood Empire Wines ceased to exist, but Italy Industries was transformed into American Industries and continued to make bulk wines there until 1972, when it was bought by Schlitz Brewing Company. The name, "Geyser Peak," was retained and was later bought by Henry Trione. See Geyser Peak.

BALAGNA WINERY
Brand Name: Il Santo Cellars
Los Alamos, New Mexico

John Balagna is the grandson of Domenic and Domenica Balagna and Joseph and Caterina Vezzetti. The Balagnas were born in the Piedmont and emigrated to the United States in 1883. The Vezzettis were also from Piedmont, arriving in the United States in 1882.

John Balagna (senior) and Maria Teresa Vezzetti were both born in the United States, and passed on their families' winemaking heritage to John (junior), but it was from his grandfather Joseph Vezzetti that John (junior) learned to make wine.

John recounts how his grandfather Vezzetti brought Nebbiolo cuttings from Italy and planted them at the Vezzetti home in Brookside, Colorado. The vines had to deal with the intense winters of this mountainous region, and required the Balagna and Vezzetti families to bury the pruned stalks of each vine in the ground to survive the winter. During the 1920s and 1930s, the family made wine from grapes grown in Cucamonga Valley in California.

John (senior) made wine but seldom drank it because he said it had an effect on him that he didn't like. In fact, the family has a funny story that evolved due to the father's refusal to consume alcoholic beverages. It seems that one day a high ranking member of the Catholic clergy was visiting and John's father wanted to serve him some of the grappa he had made. He got a bottle from the pantry, pulled the cork, and filled the cleric's glass. Nothing was said about the grappa during the evening and the guest left the house happy and satisfied. Then, John's mother, while she was cleaning up, went into the pantry and noticed another bottle was missing instead. She went back to dining room and told John's father that he had not served grappa at all, but Holy Water.

John (junior) tried growing French hybrid grapes in Los Alamos, but the altitude (7,200 feet) ruined his attempts. In 1972, he started a vineyard in the Jemez Mountains, but had only moderate success. While working for Los Alamos Scientific Laboratory (involved in the research on nuclear weapons) during the 1980s, he made wine from the Mission grape grown by Zia Pueblo Indians, supplemented by some Napa grapes he had flown into Albuquerque. Finally, in 1986, John had enough equipment to start his own commercial operation following his retirement from Los Alamos National Laboratories; after working at the lab for many years he needed a solid project to engage him in his retirement years.

A few years ago, to celebrate the fiftieth anniversary of Los Alamos National Laboratories, John made a wine called La Bomba Grande, a blend of Zinfandel (50%), Pinot Noir (25%), and Merlot (25%). He does not grow his own grapes but continues his practice of buying grapes only from the vintners who grow European varieties in New Mexico.

Grape varieties produced: Cabernet Sauvignon, Merlot, Zinfandel, Sangiovese, Nebbiolo, Chardonnay, Muscat Canelli, Riesling, Celeste Blanco, hybrids

Proprietary blends and other labels: Il Santo Cellars, La Bomba Grande, Dago Red, Gringo Rojo

Balagna Winery, 223 Rio Bravo Drive, Los Alamos, New Mexico 87544
phone: 505-672-3678

BALDINELLI VINEYARDS
Plymouth, California

Edward Baldinelli bought this vineyard, which dates from 1920, in partnership with John Miller. From some seventy acres, the partners made Zinfandel and Cabernet Sauvignon from 1979 until 1994, when they allowed the winery bond to lapse and they stopped making wine.

The new owner is redefining the Italian heritage of the Baldinelli winery, but has now returned to production under another name.

Grape varieties produced: Zinfandel, Cabernet Sauvignon
Proprietary blends and other labels: none

Baldinelli Vineyards, 10801 Dickson Road, Plymouth, California 95669
phone: 209-245-3398

BANCHERO WINERY

Luigi Banchero came from Italy and opened this winery in California. Unfortunately, his dreams died when Prohibition forced the winery to close. His son, Louis, reopened the Banchero Winery in 1933, upon Repeal, and operated it until 1942.

BANDIERA WINERY
Cloverdale, California

Emilio Bandiera left Lucca, Italy, around the turn of the century, poor and looking for a new opportunity in a new world. He founded the Bandiera Winery in 1937 to produce good, affordable wine for Americans (and his immigrant countrymen) to drink with every meal. Most of his wine was sold in barrels or jugs for many years, but all of the wines symbolized the Bandiera philosophy: produce good wines meant for everyday drinking at an affordable price.

Emilio's son, Ralo, and grandson kept the winery in the family until 1980 when some investors bought it under the name of the California Wine Company. In 1996, the new owners added to the property by buying Stonegate Winery in Napa Valley to make small lots of reserve style wines. But Bandiera still exists, and the original goal of making good, sound wines at affordable prices has been retained.

Grape varieties produced: Cabernet Sauvignon, Zinfandel, Merlot, Chardonnay, Sauvignon Blanc

Proprietary blends and other labels: Sage Creek

Bandiera Winery, 155 Cherry Creek Road, Cloverdale, California 95425 phone: 707-894-4295 fax: 707-894-2563

BARBOURSVILLE VINEYARDS
Barboursville, Virginia

The Zonin family has been involved in wine in Italy for seven generations. When it decided to look for vineyard land in the United States, it settled on Barboursville, Virginia, in 1976.

The Zonin family brought a specific interest in things Italian, appointing Gabriele Rausse as the winemaker— followed later by

BARTOLUCCI BROTHERS WINERY

The Bartolucci Brothers Winery was founded by a family of grape growers who decided to open a winery following Repeal in 1933. They gave up the business in 1938, but in 1942, one of the brothers, Louis, decided to restart it.

For a while, Louis Bartolucci sold wine to Petri Wine Company; then he entered into a partnership with Andrea Gusmanno of San Francisco and Harry Weiner of New York and modernized the winery. After the wine market collapse of 1947, Weiner was convicted of making black-market sales and Gusmanno went bankrupt. Once again, Louis Bartolucci was forced to reorganize to keep the winery. He did so, and made a successful family business that survived into the 1960s.

In 1971 the Bartolucci Winery was bought by Oakville Vineyards. When Oakville Vineyards failed in 1976, the Bartoluccis bought back the winery. Louis Bartolucci has since turned the operation into the Mont St. John Cellars in Napa. See Mont St. John Cellars.

BASIGNANI WINERY
Sparks, Maryland

Bert Basignani is a builder by trade, but pursued his amateur wine-making for years before making the jump to commercial production. In 1986 when the winery opened for business, the Basignani family was crushing outside the converted garage/winery, not unlike the scenario one might have expected of an avid amateur winemaker.

The business has since expanded and enjoys continued success, though it suffers from a lack of name recognition and from the bias against East Coast wines that afflicts many wine drinkers in America.

Two of Bert and Lynn Basignani's wines are named after their daughters, Marisa and Elena. Another wine, San Lorenzino, is named after their son.

Grape varieties produced: Cabernet Sauvignon, Chambourcin, Maréchal Foch, Chancellor, Merlot, Chardonnay, Burdin, Vidal Blanc, Seyval Blanc, Riesling

Proprietary blends and other labels: none

Basignani Winery, 15722 Falls Road, Sparks, Maryland 21152 phone: 410-472-4718 fax: 410-433-2530

BAY VIEW RANCH AND VINEYARD WINERY

This winery was opened by Felix Borreo, from Genoa, in 1888 but was closed when Prohibition struck. The Disney family bought the property years later and used the Italian varietals planted by Borreo as the basis of their very popular Silverado Sangiovese.

BELLA NAPOLI WINERY
Manteca, California

Anthony Cappello left Naples and came to the United States in 1899. He changed his name to Tony Hat (*cappello* means "hat" in Italian) and founded the Bella Napoli Winery in 1934. It is now owned and operated by his children.

Producing mostly jug wines, the Bella Napoli Winery supplies local restaurants and sells wine at the winery.

Grape varieties produced: Carignane, Grenache, Chardonnay, Chenin Blanc, Colombard

Proprietary blends and other labels: Vine-Flow, A La Sante

Bella Napoli Winery, 21128 South Austin Road, Manteca, California 95336 phone: 209-599-3885

BERNARDO WINERY
San Diego, California

Vincent Rizzo was born in Sicily into a family that had been making wine for hundreds of years. The stories of the New World convinced him to leave home and seek his future in America, which he did at the age of fourteen. He survived by working many different types of jobs, including owning several restaurants, then decided to get back into winemaking.

The Bernardo Winery originally opened in 1889 as a partnership of five Italian businessmen. This arrangement dissolved and the winery was bought in 1918 by Ferrari-Lanza. Then, in 1928, Vincent Rizzo bought it, and the winery has remained in the Rizzo family ever since. Vincent's son, Ross, born in 1939, is the current owner and winemaker.

Since the winery was purchased while Prohibition was still on, the Rizzo family made a living selling sacramental wine and selling fresh grape juice to home winemakers. Ross took over the operation in 1962 and continued with the Rizzo tradition of making wines Old World style. The winery is reportedly assembling a wine museum based on the antique winemaking equipment that has gathered at Bernardo Winery since its inception more than a hundred years ago.

Grape varieties produced: Ruby Cabernet, Barbera, Cabernet Sauvignon, Zinfandel, Grenache, Chardonnay, Pinot Blanc, French Colombard, Chenin Blanc, Johannisberg Riesling, Gewürztraminer, Muscatel, port, sparkling wine

Proprietary blends and other labels: none

Bernardo Winery, 13330 Paseo del Verano Norte, San Diego, California 92128 phone: 619-487-1866

ROBERT BIALE VINEYARDS
Napa, California

Pietro Biale was born in 1892 in a town near Genoa, called Santa Giustina. He grew up learning about horticulture and the proper care of crops, and grape cultivation was a special interest.

Pietro went to the United States and settled in California during Prohibition. It was during those years that he began dreaming of farming his own vineyard and making his own wine. In 1937 Pietro and his wife, Christina, planted a vineyard to Zinfandel just north of the city of Napa. Unfortunately, Pietro was killed in an explosion in a rock quarry in Napa in 1942, but Christina and their only son, Aldo, kept the vineyard going.

Aldo was committed to making the Zinfandel vineyard a success, and producing a Zinfandel wine that his father would have been proud of. Today, the vineyard is owned by Aldo and the winery is named after his son, Robert Biale, though there is a vineyard-designated wine from Aldo's vineyard.

Grape varieties produced: Zinfandel, Sangiovese, Petite Syrah

Proprietary blends and other labels: none

Robert Biale Vineyards, P.O. Box 5327, Napa, California 94581 phone: 707-257-7555

BIANCHETTI WINERY
Amador County, California

John Bianchetti's family had came from Italy in the 1850s and settled in Amador County. Later, John and his wife, Marie, bought 160 acres of land and farmed vegetables and grapes.

When John died in the 1890s, Marie and her sons planted grapevines for the production of wine for their own use. Unfortunately, they chose the Mission grape, which was no longer considered suitable for fine wine. When Prohibition ended, they decided to enter the commercial wine market and erected a winery building.

The business became the Bianchetti Brothers and continued to produce wine for commercial sale into the 1960s. The Bianchetti Winery no longer exists.

BIANCHI VINEYARDS AND WINERY
Kerman, California

In the 1970s the Bianchi family bought Morello Cellar, a wine storage facility that was built in 1938. They modernized the facility and turned it into the Villa Bianchi Winery, later renaming it the Bianchi Vineyards and Winery.

Today, Bianchi is a major producer of premium varietal wines in the San Joaquin Valley, with a capacity of well over one million gallons. The production was formerly in generic wines, but in recent years Bianchi has moved toward premium European varietals.

Grape varieties produced: Cabernet Sauvignon, Zinfandel, Merlot, Ruby Cabernet, Lambrusco, Chardonnay, Chenin Blanc, Sauvignon Blanc, French Colombard

Proprietary blends and other labels: none

Bianchi Vineyards and Winery, 5806 North Modoc Avenue, Kerman, California 93630 phone: 209-846-7356

BRAGNO WINE COMPANY
St. Helena, California

Frank Bragno owned the Bragno Wine Company, as a distributor for Italian Swiss Colony in Illinois. The 1943 purchase of Italian Swiss Colony by National Distributors swept away Bragno's distributorship, so he decided to buy a winery of his own.

He entered into deals to buy Riverbank Wine Company near Modesto, then the giant Alta Winery and Distillery. For reasons that are no longer clear, he got cold feet and backed out of these deals, and those wineries went to other buyers. Instead, Bragno bought the Larkmead Winery in partnership with Harry Blum of Blum and Company. In 1946 when Bragno fell behind in his loan payments to Blum, Blum bought him out.

There is currently no Bragno Wine Company.

JFJ BRONCO WINE COMPANY
Ceres, California

The Franzia family had built a very profitable generic wine business that they sold to the Coca-Cola Company in the early 1970s. However, some members of the family were still interested in making wine, so they decided to start all over again—where their grandparents had begun when they started the Franzia wine empire.

John Franzia, Jr., and his cousins, brothers Fred T. and Joseph S. Franzia, were divested of their family name as a product identifier when Coca-Cola bought the Franzia wine business. So, in 1973, they used their initials to name their new venture JFJ then added "Bronco" to complete the name.

Today, the Bronco Wine Company has its own vineyards and state-of-the-art facilities, producing mostly bulk wines that are sold extensively in sixty-five countries as well as distributed throughout the United States.

Grape varieties produced: numerous, mostly in bulk production
Proprietary blends and other labels: none
JFJ Bronco Wine Company, 6342 Bystrum Road, Ceres, California 95307 phone: 209-537-5718 fax: 209-537-0550

BUCCIA VINEYARD
Conneaut, Ohio

Fred Bucci's grandfather came from Italy. While still working as the County Tax Assessor, Fred decided to start making wine in his basement. He planted vines in 1975 and started making wine, "the old fashioned way," in 1978.

When he went commercial, he added an *a* to his name, thinking this would make it easier for the public to pronounce and remember.

Grape varieties produced: Aurore, Baco, Seyval Blanc

Proprietary blends and other labels: none

Buccia Vineyard, 518 Gore Road, Conneaut, Ohio 44030
phone: 216-593-5976

CADENASSO WINERY
Fairfield, California

The Cadenasso family, from Genoa, moved to the United States in 1906. The first Cadenasso arrived in San Francisco three days before the Great Earthquake, but he was not deterred by the disaster. While watching all the destruction around him, he held fast to his dream of owning a winery.

Like many Italian immigrants, he was broke when he arrived, but the Cadenassos were in the wine business within a week of their 1906 arrival. The Cadenasso Winery was formed soon thereafter and has stayed in the family since.

Grape varieties produced: none identified

Proprietary blends and other labels: none

Cadenasso Winery, P.O. Box 22, Fairfield, California 94533
phone: 707-425-5845

CAFARO CELLARS
St. Helena, California

Joe Cafaro's grandparents on both sides lived in Adelfia-Canetto in southern Italy. In 1914 both families emigrated to the United States. His paternal grandfather made wine during Prohibition, and he must have had quite a stash. The Volstead Act permitted the production of up to two hundred gallons of wine per year per head of household—a limit that still stands today. But Joe's grandfather must have been making more than his limit because he hid the barrels in the ground under the tomato plants.

The next generation of Cafaros didn't continue the winemaking routine and it would have been lost if Joe hadn't developed an interest in making wine "the way my grandfather did."

Joe Cafaro went beyond the simple backyard-and-basement routine, though. He worked as a winemaker at Chappellet, Keenan, and Acacia, and later consulted at Robert Sinskey Vineyards, Oakville Ranch Vineyards, Dalla Valle Vineyards, and Lewis Cellars before he started his own label in 1986. The pull of having his own winery might have been matched by the push of the business at Acacia, where he last worked before opening his own operation. It seems that from 1983 through 1984, Acacia was on the market and, in 1985, things began to come apart quickly. When The Chalone Group took over, Joe was ready to start his own winery, which he did in 1986.

Joe prefers to bottle all of his wines as 100 percent varietals, but he does blend the same varieties from different regions of Napa Valley.

Grape varieties produced: Cabernet Sauvignon, Merlot
Proprietary blends and other labels: none
Cafaro Cellars, 1591 Dean York Lane, St. Helena, California 94574 phone: 707-963-7181

CAGNASSO WINERY
Marlboro, New York

Joseph Cagnasso came to California from northern Italy—by way of Mexico—to work for the Gallo wine empire. In 1972 he moved to New York to take a job with the Brotherhood Winery. In 1977 he opened a winery of his own.

Grape varieties produced: none identified
Proprietary blends and other labels: none

Cagnasso Winery, Route 9W, Marlboro, New York 12542 (no number listed)

CALVARESI WINERY
Reading, Pennsylvania

Tom Calvaresi learned from his grandfather how to make wine, but he went beyond his grandfather's operation and now produces about ten varieties of wine. According to Anthony Dias Blue, the Calvaresi winery "is still reached by walking down the Calvaresi cellar stairs."[1]

Grape varieties produced: none identified
Proprietary blends and other labels: none

Calvaresi Winery, 832 Thorn Street, Reading, Pennsylvania 19601 phone: 215-373-7821

CAMBIASO WINERY
Healdsburg, California

This winery was started by Giovanni and Maria Cambiaso in 1934 near Healdsburg, California. In the 1940s the operations were taken over by their children, who started replacing the Carignane with Cabernet Sauvignon.

In 1972 the winery was sold to the Likitprakong family from Thailand, and the name was changed to Domaine St. George Winery. The Cambiaso Winery label no longer exists.

CANYON ROAD WINERY
Geyserville, California

Julius Nervo emigrated from Venice soon after the turn of the century and built a winery called Venezia Winery in 1908. The name was changed to Nervo several years later. The winery stayed in the family for seventy-five years before being sold to the Schlitz Brewing Company. In 1982 Schlitz sold this property and Geyser Peak to the Trione family. It is now owned by Fortune Brands.

The Triones bottled Nervo wine for several years but then opened Canyon Road Winery on the property, and transformed the Nervo production into the Canyon Road production.

The Triones also created a label called Venezia, specializing in super-premium wines and using Julius Nervo's alternate name for his winery.

Grape varieties produced: Cabernet Sauvignon, Merlot, Chardonnay, Sauvignon Blanc

Proprietary blends and other labels: none

Canyon Road Winery, 19550 Geyserville Avenue, P.O. Box 25, Geyserville, California 95441 phone: 707-857-3417 fax: 707-857-3545

CAPARONE WINERY
Paso Robles, California

Dave Caparone's grandfather came to the United States from Italy in 1899 and worked as a coal miner in Pennsylvania. Dave's father had it a little better, graduating from college in the 1920s as an electrical engineer.

Dave began work with Nebbiolo in 1979, with Sangiovese in 1982, and with Aglianico in 1989. Nebbiolo was obtained from the University of California at Davis, which had obtained the original plant material from the University of Turin in 1973.

Caparone Winery was founded in 1979 and produces Nebbiolo, Sangiovese, Aglianico, Cabernet Sauvignon, Merlot, and Zinfandel.

The wine from Caparone Winery is sold at the winery and through Trader Joe's.

Grape varieties produced: Cabernet Sauvignon, Merlot, Sangiovese, Aglianico, Zinfandel, Nebbiolo

Proprietary blends and other labels: none

Caparone Winery, 2280 San Marcos Road, Paso Robles, California 93446 phone: 805-467-3827

CARRARI VINEYARDS
Los Alamos, California

Ferruccio Carrari moved his family to Argentina around the beginning of the twentieth century to work on the railroad. A few years later, in 1906, he was killed while working on the railroad. The same year, his son Miguel was born, and his mother returned to Italy to raise him.

About 1923 Miguel returned to Argentina so he could avoid the military draft under Mussolini. In 1929 Miguel Carrari came to the United States. He first worked for Henry Ford, then came to California to work in wine and grape growing businesses. From 1930 till 1933 he worked in Guasti Vineyards. By then, Secondo Guasti had died (1927) and Guasti's son was in charge.

Miguel sold produce in Los Angeles, then leased his own vineyards in 1938. By 1940 he had become a full-time grape grower, naming his business the Hillside Vineyard Company.

Miguel's son Joe was born in 1934. Joe was already picking grapes for his father at five years old. After a stint in the military, Joe went to Argentina to try farming with his brother. They lost everything, so Joe returned and got into the grape-growing business in Napa Valley, where he planted the Winery Lake Vineyard. Joe then went to work for Paul Masson Vineyards as manager in Soledad, California. While there, he planted about twenty-seven hundred acres of vines.

In 1972 Joe started developing vineyards for other people. In 1974 he bought his first acreage and started the Vineyard Development Company, called "Vidico." In 1984 he decided to start his own label, and named it Carrari Vineyards. Today, the Carrari Vineyards wines are marketed only in California. During his career, he has planted over six thousand acres of vineyards in California.

He does not produce his own wine, but has contracts with others to produce it for him.

Joe makes a red wine, blended from Cabernet Sauvignon, Petite Syrah, and Zinfandel, which he irreverently calls Dago Red. He explains the use of the term by referring to one popular story of the origin of "dago." According to the story, it seems that on one of his return trips to the New World, Cristoforo Colombo brought his son, Diego. When the American Indians could not pronounce "Diego," the name became "Dago." In time, the word was used to refer to any of the men traveling with Colombo. As Joe Carrari fondly says, "I'd rather be called a son of Columbus than a son of a bitch." His wine won a Gold Medal at the 1985 Orange County Fair.

Grape varieties produced: Nebbiolo, Sangiovese, Barbera, Freisa, Dolcetto, Grignolino, Muscat Canelli, Pinot Grigio, Orange Muscat, Chenin Blanc, Sauvignon Blanc, Chardonnay, Semillon, Petite Syrah, Merlot, Cabernet Franc, and Cabernet Sauvignon.

Blends and proprietary wines: Dago Red

Carrari Vineyards, 439 Waite Street, Los Alamos, California 93440 phone: 805-344-4000

CASA LARGA VINEYARDS
Fairport, New York

Andrew Colaruotolo was a stonemason who came from Gaeta, Italy, in 1950 when he was eighteen years old. He loved to tell stories about his grandmother working in the vineyard in Italy. Having learned to make wine in Italy, Andrew kept up the Italian custom in the United States and, in 1974, he began planting vines to supply the wine for his family. His crop exceeded the two hundred gallons permitted for home winemaking, so in 1978 he applied for a license and started making his wine for sale.

Although the Finger Lakes region is not considered a good place for the finer European varieties, Andrew planted Chardonnay and Johannisberg Riesling and immediately started winning medals. The winery also participates in, or sponsors, a number of events throughout the year, such as Roman Days in Spring, and it has an extensive gift shop and hosts wine tastings in its Tirage Room.

Grape varieties produced: Cabernet Sauvignon, Petite Noir, Pinot Noir, de Chaunac, Chardonnay, Vidal Blanc, Gewürztraminer, Johannisberg Riesling, Aurora, Blanc de Blanc Brut, Muscat d'Ottonell

Proprietary blends and other labels: Tapestry (Cabernet Sauvignon and de Chaunac), Brut d'Ottonell

Casa Larga Vineyards, 27 Emerald Hill Circle, Fairport, New York 14450 phone: 716-223-4210

CECCHETTI SEBASTIANI CELLAR
Rutherford, California

The Cecchetti Sebastiani Cellar was formed by a partnership between Roy Cecchetti and his brother-in-law, Don Sebastiani, in 1985. This was before Don took over operations at the Sebastiani family, and he joined with Roy Cecchetti so that he could be in control of his own wine enterprise.

The family history of the Sebastiani family is discussed elsewhere in this book, but Cecchetti's family also recently emigrated from Italy. The Cecchetti family hails from Lucca, a prime agricultural spot in Tuscany, known mostly for its olive oil and other specialty foods. In fact, the Cecchetti family still makes wine and olive oil in Tuscany. Some of this olive oil is bottled under the CSC label and is imported by Cecchetti Sebastiani and marketed in the U.S.

The Cecchetti Sebastiani Cellar also produces wine under the labels Quatro and Pepperwood Grove, making about seventy-thousand cases under the latter name.

Grape varieties produced: Cabernet Sauvignon, Merlot, Pinot Noir, Cabernet Franc, Zinfandel, Chardonnay

Proprietary blends and other labels: Pepperwood Grove, Quatro
Cecchetti Sebastiani Cellar, 8440 St. Helena Highway, Rutherford, California 94573 phone: 707-996-8463 fax: 707-966-0424

CELLA VINEYARDS
California

Brothers John Battista Cella and Lorenzo Cella came from Bardi in northern Italy to America in 1898. They worked first as waiters in New York, then invested some money and a lot of effort in building up a grocery business before venturing into wine production. Just before Prohibition hit, they bought the Scatena Winery in California from Dante Forresti. John Battista ran that operation while Lorenzo stayed in New York to handle sales.

John Battista decided to move the family business and he bought the old Santa Lucia Winery near Fresno, renaming it the Roma Winery. In 1942 this and other properties were acquired by Schenley Distillers. Although John Battista continued to work there for a while, he later resigned and, in 1944, bought the Rusconi Vineyard and renamed it Cella Vineyards. After expanding the operation to twelve million gallons, the property was later sold to United Vintners, and then again to Heublein.

CILURZO WINERY
Temecula, California

Vincenzo Cilurzo tells the story of how his father made wine each year in Syracuse, New York. His father would save his change all year and, at harvest time, Vincenzo and his sister would break open the bank and determine how much they had for grapes that year. He tells stories about how his father and friends used to get together and open their homemade wines and crack nuts and argue all night about whose wine was best.

Vince didn't take up commercial winemaking right away. In fact, he first had a very successful career as a lighting director for television before trying his hand at winemaking. In that first career, he worked for ABC for about twenty years, with opportunities to work with celebrities like Merv Griffin, Frank Sinatra, and Debbie Reynolds. His assignments included the Jeopardy show (for twelve years) and the Academy Awards. He still works in Hollywood and has won an Emmy Award for his work.

Viticulturists Vincent Cilurzo and Dick Break discovered the Temecula microclimate.

In 1967 he bought property in Temecula. After studying the soil for nearly a year, he planted premium varietal grapes in 1968, making his the first *Vitis vinifera* varieties in the Temecula area. By 1978 he was ready for commercial production, making Petite Syrah and Cabernet Sauvignon, and has since expanded the list to include several more wines.

He grows his own grapes and buys more, though only from Temecula.

Vince tells the story of how he inadvertently left some Petite Syrah on the vine too long. They turned the accident into an experiment and now make a late-harvest Petite Sirah as a dessert wine, though it does not have very high alcohol.

Vince's son, Vinnie, has followed in his father's footsteps and recently opened a microbrewery in California.

Grape varieties produced: Cabernet Sauvignon, Zinfandel, Merlot, Petite Syrah, Sauvignon Blanc, Chardonnay, Chenin Blanc, Johannisberg Riesling, Muscat Canelli

Proprietary blends and other labels: Vincheno (a blend of red and white grapes, named after his son, Vinnie, and daughter, Chenin) *Cilurzo Winery, 41220 Calle Contento, Temecula, California 92592 phone: 909-676-5250 fax: 909-676-7458*

DAVID COFFARO VINEYARD AND WINERY
Geyserville, California

David Coffaro was born and raised in San Francisco. He spent several years exploiting his talent for finance and stock trading, and his success helped him afford expensive wines. But he tired of the corporate, high-finance world and decided to move to Sonoma County and become a vineyardist. His first plot of land had some old Zinfandel vines, to which he added Sauvignon Blanc and Cabernet Sauvignon.

In the beginning, he sold his crop to wineries like Nalle and Dry Creek Vineyard, and made some wine for home use with what was left over. Coffaro also tells how his wife's salary as a legal secretary kept them going while he explored his winemaker's fantasy. But, in August 1994, he crossed the line from vineyardist to winemaker and turned his garage into the winery. The equipment consists of an old stemmer, a basket press with a one-ton capacity, a crusher that is small and slow, a bottle filler, and a corker.

Coffaro's most prized product is the Estate Cuvée, a propriety red wine blending premium grapes such as Zinfandel, Cabernet Sauvignon, Merlot, Carignane, and Petite Syrah. But Coffaro works hard to keep the cost down so consumers can enjoy his wines, including not paying himself a salary. This is truly a labor of love.

Grape varieties produced: Zinfandel, Cabernet Sauvignon, Merlot,

Sauvignon Blanc (late harvest only), Carignane, Petite Syrah
  Proprietary blends and other labels: Estate Cuvée
David Coffaro Vineyard and Winery, 7485 Dry Creek Road, Geyserville, California 95441 phone: 707-433-9715 fax: 707-433-6008

CAMILLO COLOMBANO WINERY
Morgan Hill, California

Camillo Colombano came from Italy in 1913. His goal was to make wine from the Barbera vines he planted near Morgan Hill, California.

He founded his winery in 1923, but sold it to the Pedrizzetti family in 1945. Since its sale, it has ceased to exist under the Camillo Colombano name. See Pedrizzetti.

ANTHONY CAMINETTI WINERY
Amador County, California

The Caminetti family came to the United States during the early Gold Rush days, but did not enter the wine business right away. Anthony Caminetti was born in 1854 in Jackson Gate in Amador County, California, and, in the 1880s, he started making wine from Zinfandel.

Anthony was considered a well-educated vintner. He approached winemaking with a scientific skill and intended to improve the standards of quality and cleanliness in the winemaking process.

His educational background led Anthony into a career in politics, which culminated in Anthony's being elected to Congress in 1890. However, instead of wine-related legislation, Caminetti is best known for the Caminetti Act, which dealt with reopening of hydraulic placer mines. In 1888, he and State Senator Boggs founded a wine syndicate, based on Boggs's purchase of forty acres of vineyard land and Caminetti's winemaking expertise. Caminetti sent samples of the wines to the University of California for tasting and analysis, receiving positive comments for his efforts. Unfortunately, Caminetti and Boggs wine enterprise faded from view after that. The winery no longer exists.

A. CONROTTO WINERY
Gilroy, California

Anselmo Conrotto built this winery in 1926, using the gravity-flow design that was made popular in the late nineteenth century. He passed on control of the winery to his son, who later sold it to Anselmo's daughters and their husbands.

Over the years, most of the product was sold to local and San Francisco restaurants. The current owners have reduced their market and sell jug style wines to old and new customers and grapes to their old home-winemaking friends.

Grape varieties produced: none identified

Proprietary blends and other labels: none

A. Conrotto Winery, 1690 Hecker Pass Highway, Gilroy, California 95020
phone: 408-842-3053

COSENTINO WINERY
Yountville, California

Mitch Cosentino has an extensive history as a wine educator, including stints as an instructor of enology at Modesto Junior College and as a guest lecturer at U.C. Davis, Sonoma State College, and Chico State University. He has also served as a judge for many years. These experiences are all folded into a personality dedicated to the motto of quality over quantity. True to the Italian belief that winemaking is equal parts science and art, Cosentino says: "I want the art driving the business, not the business running the art."

In 1981 he started Crystal Valley Cellars in Modesto. In 1989 he moved to Yountville and opened the Cosentino Winery. His wines are so good that one has been chosen for service at the White House. On March 6, 1990, a date that also happens to be Cosentino's grandmother's birthday, the Cosentino Cabernet Franc was served by President and Mrs. Bush to the Prime Minister of the Italian Republic.

Cosentino has developed a vigorous program using Italian varietals, including Sangiovese and Nebbiolo. Most of the grapes vinified at Cosentino Winery are purchased, except for a small quantity of Merlot, which is grown on the property. Mitch Cosentino took on investors to expand the operation, which now is owned by Vintage Grapevine, Inc.

The origin of the M. Cos alternate label is interesting. It seems that Mitch, known for years to his friends as "Cos," decided to put his nickname on the label of a wine. Unfortunately, a very famous Bordeaux estate, Cos d'Estournel, took umbrage at what it thought was an infringement on its property name, and sued Cosentino. Mitch relented, and changed the name to M. Cos.

Grape varieties produced: Cabernet Sauvignon, Cabernet Franc, Merlot, Zinfandel, Sangiovese, Pinot Noir (from three different appellations), Chardonnay, Sauvignon Blanc, Gewürztraminer, Semillon, Vin Santo

Proprietary blends and other labels: M. Cos (a Cabernet blend), The Poet (Red Meritage), The Novelist (Sauvignon Blanc and Semillon), The Sculptor (sur lie Chardonnay), The Zin (Zinfandel), Il Tesoro (Sangiovese), Il Chiaretto (Chianti Classico style), The Sem (Semillon), Tenero Rosa (Zinfandel, Mataro, Napa Gamay)
Cosentino Winery, 7415 St. Helena Highway, Yountville, California 94599 phone: 707-944-1220 fax: 707-944-1254

H. COTURRI & SONS
Glen Ellen, California

The Coturris have been making organic wines since 1979. The present owner, Tony, has insisted on using organic fertilizers, natural yeasts (instead of cultured wine yeasts), and open-top fermenters (instead of temperature-controlled, sealed containers).

Reconditioned French oak barrels are used, and the wines are neither fined nor filtered, preserving the natural texture and essential components of the wine. As James Laube says: "Few wineries have divided critics as Coturri has."[2] Such primitive methods as those described above can produce awful wines, troubled by inconsistency. But Coturri has also had many very interesting wines and, if he's successful at this "return to nature," he could make a strong statement about organic farming and traditional winemaking.

Grape varieties produced: Zinfandel, Cabernet Sauvignon, Pinot Noir, Merlot, Sangiovese

Proprietary blends and other labels: none

H. Coturri & Sons, P.O. Box 396, Glen Ellen, California 95442 phone: 707-525-9126 fax: 707-542-8039

CRESCINI WINES
Soquel, California

Rich Crescini's maternal grandparents came from Asti in 1910, and his paternal grandparents arrived from Carrara the same year. Both sides settled in Santa Cruz. His maternal grandparents made two or three barrels of wine per year in the 1920s and 1930s. His parents' generation did not make wine, but his father made vinegar commercially, selling some to the U.S. Navy.

Like many first- and second-generation Italian immigrants, Rich started making homemade wine in 1970s. He took some basic community college courses in winemaking to get started and, by 1980, he had already bonded a winery. Rich and his wife, Paule, run the winery themselves, although Rich's mother runs the bottling line.

He buys all his grapes from other growers and concentrates his efforts on the winery, rather than dividing that attention with tending a vineyard. He makes about eight hundred cases a year. All the wine is sold at the winery, with its upstairs tasting room, and bocce ball court and horseshoe pits in the park area.

Grape varieties produced: Cabernet Sauvignon, Cabernet Franc, Zinfandel, Petite Syrah, Carignane

Proprietary blends and other labels: Volare (blend of Petite Sirah, Zinfandel, and Carignane; FiFi (a blend named after his cousin, whose nickname was FiFi, made primarily of Petite Sirah, Carignane, and Zinfandel)

Crescini Wines, 2621 Old San Jose Road, Soquel, California 95073 phone: 408-462-1466

D'AGOSTINI WINERY (SOBON ESTATE)
Plymouth, California

In 1914 Enrico D'Agostini purchased the winery owned by his brother Emelio and Vincenzo Fioravanti, and Giuseppe Gualtieri that was founded in 1856 by a Swiss immigrant, Adam Uhlinger. As soon as possible, D'Agostini began buying out his partners and soon the winery was his, and he renamed it D'Agostini Winery.

During Prohibition, Enrico held on to the property by selling grapes for table consumption and to home winemakers. The property stayed in the family as the D'Agostini Winery until the late 1980s. In 1989, Leon and Shirley Sobon, who had founded Shenandoah Vineyards in 1977, bought the D'Agostini property and renamed it Sobon Estate. The D'Agostini family still lives close by, keeping a proud eye on the new owners, and giving tours during special weekends.

Grape varieties produced (as Sobon Estate): Zinfandel, Syrah, Cabernet Franc, Viognier

Proprietary blends and other labels: none

D'Agostini Winery (Sobon Estate), 14430 Shenandoah Road, Plymouth, California 95669 phone: 209-245-6554 fax: 209-245-5156

DALLA VALLE VINEYARDS
Oakville, California

Gustav Dalla Valle was born in Italy into a family with more than one hundred years in the wine business. By 1953 he was living in America and he founded Scuba-Pro, a scuba-gear company, the outgrowth of his passion for scuba diving. His biography is full of stories of how a shark nearly bit off his foot or how he struggled to free his head from the mouth of a blue shark.

Fortunately for all those who love wine, Gustav returned to wine when he purchased some land in Napa Valley.

In 1982 Gustav and his wife Naoko moved to Napa and purchased twenty-five acres of vineyard land. He soon planted Cabernet Sauvignon, Cabernet Franc, and Merlot. In 1986, the first year of real production, they were advised by Joe Cafaro, who had previously worked at Keenan and Sinskey wineries. Upon Gustav's death, the winery was passed on to Naoko.

The Cabernet Sauvignon, Pietre Rosse, and Maya wines that Dalla Valle produces have scored very high marks, and match Gustav's penchant for perfection.

Grape varieties produced: Cabernet Sauvignon, Cabernet Franc, Sangiovese, Merlot

Proprietary blends and other labels: Pietre Rosse (Sangiovese, Cabernet Sauvignon, and Cabernet Franc), Maya (Cabernet Sauvignon blended with Cabernet Franc)

Dalla Valle Vineyards, 7776 Silverado Trail, Oakville, California 94562 phone: 707-944-2676 fax: 707-944-8411

DELICATO VINEYARDS
Manteca, California

In 1924 Gaspare Indelicato and his brother-in-law, Sebastiano Luppino, moved to the San Joaquin Valley and bought a dairy farm. The following spring they planted a vineyard on the land and made a business of selling grapes to home winemakers on the East Coast. In an ironic twist, their business took a bad turn after Prohibition ended because the bottom fell out of the home-winemaking market that had

The Delicato Winery, celebrating its Golden Anniversary, is located in Manteca, ninety minutes east of San Francisco.

exploded during Prohibition. This relatively sudden change produced another irony: Many of the vineyards that were kept and nurtured during Prohibition were in danger of being uprooted when commercial wine was again legal, because the vineyard land had been planted for the amateur market.

Left with little choice, in 1935, they converted their operation from grape selling to winemaking by buying the basic equipment and settling into a hay barn. Members of Indelicato and Luppino families lived together in a small farmhouse. Their first vintage totaled only 3,451 gallons.

Frank, Vincent, and Anthony Indelicato of Delicato Vineyards sit amongst several of their forty million gallons of wine.

Today, their capacity exceeds forty million gallons. But it continues to be family owned and operated. Since the word indelicato means "indelicate," the wine business adopted a more delicate name.

Each year, the winery sponsors a grape stomp that raises money for local charities. The competition has several categories, from "peewee" to "mixed doubles" and has collected thousands of dollars for the charities.

Grape varieties produced: Cabernet Sauvignon, Zinfandel, Merlot, Chardonnay, Johannisberg Riesling, Chenin Blanc, French Colombard, Fume Blanc, and vintage port.

Proprietary blends and other labels: California Sauterne (under Sam Jasper label), Sam Jasper
Delicato Vineyards, 12001 South Highway 99, Manteca, California 95336-9209 phone: 209-239-1215 fax: 209-239-8031

DELMONICO'S
Brooklyn, New York

Gerald Della Monica came from Italy before Prohibition, but it wasn't until 1935 that the family got involved in wine. Then, his son, Joseph, started Delmonico's. With no vineyards, he bought grapes from the surrounding areas for his supply.

Today, the family has continued its winemaking but most of the wine is sold in bulk to other wineries.

Grape varieties produced: none identified

Proprietary blends and other labels: none

Delmonico's, 182 15th Street, Brooklyn, New York 11215 phone: 718-768-7020

DIGRAZIA VINEYARDS
Brookfield, Connecticut

Paul V. DiGrazia planted forty-five acres in 1978 and, in 1984, entered the commercial wine market selling four brands of wine. The production has now reached seven thousand cases, including twenty-nine different wine products.

The vineyard is planted to French hybrid grapes exclusively, and the winery turns out a wide array of wines from dry to sweet, no-sulfite wines, late harvest, ice wines, dessert wines, white port, and ruby port.

Grape varieties produced: Seyval Blanc, Ravat, Vidal Blanc, white port, assortment of red grapes, ruby port, honey wine

Proprietary blends and other labels: none

DiGrazia Vineyards, 131 Tower Road, Brookfield, Connecticut 06804 phone: 204-775-1616

DOMAINE SAINT GREGORY
Ukiah, California

This property is owned by Greg Graziano, who also owns Monte Volpe Vineyards. Graziano uses Domaine Saint Gregory to grow and vinify French grape varieties to complement the Italian varieties and Italian style of wines produced at Monte Volpe.

See Monte Volpe for a more complete history of the Graziano family.

Grape varieties produced: Chardonnay, Pinot Noir, Pinot Blanc, Pinot Gris

Proprietary blends and other labels: none

Domaine Saint Gregory, 4921 East Side Road, Ukiah, California 95482 phone: 707-463-1532 fax: 707-462-8951

DONATONI WINERY
Inglewood, California

Hank Donatoni spent thirty-six years flying for United Airlines, so it should come as no surprise that, when he decided to follow his dream of making wine, he would choose a building right at the end of the Los Angeles Airport runway for his winery. That he did in 1979, while he still was flying, though he now is retired.

He brings his Italian winemaking heritage with him. Like so many Italian Americans in the early 1900s, Hank's father was born in the States, then returned to Italy to grow up. Hank's paternal grandfather was a winemaker near Verona, and passed on his affinity for the grape through the generations.

Hank buys all his grapes from vineyardists in the Paso Robles area and specializes in the French varieties. Most of his wine is sold to an Italian restaurant in a hotel in Kona, Hawaii.

Grape varieties produced: Cabernet Sauvignon, Chardonnay

Proprietary blends and other labels: none

Donatoni Winery, 10604 South La Cienega Blvd., Inglewood, California 90304 phone: 213-645-5445

ESTRELLA RIVER WINERY
Paso Robles, California

This winery has passed through several hands since its birth in 1977. It was started by Cliff Giacobine, after his retirement from the space industry. Its first winemaker was Gary Eberle, who left in 1981 to start his own winery. In 1988, the winery was sold to Wine World Estates and renamed Meridian.

Recently, the Franzia family's Bronco Wine Company (see JFJ Bronco) revived the name and Estrella River Winery is in business once again.

Grape varieties produced: Chardonnay, Sauvignon Blanc, Petite Syrah, Zinfandel, Cabernet Sauvignon

Proprietary blends and other labels: none

Estrella River Winery, Highway 46 East, Paso Robles, California 93446 phone: 805-238-6300

FACELLI WINERY
Woodinville, Washington

Lou Facelli learned to make wine from his grandfather in Santa Cruz, California. But in 1973 he decided to take his family away from the busy life on the West Coast and they settled in Wilder, Idaho, looking for a rustic answer to life. He made wine there, and opened the Louis Facelli Winery in Wilder in 1981. In 1986, he decided to take the plunge and move to better property in Washington.

First, Facelli worked at the Salmon Bay Winery, then Haviland Winery, before opening his own winery. He has kept the business family owned and operated, and buys all his fruit from the Yakima and Columbia Valleys in Washington. In 1996, Facelli purchased new equipment to expand the size of the family business. With the winery expansion, Facelli is looking to expand into new markets.

Grape varieties produced: Cabernet Sauvignon, Merlot, Pinot Noir, Chardonnay, Sauvignon Blanc

Proprietary blends and other labels: none

Facelli Winery, 16120 Woodinville-Redmond Road, NE, Woodinville, Washington 98072 phone: 206-488-1020 fax: 206-488-6383

FERRANTE WINERY
Geneva, Ohio

Winemaking is not new to Ohio, as the state supports forty wineries. One of the oldest is the Ferrante Winery.

Anna and Nicholas Ferrante started the family business when they opened a winery near Cleveland in 1937. Their sons, Peter and Anthony, continued the family enterprise by building a new winemaking facility in the 1970s, and adding a restaurant in the 1980s.

Unfortunately, a fire swept through the restaurant in 1994, stopping at the firewall that separated the dining rooms from the winery, cellar,

The Ferrante Winery & Ristorante is one of Ohio's largest family-owned wineries. They have a full-service Italian restaurant to showcase their wine.

and warehouse. Rededicating themselves to establishing the Italian-style ristorante that had been part of their plans, the family rebuilt the restaurant and the combined family operation became known as the Ferrante Winery and Ristorante.

Grape varieties produced: Pinot Noir, Cabernet Sauvignon, Merlot, Chardonnay, Johannisberg Riesling, Vidal Blanc, Catawba, Rose

Proprietary blends and other labels: none

Ferrante Winery, 5585 Route 307, Geneva, Ohio 44041 phone: 216-466-8466 fax: 216-466-7370

FERRARA WINERY
Escondido, California

The family business was started by Gaspar and Vera Ferrara, third-generation Italian Americans. This was during the days of Prohibition, so they were limited to farming vineyards, one thousand acres of them.

The next generation of the Ferrara family turned the grape growing into winemaking. Today, the wines from Ferrara Winery are only sold at the winery.

Grape varieties produced: none identified

Proprietary blends and other labels: Ferrara Wine Cellars

Ferrara Winery, 1120 West 15th Avenue, Escondido, California 92025 phone: 619-745-7632

FERRARI-CARANO WINERY
Healdsburg, California

The Ferrari-Carano Winery is fairly new to California, by Italian American standards, but Don and Rhonda Carano have built a spectacular facility and they produce wines of great breeding and finesse. To make their wines, they hired George Bursick, who got started in wine by making it for himself at home. But Bursick's credentials are now among the best, and his wines consistently win medals and accolades from critics throughout the wine press.

Don and Rhonda Carano of the Ferrari-Carano Winery own The Villa Fiore in Dry Creek Valley, a twenty-five thousand square foot hospitality center.

Founded in 1981, Ferrari-Carano was named for Don's paternal grandmother (Ferrari) and his family name. Don and Rhonda, who made their money in the hotel and casino businesses, can afford the very best and they lavish attention and money on their Sonoma County operation. Don has joined his experience as a lawyer with

Rhonda's experience in food and nutrition to make Ferrari-Carano a culinary masterpiece.

They originally bought a parcel of land in the Alexander Valley with a restored 1904 farmhouse and thirty acres of grapes. But while Don and Rhonda were both attending viticulture seminars at U.C. Davis, they couldn't resist buying more vineyard land.

In 1996 they opened the Villa Fiore, a fantastic, twenty-five-thousand-square-foot Italianate hospitality center in Dry Creek Valley. The building, which is surrounded by five acres of elaborately landscaped gardens, includes a two-thousand-square-foot tasting room and wine shop, temperature-controlled cellar with vaulted ceilings and iron grill-work doors for Ferrari-Carano's collection of specialty wines, an exhibition kitchen with a wood-burning oven and French rotisserie, and other beautiful furnishings. The second floor of Villa Fiore houses the staff offices and a large conference room with multimedia capabilities.

Grape varieties produced: Cabernet Sauvignon, Merlot, Sangiovese, Zinfandel, Chardonnay, Sauvignon Blanc, Semillon

Proprietary blends and other labels: Siena (Cabernet Sauvignon, Sangiovese, Merlot, Malbec), Tresor (Cabernet Sauvignon, Merlot, Cabernet Franc, Malbec, Petite Verdot), Eldorado Gold (Semillon, Sauvignon Blanc)

Ferrari-Carano Winery, 8761 Dry Creek Road, P.O. Box 1549, Healdsburg, California 95448 phone: 707-433-6700 fax: 707-431-1742

FERRIGNO VINEYARDS AND WINERY
St. James, Missouri

Richard and Susan Ferrigno started this winery by converting a dairy barn into a winery and tasting room and planting French hybrids on land that had previously supported only Concord grapes. The couple each gave up their jobs to do this, and their business has slowly grown to include buffet dinners in their wine garden, and plans to build a bed and breakfast facility.

Grape varieties produced: none identified

Proprietary blends and other labels: none

Ferrigno Vineyards and Winery, Box 2346, Route 2, St. James, Missouri 65559 phone: 314-265-7742

J. FILIPPI WINERY
Mira Loma, California

The legendary Secondo Guasti, founder of the Italian Vineyard Company.

In 1904 Giovanni Filippi traveled to the United States and worked as a mason for the legendary Secondo Guasti, helping to build the Italian Vineyard Company. He returned to Italy, but his son, Antonio, emigrated to America and started growing grapes and citrus fruit.

In 1920 Giovanni and his son Joseph left Schio, Italy, for good, when Joseph was eighteen. They traveled to Cucamonga Valley in California and soon entered the agriculture business, growing grapes and citrus fruits. In 1922, the Filippi family opened the G. Filippi Ranch, and in 1934 renamed it the Joseph Filippi Winery, in Fontana-Mira-Loma, and entered into commercial winemaking. The vineyards grew to include Zinfandel, Grenache, Alicante, Mission, Chasselas, and Burger.

In 1967 the Filippi family added the Thomas Winery to its holdings. Built in 1839, the Thomas Winery is considered California's oldest winery.

Grape varieties produced: Cabernet Sauvignon, Gewürztraminer, Zinfandel, French Colombard, Grenache, Carignane, Chardonnay, Sauvignon Blanc, sherry, port

Proprietary blends and other labels: Joseph Filippi, Chateau Filippi, Thomas Vineyards, Old Rancho, Pride of Cucamonga, Guasti, California Chianti

J. Filippi Winery, P.O. Box 2, Mira Loma, California 91752
phone: 909-899-5755 fax: 909-428-6264

FIORE WINERY AND LA FELICETTA VINEYARD
Pylesville, Maryland

Mike and Rose Fiore were born in Lamezia Terme in southern Italy. Rose's father was in the grape business and Mike's family had been involved in winemaking. Mike grew up making wine in Italy before emigrating to America in 1962.

Originally, the Fiores didn't intend to get involved in winemaking, since Mike was convinced that the business had caused his family in Italy much hardship. But their memories of Italy and of the grape harvest and winemaking changed their minds. In 1975 they purchased a small farm in Maryland and planted grapevines for their own use.

Then, the small vineyard turned into a big vineyard and the Fiores were left with more grapes than they could possibly ever use. A grape glut made it difficult to sell the grapes to pickers interested in making their own homemade wine, so Mike and Rose decided to turn their small vineyard, which had become a large vineyard, into a small winery—which in time, turned into a large winery. They managed the growth from fifteen hundred gallons to fifteen thousand while both were still working full-time jobs. Recently, Rose switched to full-time winery work, while Mike has retained the job he has held for many years with the local utility company.

The winery has continued to be a family project, employing the efforts of their son and friends, as well as a few part-time employees who fill in the gaps during the busy seasons.

Grape varieties produced: Cabernet Sauvignon, Chambourcin, Chancellor, Chardonnay, Vidal, Cabernet Franc, Merlot, and an experimental patch of Sangiovese and Nebbiolo

Proprietary blends and other labels: none

Fiore Winery and La Felicetta Vineyard, 3026 Whiteford Road, Pylesville, Maryland 21132 phone: 410-879-4007 and 410-836-7605

FOPPIANO VINEYARDS
Healdsburg, California

Giovanni ("John") Foppiano left Genoa, Italy, in 1862 to come to America. He traveled by ship to Panama, walked across the isthmus and boarded a ship to San Francisco. He came in search of gold, but had only moderate success. He ended up in Healdsburg in 1864. Turning to farming fruits and vegetables was a natural shift, and he sold these from his wagon to the people in Sonoma County. Several years later, he went back to Italy to find a bride. He married Rosa Rosasco and brought her back to his home in America where they raised nine children. Their son, Louis A., was born in 1877.

In 1896 John purchased Riverside Farm, a working winery, with his son, Louis. Their business originally included delivering wine to the restaurants in San Francisco, especially the North Beach district that was heavily populated by Italians. According to records, John said: "I see so many of my countrymen arrive in this beautiful community every year. They want good wine, like they had at home, in Italy. I want to make this wine for them."

A significant chapter in the Foppiano family history occurred in 1910. John had lost faith in the future of wine as a family business. After several disagreements with Louis A. about the finances of the winery, John threatened to sell the business. Louis A. secretly borrowed money from his wife's family and bought the Foppiano business. John considered this a disloyal act, and stopped speaking to his son until just before John's death. The same year, 1910, Louis Joseph Foppiano was born.

When Prohibition hit, Foppiano Vineyards had eighty thousand gallons of the 1918 vintage on hand. In 1926 federal agents raided the winery (possibly due to Louis A.'s continuing to sell

Louis Foppiano, Sr. holding daughter, wife Matilda and sons at old winery on Highway 101, circa 1910.

wine out the back door of the winery), but allowed townspeople to bring their jugs to Foppiano to fill them up with the wine on reserve. Unfortunately, this still didn't deplete the Foppiano supply, so the Foppiano family was forced to dump thousands of gallons of wine into the nearby creek.

Throughout Prohibition, the Foppiano Wine Company sold grapes to home winemakers in San Francisco and cities in the East. To supplement this income, Louis A. returned to the farming occupation his father had started before the Foppiano Vineyards were planted, but he continued growing grapes for sale to home winemakers. Louis A. died in 1924.

When Prohibition ended, Louis J. was 23, but he planned to rebuild the family wine business. He produced eighty-five thousand gallons of wine in 1933, though he said in the 1990s that he knew "about as much about winemaking then as I do about nuclear power now." In 1937 Louis J. tore down the old winery and built a new one and started bottling wines under the Foppiano label. In 1946 Foppiano bought the Sotoyome Vineyard adjacent to the Riverside Farm. Today, while making many good wines, the Foppiano Winery is best known for its consistently excellent Petite Syrah.

Louis J. founded the Sonoma County Wine Growers Association in 1946 to help the industry during the years after Repeal. He was also a founding member of the California Wine Institute.

Grape varieties produced: Cabernet Sauvignon, Zinfandel, Petite Syrah, Merlot, Chardonnay, Sauvignon Blanc

Proprietary blends and other labels: Louis J. Foppiano, Fox Mountain, Riverside Farm

Foppiano Vineyards, 12707 Old Redwood Highway, Healdsburg, California 95448 phone: 707-433-7272 fax: 707-433-0565

FORTINO WINERY
Gilroy, California

Ernest Fortino was born in Calabria, Italy, and grew up to be the fourth generation of winemakers in the Fortino family. He came to America in the 1960s and, since he didn't know English, he worked in the fields to make a start on his new life. In time, he got a job working at the Bargetto Winery as their winemaker. He met and married Marie, also from Italy, while working at Bargetto. Together, they saved up enough during that job to start their own business: a winery.

The Fortino family bought and rebuilt the Cassa Brothers Winery in Gilroy, California, in 1970. They committed to making small lots of hand-crafted wines, in the manner of the Old World. Ernie Fortino has said that winemaking is not lab work. "We tasted the grapes," he said, "We had to work with God."

Now, Gino and Teri Fortino are in charge of operations. They make mostly Italian-style wines from a variety of grapes, and they even produce a wine called Chianti and another called Burgundy Reserve. True to their Italian heritage, the Fortinos

have incorporated food into the business, by adding a deli onto the winery and selling bread, meat, and cheese for a picnic under the trees.

Grape varieties produced: Cabernet Sauvignon, Zinfandel, Pinot Noir, Petite Syrah, Barbera, Ruby Cabernet, Grenache, Malvasia, Carignane, Charbono, Chardonnay, Riesling

Proprietary blends and other labels: none

Fortino Winery, 4525 Hecker Pass, Gilroy, California 95020 phone: 408-842-3305 fax: 408-842-8636

FRANZIA WINERY
San Joaquin Valley, California

Giuseppe Franzia came from Genoa in 1893 and worked in San Francisco for fifty cents an hour until he had saved enough money to plant a vineyard. In 1915, he bought the Ripon Winery, but closed it when Prohibition hit.

The Franzia sons maintained the vineyard throughout Prohibition, then opened a new winery following Repeal, called Franzia Brothers. Most of the wine was sold in bulk, but during World War II, they committed to bottling their own wines. This switch in plan caused some disagreement among the brothers and, in 1971, they sold the operation to eastern investors.

In 1973 the Franzia Winery was sold again, this time to the Coca-Cola Company. Then, in 1981, The Wine Group, headed by Arthur Ciocca, bought the Franzia operation, which, by then, had become little more than a label in a much longer line of other wine products.

The next generation of the Franzia family got re-involved with wine under the label JFJ Bronco. See JFJ Bronco.

FRASINETTI WINERY
Sacramento, California

James Frasinetti came from Italy in the late 1890s and settled in Sacramento. He started making wine in 1897 and delivered the bulk of his product to Sacramento in horse-drawn wagons for sale. During that time, the Frasinetti vineyard reached four hundred acres. In addition to the wine the family produced, they also shipped grapes to the East Coast to supply the home-winemaking market there.

During Prohibition, the Frasinettis switched to making altar wine and selling their grapes for table consumption. This was, no doubt, supplemented by the market they had already established with home winemakers in the East. Things got a little better after Prohibition ended, and the vineyard land was expanded.

The next few decades saw little change in the Frasinetti holdings. As the third generation took over in the 1970s, though, the Frasinetti Winery began to take on a new look. They got rid of some of the redwood vats and bought oak barrels, and tried to apply Old World techniques to New World lessons.

In recent years, the Frasinetti family has increased the oak cooperage and added stainless steel tanks for fermentation. The winery still produces an extensive line of wines at friendly prices. All product is sold at the winery and in their restaurant.

Grape varieties produced: Cabernet Sauvignon, Merlot, Zinfandel, Cerasolo, Chardonnay, Sauvignon Blanc, Chenin Blanc, Johannisberg Riesling, and several dessert wines and a port

Proprietary blends and other labels: none

Frasinetti Winery, 7395 Frasinetti Road, Sacramento, California 95828 phone: 916-383-2444 fax: 916-383-5825

GABRIELLI WINERY
Redwood Valley, California

The Gabrielli family lived in the Marches region in Italy, making wine in their town of Capradosso. In 1915 Saverio Gabrielli came to America and settled in Pennsylvania. Although there was no commercial wine production then, the family made wine at home from California grapes shipped to Philadelphia, including Alicante Bouschet, Zinfandel, Muscat, Grenache, and Thompson Seedless. Sam Gabrielli remembers making wine in the family's basement in Pennsylvania, and during his youth he worked at Conestoga Winery in Pennsylvania during the harvest.

Wine was processed and stored behind these doors of the Gabrielli Winery. Winemakers then sold it to the locals in Capradosso, Italy and drank it themselves.

Sam became a carpenter, and continued to live in Pennsylvania. One day, he came across a book about winemaking in the county library. He wrote to the University of California at Davis for more information and, when he received their curriculum, decided that he wanted to study enology. So he moved to California where he met his future wife, Bernadette Yamada, and entered the enology program at Davis. After graduation, he was sidetracked into biochemical engineering research for six years, then he came back to wine.

In 1989 Sam and Bernadette and Jeff Hinchliffe started the Gabrielli Winery, relying on a U.C. Davis education in enology and a commitment to making intense wines that take advantage of the varied microclimates of Mendocino.

Grape varieties produced: Zinfandel, Pinot Noir, Sangiovese, Petite Syrah, Chardonnay, Riesling, Semillon, Chenin Blanc

Proprietary blends and other labels: Ascenza

Gabrielli Winery, 10950 West Road, Redwood Valley, California 95470 phone: 707-485-1221 fax: 707-485-1225

GAGETTA WINERY
Rutherford, California

Joseph Gagetta made wine at Lombarda Winery, the site established by Charles Forni. When Lombarda Winery was sold to the Napa Cantina Winery, Gagetta intended to take the Lombarda name for his own operation in Rutherford. But Gagetta died before he could formalize the plan, and his son, Dennis Gagetta, kept the Joseph Gagetta Winery name in Rutherford.

The winery no longer exists.

GALLEANO WINERY
Mira Loma, California

Domenico Galleano came from northern Italy in 1913 and bought Esteban Cantu's ranch in 1926, but he didn't start the winery until 1933 when Prohibition ended. The winery has stayed in the family and is currently managed by Domenico's grandson, Don Galleano. It is the oldest winery in Riverside County, California, and was designated a County Historical Landmark in 1993.

This nineteenth-century barn was part of the Galleano Winery, the oldest winery in Riverside County. It is now a county historical landmark.

Most of the wine is sold in bulk to other wineries, but the Galleanos also sell grapes, as well as wine under their own label.

Grape varieties produced: Zinfandel and others

Proprietary blends and other labels: none

Galleano Winery, 4231 Wineville Road, Mira Loma, California 91752 phone: 909-685-5376 fax: 909-360-9180

E. & J. GALLO
Modesto, California

The Gallo wine empire is precisely that: An empire. Many good things have been said about it through the years and many bad things, but the business that Ernest and Julio put together in the years following Repeal has been truly amazing.

Giuseppe "Joe" Gallo was born in 1882 in Fossano in northern Italy. Just after 1900, he left Italy for Venezuela. After a while he left there and traveled to Philadelphia, then west to Oakland. He bought land in Modesto and planted vineyards. Joe married Assunta "Susie" Bianco in 1908 and their children Ernest and Julio were born in 1909 and 1910, respectively.

The stories begin to diverge a bit at this point. Some witnesses claim that Joe Gallo teamed up with his brother, Michelo, also known as "Mike," to form the Gallo Wine Company in 1906[3] while other stories—including that of the Gallos themselves—state that Ernest and Julio didn't know anything about wine until after Repeal, learning it from pamphlets they found in the library. The difference in stories is significant, since the first suggests that Joe Gallo made wine and that Ernest and Julio knew about winemaking in their youth while the second story suggests that Joe Gallo never made wine from the many acres of vineyards he owned and that his sons had to teach themselves the process after Repeal. An intermediate interpretation of the Gallo history is offered by Adams, who writes that Ernest and Julio remembered their father making wine, but it was in the basement of their house and only for his own use.[4]

Ernest was responsible for grape sales during Prohibition and would often travel to Chicago to supply the growing home-winemaking industry there. He also opened markets on the East Coast for the Gallo grapes. Throughout the years of his partnership with his brother, Julio, Ernest would remain the preeminent salesman of the pair.

And in the years following Repeal, Ernest would return to the cities where he had hawked his grapes to sell the wine the E. & J. Gallo Wine Company was then producing.

The stories converge again after Repeal, all agreeing that Ernest and Julio Gallo applied for a winery license soon after their parents' sudden death in 1933, and just after the Twenty-first Amendment repealed Prohibition. They converted a warehouse in Modesto into their winery and started making wine as soon as the new law allowed.

In the beginning, they made bulk wine and sold much of it to East Coast distributors. Their plan was clear: make acceptable wine for a low price and capture the market for those not looking for a fine-wine experience. By doing so, they based their success on volume, and they produced a prodigious volume of wine to succeed.

In the late 1930s they started buying grapes from Dry Creek Valley to make their wine, specifically from the Frei brothers. They liked the result so much that, in 1947, they formed a partnership with the Frei brothers. In 1976 they finished the deal by buying out the Frei brothers and enlarging the winemaking facility there. The wines produced by the Gallos from that property still say Frei Ranch on the label.

The Gallo headquarters, its buildings set on landscaped ground along Dry Creek in Modesto, is an exercise in architectural civility.

Thanks to Ernest, the family wine business was tuned into market issues early. He became a marketing expert and would often visit stores all over the country to ensure that his wines were positioned on shelves just about chest level, considered to be the perfect spot since it is where the sight line and arm movements merge. He created the Carlo Rossi line of wines, named after one of the Gallo empire's historically most successful salesman, Charles Rossi—a fitting tribute from a company designed more for sales than quality in its early years. He also created Bartles & Jaymes wine coolers and is said to have been instrumental in the fabulously successful advertising campaign that launched this product line.

While Ernest was convincing the world to buy Gallo wines, Julio was staying close to home making them. He was quieter than his more energetic brother, knew more about winemaking, and was probably easier to like. Julio unfortunately died in an auto accident in 1993.

E. & J. Gallo produces a brandy, a sparkling wine called Totts and another called Eden Roc, the Andre group of cheap sparkling wines, Livingston Cellars port, Hearty Burgundy, Ripple, and Boone's Farm, among other names.

In recent years, Ernest has tried to take his company into the future. He is now marketing wines in the premium price range, with some success. Only time will tell whether he can erase a reputation that puts "Gallo" just before the word "jug wine" on the wine public's tongue.

The new Gallo generation, principally Matt and Gina, are spearheading an effort to promote Gallo of Sonoma. The new enterprise bears no relation to the jug wines of Gallo's past, concentrating instead on premium grapes from premium properties. The younger generation's dedication to wine is the same as that of Ernest and Julio, and they are building their empire in an era that looks for great wines, not just the bulk wines popular when the winery's founders opened their doors after Prohibition. By early accounts, it appears they will be as successful in the new era as their grandfather Julio and Uncle Ernest were in the old era.

Grape varieties produced: numerous

Proprietary blends and other labels: Gallo of Sonoma, Frei Ranch, Carlo Rossi, Bartles & Jaymes, Livingston Cellars, Totts, Eden Rock, Andre, Ripple, Boone's Farm, others

E. & J. Gallo, 600 Yosemite Boulevard, Modesto, California 95353 phone: 209-579-3111 fax: 209-579-4361

GEMELLO WINERY
Mountain View, California

This winery was started in 1934 by John Gemello, who wanted to make Italian-style wines. He stuck to red wines, and passed down the winery and his traditions to the next generations.

John sold the winery to his niece in 1982 and it was incorporated into the Obester Winery.

Grape varieties produced: Cabernet Sauvignon, Zinfandel, Petite Syrah

Proprietary blends and other labels: none

Gemello Winery, 2003 El Camino Real, Mountain View, California 94040 phone: 415-948-7723

J. H. GENTILI WINES
Redwood City, California

Jim Anderson's winemaking started out as a hobby, but his interest nearly turned it into a research and development project, leading him to study many different kinds of grapes. This got him into planting vines, which for a while were supplemented with purchased grapes. In 1981 he decided to get a winery bond and start producing for commercial sale. Soon thereafter, he switched from growing grapes to buying them.

He chose Gentili as the name since his mother's side of the family, the Gentilis, are Italian and his interest in winemaking came from them.

Anderson is also in the fishing business, which he came to through his father's side of the family. This is the true source of his income, and the fishing industry's difficult times at the turn of this last century have forced Anderson to put the winery on hold until things get straightened out.

Anderson still produces wine, and still has his winery bond, though he has been storing the wine until he can get back into the business with heart.

Grape varieties produced: Zinfandel, Cabernet Sauvignon, Cabernet Franc, Chardonnay, Sauvignon Blanc

Proprietary blends and other labels: none

J. H. Gentili Wines, 60 Lowell Street, Redwood City, California 94062 phone: 415-368-4740

GEYSER PEAK WINERY
Geyserville, California

The winery was founded in 1880 by Augustus Quitzow. In 1887 it was purchased by Edward Walden & Company, importers of French brandy, who wanted to make brandy at the winery. In 1908 Edward Walden lost the winery in default, after suffering great financial losses around the turn of the century. The Farmers' and Mechanics' Bank took over and leased the winery to O. J. LeBaron and W. S. Kelly, who named it Geyser Peak. In 1910 the Ciocca Lombardi Winery Company of San Francisco took over and turned Geyser Peak into one of the best-equipped wineries in California. From 1908 until 1937, the operation was known as the Geyser Peak Wine and Brandy Company.

In 1937 the Bagnani family's Italy Industries bought Geyser Peak,

renaming it Redwood Empire Wines. In 1945 Redwood Empire Wines ceased to exist, but American Industries continued to make bulk wines at Geyser Peak until the Bagnanis sold it to the Schlitz Brewing Company in 1972. Schlitz modernized and expanded the winery significantly and, in 1980, sold Geyser Peak to Stroh's Brewing Company, who held onto it for only two years.

In 1982 the Trione family bought the winery from the Stroh's Brewing Company and started to turn things around. In 1985, they dropped Summit, a line of wines packaged in collapsible plastic sacks and stored and sold in cardboard boxes. In 1989, they sold half interest in the winery to Penfolds in Australia. In doing so, they acquired the services of Daryl Groom, a winemaker who has taken Geyser Peak to the heights of the popular market. Later, the Trione family bought back the shares from Penfolds, while Groom stayed on.

Henry Trione, the family patriarch, has always had an interest in polo. His love of the sport kindled with his passion for wine when Geyser Peak became the official winery of the United States Polo Association. In 1998, the Trione family sold Geyser Peak and its subsidiary labels to Fortune Brands.

Grape varieties produced: Cabernet Sauvignon, Merlot, Cabernet Franc, Petite Verdot, Shiraz, Zinfandel, Malbec, Chardonnay, Sauvignon Blanc, Semillon, Gewürztraminer, Johannisberg Riesling, late harvest Riesling, Shiraz port

Proprietary blends and other labels: Reserve Alexandre (Meritage), Premium Vintage Red, Premium Vintage White, Canyon Road, Venezia, Fox Ridge
Geyser Peak Winery, 22281 Chianti Road, P.O. Box 25, Geyserville, California 95441 phone: 800-945-4447 fax: 707-857-3545

GINOCCHIO BROTHERS WINERY
Jackson, California

The Ginocchio brothers started making wine in 1876 in Amador County near Jackson, California. They used a traditional Italian method of drying their grapes, using the Alden Fruit Dryer that they invented for the purpose.

The traditional method is called *passito* and consists of laying the grapes out on pallets or hanging them from tree limbs to allow some of the moisture to evaporate and concentrate the sugar and flavor components in the grapes. The resulting wine is concentrated in flavor, higher in alcohol than other wines, and sometimes has a slightly port-like character.

The Ginocchio brothers wine was described as resembling port in both color and body. Apparently, it was a big success, though most of it never left Amador County. The winery is no longer in existence.

GIUMARRA VINEYARDS
Edison, California

Giuseppe Giumarra came from Sicily, worked in Toronto for a while, and then settled in Bakersfield, California. In 1946 he built a winery designed to make bulk dessert wines and concentrate, but his brother, John, got them into the table-wine business.

Most of the wine is still sold to other wineries, but the Giumarra family also became involved in a much more ambitious enterprise: the production of soft drinks such as Snapple and Arizona. This has become the concentration of the family business, though some bulk wines are still produced.

Grape varieties produced: none identified
Proprietary blends and other labels: none
Giumarra Vineyards, Edison Road and Edison Highway, Edison, California 93220 phone: 805-395-7000

GRECO WINERY
Middletown, Ohio

Anthony M. Greco left Cosenza, Italy in the 1950s to work as an engineer in the United States. He landed in New York, worked there for a while, then moved to Minnesota to continue his trade. Later he moved to Ohio, still working as an engineer.

In 1977 Greco bought twenty-five acres in Franklin, Ohio, and planted vines. Later, after retiring from his engineering career, he moved his operation to Butler County and bought another sixty-three acres to farm. Greco kept the operation going during his retirement, though his production has been decreasing throughout the late 1990s. As of this writing, he is selling off much of the wine that he has stored and aged in barrels.

Greco makes generic white and red wines and a special bottling that he calls Supremo that is aged for five years in oak.

Grape varieties produced: none identified

Proprietary blends and other labels: Supremo

Greco Winery, 6266 Hamilton-Lebanon Road, Route 63, Middletown, Ohio 45044 phone: 513-539-8768

EMILIO GUGLIELMO WINERY
Morgan Hill, California

Emilio Guglielmo, born in 1883, came to the United States from Piedmont, Italy, in 1908. He worked in a variety of jobs while making his way to the West Coast. He arrived in San Francisco in 1910, sent for his Italian sweetheart, Emilia, married her, and started making wine for friends and neighbors in the basement of their house. They moved to the Santa Clara Valley and founded the Emilio Guglielmo Winery in 1925, while Prohibition was still in force. Planning for the end of Prohibition, Emilio and Emilia started buying up vineyard land in the Santa Clara Valley near Morgan Hill, about eighty miles south of San Francisco. After Prohibition, the Guglielmo family turned commercial, but kept the business in the family.

Emilio's knowledge of both French and Italian allowed him to develop a clientele among the Italian, French, and Basque communities of San Francisco, especially the North Beach area of the city. In the

late 1940s, the business was passed on to their son, George Guglielmo, and his wife, and the business is now operated by the third generation after Emilio.

Over the years, the Emilio Guglielmo Winery has maintained its reputation for hearty, Italian-style wines.

Grape varieties produced: Cabernet Sauvignon, Merlot, Pinot Noir, Zinfandel, Sangiovese, Petite Syrah, Grignolino, Marsala, Chardonnay, Sauvignon Blanc, Johannisberg Riesling

Proprietary blends and other labels: Mt. Madonna, Emile's, Emile's Private Stock, Claret (a changing blend, recently of Zinfandel and Petite Syrah), Stars and Stripes (Chardonnay vintage 1995, also titled: America's Cup Defense)

Emilio Guglielmo Winery, 1480 East Main Avenue, Morgan Hill, California 95037 phone: 408-779-2145 fax: 408-779-3166

HECKER PASS WINERY
Gilroy, California

The Hecker Pass Winery is owned by Mario Fortino, of the family that owns the Fortino Winery just down the road. He left the family business in 1972 to set up his own winery, but retained his interest in producing wines in the Italian style.

Grape varieties produced: Cabernet Sauvignon, Zinfandel, Grenache, Carignane, Petite Syrah, Chablis, port, sherry

Proprietary blends and other labels: none

Hecker Pass Winery, 4605 Hecker Pass Highway, Gilroy, California 95020 phone: 408-842-8755 fax: 408-842-9799

CHARLES KRUG WINERY
St. Helena, California

Charles Krug came to the United States from Germany in 1847. He married Mariano Guadalupe Vallejo's grandniece and, from her dowry, he assumed control of the land where he established the Charles Krug Winery in 1861. The winery was having financial trouble in the early 1900s, and when Prohibition hit, it closed down.

For a short time after Repeal, Louie Stralla leased the facility for his Napa Wine Company; then he moved on. James K. Moffitt then bought it but soon was looking for a buyer. He was still looking when, in 1943, Cesare Mondavi was persuaded by his sons to buy the Charles Krug Winery. As Adams states, "credit for the many good and fine wines now made [at Charles Krug] belongs not to Krug, but to the Italian family named Mondavi."[5]

The Mondavis brought the business back into black ink and built it into one of the better known brands in America. This was accom-

Charles Krug's carriage house in St. Helena, California.

plished with Peter Mondavi in charge of winemaking and his brother, Robert, handling sales and marketing.

In 1966 Robert Mondavi split with the family in what has become an historic event for American wine. After twenty-three years of Robert and Peter working to establish the Charles Krug Winery, Robert set off to establish the world-famous Robert Mondavi Winery. Peter has continued to pursue fine wines at the Charles Krug estate and has had great success in maintaining the reputation that his family's fifty years of management had established.

Grape varieties produced: Cabernet Sauvignon, Pinot Noir, Merlot, Zinfandel, Sangiovese, Gamay Beaujolais, Chardonnay, Chenin Blanc, Sauvignon Blanc, Johannisberg Riesling

Proprietary blends and other labels: C. K. Mondavi

Charles Krug Winery, 2800 St. Helena Hwy, St. Helena, California 94574 phone: 707-963-5057

LARKMEAD WINERY

Larkmead Winery, earlier referred to Larkmead Vineyard, had been in existence since the 1880s, and counted many illustrious names among its owners. There was Lillie Hitchcock Coit, who donated Coit Tower to San Francisco's Telegraph Hill. Then there was Felix Salmina from Switzerland, National Distillers, the Larkmead Cooperative, and Hanns Kornell. And there was also Frank Bragno from Chicago.

After Repeal, Bragno Wine Company was the Illinois distributor for Italian Swiss Colony, but lost that source of wine when Italian Swiss Colony was bought by National Distillers. So Bragno went in search of its own winery in California, to ensure a future supply of wine and avoid another buyout. Frank Bragno bought Larkmead Winery in 1943 in a partnership with Blum and Company, offering half the stock in Larkmead in return for the financial backing to get Bragno's idea off the ground. Unfortunately, the terms of the partnership were strict, and Harry Blum's goal for Larkmead didn't match Bragno's: Blum was looking for a good return on his investment and Bragno was trying to start a business for his family's Bragno Wine Company, which by then included Bragno Imperial and Lloyd's Imported, as well as shares in Riverbank Winery.

Soon, Bragno fell behind in his payments to Blum and Company. Blum ran out of patience in 1946, and bought Bragno's shares in Larkmead in that year. Larkmead Winery no longer exists.

LEONETTI CELLAR
Walla Walla, Washington

Frank and Rose Leonetti left Calabria, Italy in 1906 and wound up in Washington State. At first, they satisfied their typically Italian need for wine at dinner by having California grapes shipped north and, together with Italian neighbors, made their own wine in those years.

Frank and Rose are remembered well by their family for the vegetables and grapes they raised. Gary Figgins, their grandson, remembers being poured a glass of wine at the age of five by Grandpa Leonetti. A severe winter in the 1950s killed most of Frank Leonetti's vines and, were it not for his grandson, Gary, the idea of Leonetti wines would also have been killed.

Gary started small, making his own wine and often experimenting with non-grape wines. In 1975 he tried Pinot Noir and, in 1976, Cabernet Sauvignon. His interest continued—and grew—but it was only in the late 1980s that Gary Figgins's already well-respected wines turned enough of a profit to allow him to devote himself full time to winemaking.

Gary has devoted himself to the production of red wines and insists that he will continue with that focus. His wines are not cheap but, by all accounts, are worth every penny. In the late 1990s, Leonetti Cellar began production of Sangiovese and is considering expanding into planting or purchasing other Italian grape varieties.

The Leonetti Cellar produces premier Washington State Cabernet, Merlot, and Sangiovese.

Grape varieties produced: Cabernet Sauvignon, Merlot, Sangiovese
Proprietary blends and other labels: none
Leonetti Cellar, 1321 School Avenue, Walla Walla, Washington 99362 phone: 509-525-1428

LOMBARDA WINERY

This winery started on property purchased and planted by John Tychson. In 1895, Antonio Forni, an immigrant from Lombardy, bought it and built the Lombarda Winery on the spot. By 1900, Forni had established himself in the wine business and invested his profits in the construction of a hand-hewn stone winery that was completed in 1906 with a capacity of three hundred thousand gallons.[6]

The property was closed during Prohibition then used briefly by Joseph Gagetta in 1932 and Walter Martini in 1933. When it was bought by the Napa Cantina Winery, Gagetta appropriated the name, which he and Martini used in a joint venture. Following Gagetta's death in 1934, Martini moved the Lombarda winery to a location just north of St. Helena. From then until 1940, Lombarda served as a processing facility, receiving bulk wine that was bottled and resold. By some accounts, ownership returned to Forni's widow, through default. Then, in 1940, it was bought and renamed Freemark Abbey.

The Lombarda Winery label no longer exists.

ANGELO MARRE WINERY

Angelo Marre came with his family from Italy in 1868. He settled in Amador County and promptly opened a boarding house. By 1877 he was making wine and brandy, serving some to his boarders, and shipping six thousand gallons to Chicago every year. By 1878 he was shipping wine to Memphis, New York, and, in 1880, Philadelphia.

In 1881 Marre opened wholesale warehouses in Chicago and New York to handle the volume of wine traffic he was involved in. He also erected a stone building in Jackson, California, to sell his wine. Today, that building is a private residence at the corner of Broadway and Bright.

MARTINELLI WINERY
Windsor, California

Giuseppe and Louisa Martinelli left their hometown in Tuscany and came to the town of Forestville in Sonoma County in 1887. Giuseppe started by planting vineyards for other wineries, then saved up enough money to buy his own. To get started, Giuseppe and Louisa cleared twelve acres of redwood trees by hand. As if that weren't enough of a challenge, the land they planted to vines in the years to come was so steep that a family elder said: "It takes a jackass to farm a hill that steep." The vineyard is now named Jackass Hill.

In 1905 they planted Zinfandel and Muscat Alexandria. Due to Giuseppe's untimely death in 1918, Leno Martinelli left school at the age of thirteen to help out at the family farm.

In 1927 Leno married Alma Bondi. Their son, Lee, took over the business in 1973 and immediately started planting more vineyards. Today, the Martinellli Vineyards include premium grape varieties, principally Zinfandel, Pinot Noir, Chardonnay, Gewürztraminer, and Sauvignon Blanc. The Pinot Noir is from the Bondi vineyard, which belonged to Lee's uncle but was merged with the Martinelli holdings on Tony Bondi's death. And the family is making great strides with its Zinfandel that is principally from the Jackass Vineyard and is labeled as such.

Grape varieties produced: Zinfandel, Pinot Noir, Chardonnay, Sauvignon Blanc, Gewürztraminer

Proprietary blends and other labels: Jackass Vineyard
Martinelli Winery, 3360 River Road, Windsor, California 95492 phone: 707-525-0570 fax: 707-525-9463

LOUIS M. MARTINI
St. Helena, California

In 1899 when Louis M. Martini was thirteen years old, he left Petra Ligure, Italy, for America. He worked with his father, Agostino, selling fish in San Francisco neighborhoods. In 1906, Agostino and Louis made their first wine in a small shed behind their house in the Bayview district of San Francisco. It spoiled, but Louis was not deterred. He decided to return to Italy to study winemaking.

He came back to California and resumed selling fish. However, now he was also making and selling wine. He followed the wisdom of his wine professor in Italy, that winemaking required careful attention, that the winery and equipment should be clean and well tended, and that fermentation should be carried out in a cool, clean environment. The Louis M. Martini Winery was "probably the first winery in the Napa Valley to invest in mechanical refrigeration," says James T Lapsley.[7] Martini's techniques were so respected that, after Prohibition, they even garnered the praise of the Treasury bureaucrats who inspected the commercial wineries.

Louis Martini of the Louis M. Martini Winery.

In 1911 father and son decided to buy a small vineyard in Pleasanton and began making more wine. In 1918 when the winery business didn't pan out, Agostino and his wife, Angelica, returned to Italy, but Louis remained in California. In 1922, while Prohibition was still in effect, Louis founded the L. M. Martini Grape Products Company. Although the company made sacramental wine, its primary business appears to have been selling grape concentrate to home winemakers. A family story says that Louis M. once sold one hundred thousand gallons of grape juice to home winemakers in one day.

When Repeal arrived in 1933, he was ready to resume winemaking operations, so he bought the Eccleston farm in St. Helena, renamed it the Louis M. Martini Winery, and devoted it to the production of dry table wines. In 1938, Louis M. bought the Mt. Pisgah Vineyard in Sonoma County which had been planted in the 1880s by Samuel Goldstein, and renamed it Monte Rosso Vineyard. By 1940, when many wineries were still bottling generic wines in jugs, Martini was making and marketing varietally based wines. A 1941 Treasury Department report on the L. M. Martini Winery referred to "W. Zinfandel," perhaps the first reference to White Zinfandel being made in California.

In 1942 Louis bought La Loma Vineyard and Stanley Ranch (which are no longer part of the Martini empire). Four additional vineyards have been added in Healdsburg, Chiles Valley, Pope Valley, and Lake County.

Louis M.'s influence in the wine industry has been profound. Not only did he establish a state-of-the-art winery in St. Helena just as Prohibition was repealed, but he was instrumental in the founding of the Wine Institute and the Napa Valley Vintners Association. He also put his name on the label in the 1930s when most of the wineries were still selling their wine in bulk. The decision created a lot of name recognition for him, but also kept on the pressure to produce good wine since the buyers would know the source of the wine.

Louis P., son of Louis M., was trained at the University of California at Berkeley and Davis and became winemaker for the family winery in 1954. Louis P. kept up the family's reputation for clean, careful winemaking when, in 1958, he installed a bottling system that would inject carbon dioxide into the bottles before corking. He was succeeded by his son, Michael, in 1977. Louis M. died in 1974.

Grape varieties produced: Barbera, Cabernet Sauvignon, Merlot, Pinot Noir, Zinfandel, Petite Syrah, Gamay Beaujolais, Chardonnay, Gewürztraminer, Sauvignon Blanc

Proprietary blends and other labels: Monte Rosso Cabernet Sauvignon, La Loma Pinot Noir, Los Vinedos del Rio Merlot
Louis M. Martini, P.O. Box 112, St. Helena, California 94574
phone: 800-321-9463 fax: 707-963-8750

MARTINI & PRATI WINES
Santa Rosa, California

Rafael Martini lived in Lucca, Italy before packing up and moving to the United States. He was from a farming family and intended to continue farming in the New World, but wine was in his blood. Like many Italians before him, he settled in the Sonoma County, finding the climate and topology so similar to his native Tuscany. He planted brussel sprouts, artichokes, and broccoli, and opened a distribution center in San Francisco to sell the produce in the city.

But Rafael also wanted grapevines. So, in 1902, he bought the Twin Fir Winery in the Russian River area near Sebastopol (built in 1881) and renamed it the R. Martini Winery. As Twin Fir and later, R. Martini, it is acclaimed as the oldest winery in continuous operation in Sonoma County.

R. Martini Winery's agricultural connections helped it survive and stay in business throughout Prohibition. In addition, Narciso, Rafael's son, took advantage of the exception made for religious wine and shipped as much as ten thousand gallons of wine per year to rabbis in New York. As Narciso's son, Elmo, is quoted as saying, "It's amazing how many more rabbis there suddenly were in New York during Prohibition."

Rafael's son, Narciso, sold the winery in 1943 to Hiram Walker, but the deal included keeping Elmo on to operate it. In 1950 Elmo and fellow

Workers at the Martini & Prati Winery transport grapes from the vineyard at harvest time in 1945.

vintner Enrico Prati bought the winery back and named it Martini & Prati.

Much of the original equipment has been preserved and provides visitors with a unique picture of the earliest times of American wine production. The Martinis' original house still stands, the first one built on Laguna Road, with its square nails and locally milled virgin redwood. The stable and bunkhouse once used by itinerant Italians working the grape crush is now the tasting room at the winery. Martini & Prati still uses huge redwood tanks—some holding as much as thirty-five thousand gallons—for storing the wine, a solution decried by many modern-day wineries but still cherished as a traditional artifact of American winemaking. Today, Martini & Prati uses twenty-five-ton open-top concrete fermentation tanks, a practice more common to the Martini and Prati families' European origins than to the New World, but one which is well suited to the production of red wines.

As a further tribute to the past, Martini & Prati invites its visitors to fill their own jugs straight from the tanks, a European practice from an era when wine production was a community endeavor and all villagers shared in the product together.

Cellar workers at Martini & Prati enjoy the fruits of their labor in 1917.

Grape varieties produced: Sangiovese, Cabernet Sauvignon, Barbera, Zinfandel, Pinot Noir, Sauvignon Blanc, Trousseau Gris, Chardonnay, Viognier, Moscato Canelli, port

Proprietary blends and other labels: Fountain Grove, Fuoco di Sant' Elmo (a proprietary red blend)

Martini & Prati Wines, 2191 Laguna Road, Santa Rosa, California 95401 phone: 707-823-2404 fax: 707-829-6151

MASTANTUONO WINERY
Templeton, California

Pasquale "Pat" Mastantuono's father came from Naples and settled in Detroit, where Pat was born. As an adult, Pat built a very successful business producing custom-made furniture near Los Angeles. Unfortunately, the L.A. crowds and the pace of life drove him away, and he sold his business and his house and moved to a ranch near Templeton where he grew grapes, grain, and walnuts.

At first, he made wine for his own consumption, experimenting with Zinfandel grapes from all over the state. In 1976 Pat started commercial wine production. This, too, was a success, and in 1983 he built a new winery. Pat produces good wines for good prices, and seems to get as much fun out of the bocce ball alleys next to the winery as out the wine business itself.

Grape varieties produced: Zinfandel, Nebbiolo, Sangiovese, Barbera, Pinot Grigio, Muscat Canelli, White Zinfandel, Champagne, port (based on Barbera), Chardonnay

Proprietary blends and other labels: Templeton Winery

Mastantuono Winery, Route 2, Box 100, Oakview Road, Templeton, California 93465 phone: 805-238-0676

MAZZOCCO VINEYARDS
Healdsburg, California

Tom Mazzocco is an ophthalmologist who had a very successful practice in southern California. He started winemaking as a hobbyist, trying first to make wine from concentrate. Unfortunately, his first carboy of "Chianti" met an ignoble end when it smashed open on the bathroom floor. He moved up to real grapes and Zinfandel, and met with success.

It was still a big leap to buying a commercial winery, but Tom and his wife, Yvonne, purchased River Lane Vineyard in the Alexander Valley in 1980. In 1984 they opened a winery in Dry Creek Valley, conducting their first crush of commercial grapes in 1985. By 1986 they were producing ten thousand cases.

Today Mazzocco Winery is very popular for its exceptional Zinfandel and consistently pleasing Chardonnay. The Cabernet Sauvignon has been more erratic in quality, but seems to get better each year.

Grape varieties produced: Zinfandel, Merlot, Malbec, Cabernet Sauvignon, Cabernet Franc, Chardonnay, Viognier

Proprietary blends and other labels: none

Mazzocco Vineyards, 1400 Lytton Springs Road, Healdsburg, California phone: 707-433-9035, fax: 707-431-2369

MELLEA WINERY
West Dudley, Massachusetts

Joe and Allie Compagnone were buying a couple acres of land for their manufacturing company in West Dudley, Massachusetts. In the process, they bought thirty acres, but deciding how to use the other twenty-eight acres was a chore. They had the soil tested and found that crops and orchards were not an option, but grapes were.

They started the Mellea Winery, named after Joe's mother, Rosina Mellea, and planted several varieties of grapes. A cranberry wine is also made, from a blend of cranberries and Riesling.

The tasting room is housed in a small rustic barn that is also the winery, looking out over the vineyards, brookside picnic area, and surrounding acreage. The winery is strictly modern, with stainless steel fermentation tanks, barrel room outfitted with French oak cooperage, and bottling line. Mellea Winery has several special events such as the New England Fall Wine Festival, but its most popular is the "I Love Lucy Grape Stomping Festival" where visitors are invited to jump into the vat and stomp away.

Grape varieties produced: Pinot Noir, Chardonnay, Vidal Blanc, Seyval Blanc, Riesling, Cayuga, Malvasia Bianca

Proprietary blends and other labels: none

Mellea Winery, 108 Old Southbridge Road, P.O. Box 1328, West Dudley, Massachusetts 01571 phone: 508-943-5166 fax: 508-949-2539

MENGHINI WINERY
Julian, California

Mike Menghini's grandfather came from Trento but didn't get involved with commercial wine in the United States. When Mike decided he wanted into the business, he worked first for San Pasqual Vineyards, Callaway Vineyards and Winery, and Filsinger Winery. Later, he and his wife, Toni, decided it was time to open their own winery.

Grape varieties produced: none identified

Proprietary blends and other labels: none

Menghini Winery, 1150 Julian Orchards Drive, Julian, California 92036 phone: 619-765-2072

MILANO WINERY
Hopland, California

This winery was founded by Greg Graziano and Jim Milone in 1977. Greg's family was from Asti in northern Italy and Jim's family was from Brindisi in southern Italy. The winery was an old hop kiln that had been built by Jim's grandfather and father in the 1940s, but which went largely unused until Greg and Jim reconditioned it.

In 1980 the partnership dissolved. Jim kept Milano Winery and Greg went on to become the winemaker at several estates before opening his own Domaine Saint Gregory and Monte Volpe wineries. See Domaine Saint Gregory and Monte Volpe.

Grape varieties produced: Cabernet Sauvignon, Zinfandel, Merlot, Chardonnay

Proprietary blends and other labels: none

Milano Winery, 14594 S. Highway 101, Hopland, California 95449 phone: 707-744-1396

MILANI WINERY

This winery was started by an Italian immigrant named Milani. By 1904 he had grown disaffected with the wine business and sold the vineyard and winery to Samuele Sebastiani. The Milani Winery no longer exists under this name.

MOCERI WINERY
San Carlos, California

Frank Moceri was the distributor for Santino Wines when he decided to form a negociant house to buy wine and blend and bottle it under his own name.

Grape varieties produced: Cabernet Sauvignon, Chardonnay, Sauvignon Blanc

Proprietary blends and other labels: none

Moceri Winery, 1724 Laurel Street, San Carlos, California 94070

ROBERT MONDAVI WINERY
Oakville, California

Robert Mondavi is the most famous member of a fine family of American wine. His father, Cesare, emigrated from Sassafarento in 1906 and settled in Minnesota. In 1918 the Italian Club of Minnesota convinced Cesare to search California for a source of grapes for their home winemaking. He liked California so much, he moved his family there in 1923. In 1936 the Mondavis bought Sunnyhill Winery and renamed it Sunny St. Helena Winery. Three years later, they needed more space, so they rented the DiMarco Winery on Spring Street in St. Helena, then in 1941 they expanded again and leased the Gagetta Winery in Rutherford.

By 1940 the Mondavi family owned a controlling share of the Acampo Winery, which would be sold in 1943 to finance bigger operations. When the Charles Krug Winery was put up for sale in 1943, Robert began his now-illustrious career by convincing his father to buy it. In 1946 the Mondavis sold their remaining interest in Sunny St. Helena Winery to Martin Stelling, Jr., and concentrated on production at Charles Krug.

Cesare assigned his sons separate responsibilities: Robert would handle sales and marketing while Peter was responsible for winemaking. Robert applied his still-conspicuous flair for public relations and traveled throughout the country selling the Krug wines. But he believed that California wines could be the equal of those from Europe, so disagreements often arose over the quality of the wines his brother was producing.

When Cesare died in 1959, control of the winery passed to his widow. Robert was still doing sales and Peter was still making the wine. In 1965 Cesare's heirs fought over the future of the Charles Krug Winery they had run as a family business since purchasing it. Finally, the feud became cataclysmic: Robert was voted out of an active role in the family business, and he left Charles Krug Winery.

In 1966 Robert broke ground on his new winery, the Robert Mondavi Winery. Here, he could insist on things being done his way, which included heavy research into vineyard management, soil types, and winemaking processes, later choosing specific vinification techniques for each varietal. It is now probably the best-known American winery anywhere in the world. It achieved that status by exploring every niche of the wine market, but steadfastly insisting on quality wines even when they were bottled in jug sizes, and by establishing numerous separate labels to promote its product and serve every interest.

The winery's success is also dependent in no small way on its founder's dream. When Robert Mondavi separated from his family's business at the Charles Krug Winery, he set his sights on nothing less than revolutionizing the way Americans think about, and drink, wine.

Like his father before him, Robert Mondavi employed his sons, Michael and Tim, in separate segments of the business and was intent on continuing the Italian tradition of making his a family business. And he continued to employ highly qualified people to achieve his dream. He bought vineyard land to add to his empire, thereby creating new labels such as Woodbridge, a popular, low-priced varietal program. He also experimented with the many types of grapes available in California. His wine program supports a growing research project into the ideal vines for microclimates.

In 1979 he joined forces with the Rothschilds of Chateau Mouton-Rothschild to produce a wine called Opus One, which blends Cabernet Sauvignon with smaller percentages of Cabernet Franc, Merlot, Malbec, and Petit Verdot in traditional Bordeaux fashion. The wine is lavished with attention, including the most expensive grapes and equipment, and has always shown very well. It was Mondavi's crown-

ing achievement, until his life and schedule were taken over by his obsession with the meaning and role of wine in everyday life.

In the 1990s Mondavi combined with the Frescobaldi family of Italy to produce Luce, a blend of Sangiovese and Merlot, and later added Lucente, a blend of the same grapes. Mondavi has also entered into a project with the Chadwick family in Chile to produce and market Caliterra.

Ever since he entered the wine business as a youngster helping his father, Robert Mondavi believed that wine was not only healthy for the average person, but that it was a logical and pleasing component to every day life. His father started his wine business with that thought in mind, and Robert has carried on the philosophy. With those basic beliefs, Robert has encouraged the consumption of wine in moderate amounts. He formed what is now known as The Mission, a program to educate the American public about the good and healthful aspect of wine consumption. In doing so, he has raised the ire of the Bureau of Alcohol, Tobacco, and Firearms many times. He has asked for—and been denied—permission to print positive statements about the healthy benefits of drinking wine on his labels, even resorting to quoting Thomas Jefferson. The BATF has turned down each request.

But Robert Mondavi has never slowed down. In recent years, he had turned over all winery operations to his sons and daughter, Marcia, so he can concentrate his efforts on his Mission. He still travels extensively and speaks to anyone who will listen about the historical and cultural significance of wine and the healthful benefits of moderate consumption. A picture of health at more than eighty years old, he is one of The Mission's best emissaries.

Robert Mondavi's wines are also a testament to the drive and vision he inherited from his father. They have won many awards and pleased many palates, from connoisseurs to initiates.

Grape varieties produced: Cabernet Sauvignon, Cabernet Franc, Merlot, Pinot Noir, Malbec, Petit Verdot, Zinfandel, Gamay Beaujolais, Chardonnay, Sauvignon Blanc, Johannisberg Riesling, Chenin Blanc, Muscato

Proprietary blends and other labels: Opus One (Cabernet Sauvignon, Merlot, Cabernet Franc, Malbec, Petite Verdot), Woodbridge, Vichon, Byron, La Famiglia de Robert Mondavi
Robert Mondavi Winery, P.O. Box 106, Oakville, California 94562 phone: 800-MONDAVI

MONT ST. JOHN CELLARS
Napa, California

This winery is owned by the Bartolucci family and is an outgrowth of the original Bartolucci Winery. The original property was started, closed, and started again throughout the 1930s and 1940s, then sold to Oakville Vineyards in the 1970s. When Oakville Vineyards failed in 1976, the Bartoluccis bought back the winery.

Louis Bartolucci opened Mont St. John Cellars in 1979 and produces a variety of wines from traditional European grapes.

Grape varieties produced: Cabernet Sauvignon, Merlot, Pinot Noir, Chardonnay

Proprietary blends and other labels: none

Mont St. John Cellars, 5400 Old Sonoma Road, Napa, California 94588 phone: 707-255-8864

MONTE VOLPE VINEYARDS
Ukiah, California

This winery was started by Greg Graziano, the owner of Domaine Saint Gregory (see Domaine Saint Gregory). The Domaine wines are intended to be French in style, but the wines grown at Monte Volpe are strictly Italian.

The Graziano family came from Asti in northern Italy in the late 1800s. Vincenzo Graziano worked in the coal mines of Pennsylvania in the early years and only later made it to California, finding work as a gardener. In 1910, Vincenzo bought land in Mendocino and started growing grapes. When he died in the 1960s, he left his vineyard land of approximately 250 acres to his children.

In 1970 Joseph Graziano, Vincenzo's son, died. Joseph's son, Greg, was already making wine for himself and, in 1977, started Milano Winery in an old hop kiln with Jim Milone (see). He has since sold his shares to Milone, who continues to operate the Milano Winery.

Greg's plan for Monte Volpe was to concentrate on Italian varietals. He drew his experience from stints at Baccala, Tyland, and Olson wineries, and his former position as winemaker for La Crema and Hidden Cellars wineries.

Grape varieties produced: Sangiovese, Barbera, Nebbiolo, Pinot

Bianco, Moscato, Tocai Friulano, Arneis, Pinot Grigio, Dolcetto
Proprietary blends and other labels: none
Monte Volpe Vineyards, 4921 East Side Road, Ukiah, California 95482
phone: 707-463-1532 fax: 707-462-8951

MONTEVINA WINERY
Plymouth, California

Montevina Winery, the first winery established in the Amador foothills since Prohibition, was established in the Shenandoah Valley in 1970. The vineyard was planted to Zinfandel, Barbera, and Sauvignon Blanc. Cary Gott, who owned the vineyard at that time, took the advice of Darrell Corti and also planted Italian varietals such as Sangiovese and Nebbiolo. In 1982 Gott left and the winery entered a period of decline.

Bob Trinchero, from Sutter Home Winery, became interested in vineyard land in Amador County when, in 1968, he tasted a Zinfandel made from grapes grown on the Deaver Ranch Vineyard in Amador's Shenandoah Valley. He purchased twenty tons of Zinfandel and released his first Amador County Zinfandel in 1971. The Trinchero family continued to make Zinfandel from Amador County grapes for twenty years. In 1988, the Trincheros bought Montevina Winery, to get a foothold in Amador County. They added vineyard land and planted additional Italian varietals such as Refosco and Aleatico. Grapes from the more than one-hundred-year-old vines on the Deaver Ranch property are still used to make the Sutter Home Reserve Zinfandel.

The Trinchero family has launched an ambitious program at its Delta Ranch to study nearly fifty varieties of Italian grapes and clones, including Greco, Aglianico, Canaiolo, Cortese, Dolcetto, Malvasia, Vernaccia, and Teroldego. Their experimental vineyards include many grape varieties that are no longer cultivated in Italy, such as Malvasia Rovasenda and Neiretta Verzuolo. Their program was inspired by the recognition that the Amador County climate closely resembles that of Tuscany in central Italy. As the Montevina Gazetta says: "Montevina promises to become the epicenter of the Italian movement in California."

In 1992 Montevina Winery switched to organic farming to protect its workers and the environment. This technique involves the use of cover crops such as dill, fennel, mustard, and other plants between the rows of vines to control vineyard pests such as mites and leafhoppers.

The cover crops are also known to invigorate the grapevines and add organic matter to the soil. Montevina Winery also applies environmental concerns to the winery, where a high percentage of recycled materials are used in packaging, storing, and shipping.

Grape varieties produced: Zinfandel, Sangiovese, Nebbiolo, Refosco, Barbera, Aleatico, Aglianico, Teroldego, Freisa

Proprietary blends and other labels: Montanaro (Barbera, Zinfandel); Matrimonio (Sangiovese, Barbera, Nebbiolo, Refosco, Zinfandel); Brioso (100% Zinfandel), Terra d'Oro (see also Sutter Home Winery)

Montevina Winery, 20680 Shenandoah School Road, Plymouth, California 95669 phone: 209-245-6942 fax: 209-245-6617

MOUNT PALOMAR WINERY
Temecula, California

John Poole spent years in the radio business, as the owner of KBIG in Catalina Island, before making the switch to wine.

In 1969 he planted the vineyards for Mount Palomar Winery, but the winery itself wasn't started until 1975. In 1977 a wine tasting room was added, and the facility has been expanded several times since then, a tribute to its success.

The experience at Mount Palomar has been as much an experiment. Poole was joined by his son, Peter, a university-trained botanist, and Mario Moramarco, viticulturist, with whom he worked to find new vineyard and winery techniques to enhance the quality and taste of the wine. Premium Italian varietals like Sangiovese and Cortese were planted and bottled under the label Castelletto, using Peter's mother's maiden name for the new line of wines. Similarly crafted, Mediterranean-styled wines have been so successful that the Mount Palomar winery now carries a line of wines called Le Mediterranée.

Grape varieties produced: Sangiovese, Carignane, Petite Syrah, Cortese, Chardonnay, Viognier, Rousanne, Marsanne, Orange Muscat, Tannat, Sauvignon Blanc, Johannisberg Riesling, port

Proprietary blends and other labels: Castelletto, Le Mediterranée

Mount Palomar Winery, 33820 Rancho California Road, Temecula, CA 92591 phone: 909-676-5047 fax: 909-694-5688

NERVO WINERY
Geyserville, California

Nervo Winery was founded in 1908 by Julius Nervo, who had emigrated from Venice soon after the turn of the century. The winery stayed in the family for seventy-five years before being sold to the Schlitz Brewing Company. In time, Schlitz sold this property and Geyser Peak to the Trione family. It is now owned by Fortune Brands.

The Triones bottled Nervo wine for several years but recently founded Canyon Road, a new winery and new label, on the site of the former Nervo Winery. The Nervo Winery no longer exists under this name.

NIEBAUM-COPPOLA ESTATE WINERY
Rutherford, California

Francis Ford Coppola first became famous for making movies, with blockbuster hits like the *Godfather* series, *Apocalypse Now*, *The Conversation*, and *Bram Stoker's Dracula* heading the list. But, in 1975, he launched himself into a new career, one that fired his imagination as much as the blankness of a silver screen.

The original Inglenook Ranch was founded by Napa banker W. C. Watson in 1871 and was planted to equal amounts of black malvoisie and zinfandel. Watson sold the vineyard to Serranus Clinton Hastings, who sold it to Gustave Niebaum in 1880. Niebaum purchased adjoining acres and, by 1881, had amassed an estate of more than one thousand acres. Niebaum (originally spelled Nybom), a

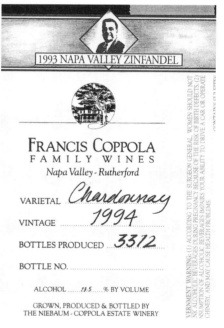

Finnish sea captain, wanted to establish a vineyard that could produce European-style wines. He visited Bordeaux and brought back Cabernet Sauvignon and Cabernet Franc vines—the clones of which are still planted on the estate to this day. Winery records show Niebaum was the first in America to estate bottle his wines in order to maintain quality, a philosophy that paid off in awards won worldwide at expositions in Paris, Melbourne, and even Bordeaux.

Gustave Niebaum died in 1906 and, when his wife died in 1936, the estate passed to his grandnephew, John Daniel, Jr. Daniel continued winning medals, if not necessarily making a profit, and the Niebaum Cabernet Sauvignon solidified the property's reputation as one of Napa's premier wineries. Unable to escape financial troubles, Daniel sold Inglenook to United Vintners in 1964. He died in 1970.

Coppola bought into the estate in 1975, adding his name to that of the original owner and calling it Niebaum-Coppola. He got over fifteen hundred acres of land, the winery, and the Victorian mansion that had been owned by Niebaum. In his own words, Coppola described his modest goals as making "enough wine to drink and pretend I was my grandfather," but modest goals were foreign to Coppola. In 1995, he bought the remainder of the estate, then owned by Heublein, and fulfilled his dream of reunifying the property once owned, and made famous, by Gustave Niebaum.

From 1982 to 1990, André Tchelistcheff advised Coppola and made his impact most conspicuous in the estate's premier wine, Rubicon. But Coppola turned Zinfandel, which had been continuously planted on the property since the 1850s, into a family landmark. At first, he made only a couple of barrels of Zinfandel, then, in 1990, released Edizione Pennino, a Zinfandel named after his maternal grandfather and namesake, Francesco Pennino. The label highlights Coppola's Italian-American roots, with one side depicting the Bay of Naples and the other depicting the Statue of Liberty. To complete the symbolism, Edizione Pennino is released every year on Columbus Day.

Coppola stresses dry farming and does not use pesticides or herbicides. His other endeavors include the production of olive oil from his own trees in Napa and the distillation of grappa from the grape pomace from his winery. Coppola also markets a line of wines called the Francis Ford Coppola Family Wines, including a Chardonnay and separate bottlings of the components of Rubicon: Cabernet Sauvignon, Cabernet Franc, and Merlot. He is also a partner in the San Francisco restaurant, Rubicon.

Grape varieties produced: Cabernet Sauvignon, Cabernet Franc, Merlot, Zinfandel, Chardonnay, Viognier

Proprietary blends and other labels: Rubicon (a blend of Cabernet Sauvignon, Cabernet Franc, and Merlot.); Edizione Pennino (Zinfandel from the rust-red soils of Rutherford); Francis Coppola Family Wines; Gustave Niebaum Commemorative

Niebaum-Coppola Estate Winery, P.O. Box 208, Rutherford, California 94573 phone: 707-967-3450 fax: 707-963-9084

A. NONINI WINERY
Fresno, California

Antonio Nonini emigrated from Northern Italy to the United States in 1900. When he decided it was time to marry, he followed Italian tradition and returned home in 1910 to claim his bride, Angiolina. Their first son, Reno, was born in 1914 in Fresno, California, and would later become the driving force behind A. Nonini Winery, founded in 1936.

Vines were first planted in 1918, and Zinfandel vines were added in 1921. The Nonini's vineyards also include Barbera, Alicante Bouschet, and Palomino grapes. Each of the wines produced at A. Nonini Winery are 100 percent of the varietal specified on the label. Many of the redwood tanks that are still used by the winery date back to the time of its founding, and the grape crusher, basket presses, and filtration equipment have been in use for over fifty years.

Reno was followed into the wine business by his son, Tom, who is the general manager, and Reno's grandson, James.

Grape varieties produced: Zinfandel, Barbera, Alicante Bouschet, Palomino

Proprietary blends and other labels: none

A. Nonini Winery, 2640 N. Dickenson Avenue, Fresno, California 93722 phone: 209-275-1936

OAKVILLE WINERY
Oakville, California

First built by the Bartolucci brothers following Repeal, the Oakville Winery (also known as the Bartolucci Brothers Winery) was abandoned in 1938. Louis Bartolucci reopened it in 1942, installed new equipment, and made a business of selling bulk wine to large commercial wineries, like Petri Wine Company.

Louis Bartolucci's concept was so successful that he was approached with a plan to bottle and market his wines himself, without selling them in bulk. He bit, and might have been successful if one of his partners hadn't been convicted of a felony, if the wine market hadn't collapsed in 1947, and if his other partner hadn't gotten into trouble with creditors. Louis Bartolucci once again bailed out the Oakville Winery, this time by a reorganization that employed his brothers, and used a short crop in 1949 to boost the value of his bulk wine.

The success of those few years following dissolution of the partnership put Bartolucci on the road to profit, and the Oakville Winery survived into the 1960s. It no longer exists.

OLIVETTO WINERY
Healdsburg, California

The Olivetto Winery in Healdsburg, California was first owned by the families of Franceschini and Lorenzini. It was one of the early gravity-fed wineries in the region, with its fermentation room on the top floor and storage cellar below.

In 1930 the winery was bought by Rachele Passalacqua, the wife of Frank Passalacqua, whose first winery perished with the fire that destroyed his mansion in Healdsburg. But Rachele had more luck with her winery, operating it as Sonoma County Cellars, and passing it on to her children upon her death. The winery is currently leased to the E. & J. Gallo Company, but does not exist under its own name.

PAPAGNI VINEYARDS
Madera, California

Demetrio Papagni was the third generation of winemakers in his family in Bari when he left in 1912 to settle in California. In 1920 he planted vineyards and had a healthy business in selling grapes and juice to home winemakers in California and the East Coast. The family business continued along these lines until Demetrio's son, Angelo, stepped in.

Angelo decided fine table wines were the thing to make, and he was convinced that such fine wine was possible in Madera County. He built a winery in 1973 and began producing a line of premium wines that, according to Adams, "has astonished the wine world and contradicted the opinions of experts" regarding the possibilities of wine from that area.[8] He makes still and sparkling wines, and ages his reds in fifty-gallon oak barrels.

Grape varieties produced: Zinfandel, Barbera, Alicante Bouschet, Chenin Blanc, Sparkling Moscat

Proprietary blends and other labels: Moscato d'Angelo
Papagni Vineyards, 9505 Road 30 1/2, Madera, California 93638 phone: 209-485-2760

PARDUCCI WINE CELLARS
Ukiah, California

In 1921 Adolph Parducci bought vineyard land in Mendocino County. The family's pre-Prohibition operation consisted of tending vineyards and selling grapes. During Prohibition, they sold sacramental wine, and grapes and grape juice to home winemakers. But the Parduccis also took advantage of circumstances created by Prohibition and bought winemaking equipment at near-bankruptcy prices and transferred it to their Home Ranch.

In 1932 as the tide of Prohibition was ebbing, the Parduccis began full-scale wine production. On August 9, 1933, several months before Prohibition ended, Adolph and his son John filed an application with the Treasury Department for a license to "manufacture, possess, and sell" wine.

In 1960 Adolph passed control of the winery to his sons, with John as the winemaker. It was under John's leadership that the Parducci Winery proved that Mendocino County was capable of making excellent wines. In the mid-1970s the family needed cash and sold the winery to Teachers Management and Investment, Inc., retaining the right to run the winery. Unfortunately, disputes with TMI, Inc., resulted in the loss of family control and the assumption of total authority over Parducci Winery by TMI, Inc., in 1995.

Grape varieties produced: Cabernet Sauvignon, Zinfandel, Gamay Beaujolais, Pinot Noir, Merlot, Charbono, Carignane, Petite Syrah, Chardonnay, Sauvignon Blanc, Chenin Blanc, Johannisberg Riesling, Gewürztraminer, Muscat Canelli

Proprietary blends and other labels: Vintage Red (Carignane,

(To be used only in connection with applications for original basic permits of the "A," "K," "L," "P," "B," or "Industrial Alcohol Plant, Bonded Warehouse, Denaturing Plant" classifications)

Form 80
TREASURY DEPARTMENT
BUREAU OF INDUSTRIAL ALCOHOL
November, 1930

REPORT ON APPLICATION
OFFICE OF SUPERVISOR OF PERMITS

San Francisco, California
(City and State)

Application received ...8-9-33....
(Date)

Name of applicant ...... ADOLPH B. PARDUCCI AND JOHN A PARDUCCI, D.B.A.
(Insert name or names shown in application)

Trading as .... PARDUCCI & SON

Address ..Rt. 2, Box 628, Ukiah, Mendocino County, Calif. Bond, S.1,000.00
located about 3½ miles north of Ukiah, ½ mile West of the Redwood
Application to ..manufacture, possess and sell.................................Highway
(State exact acts for which permit is desired)

Has applicant, partner, or officer or principal stockholder of corporation ever applied for, held, or been connected with a permit under the National Prohibition Act? If so, indicate references to pertinent information in office files which inspector should review.

REMARKS: Mails and Files reports no previous
record. Bond $1000 on file. No
prehearing will be held.
Please determine if bonded winery
heretofore operated at this   ENCLS: 1404 - 8-1-33
location.   698 in triplicate
                                             Plan in trip. dated 8-1-33
                                             1511 card

NOTE—Permit clerk will examine office files thoroughly and fill in all items above where information is available, and also Inspection Request, immediately below.

INSPECTION REQUEST

To CHIEF INSPECTOR: Date .... September 12, 1933
It is requested that inspection be made relative to the above application.

_____
Permit Clerk.

INSPECTION ASSIGNMENT

To ....   Date ....
(Inspector or inspectors)
You are directed to make an inspection relative to the above application and to submit your report on the following pages of this form.

8-15499   Chief Inspector.

Cabernet Sauvignon, Cabernet Franc, Zinfandel, Grenache), Bono-Sirah (Charbono, Petite Syrah, Carignane), Vintage White (French Colombard, Sauvignon Blanc, Riesling, Chenin Blanc, Flora, Gewürztraminer, Chardonnay, Muscat Canelli)
Parducci Wine Cellars, 501 Parducci Road, Ukiah, California 95482 phone: 707-463-5350 fax: 707-463-5379

PASTORI WINERY
Cloverdale, California

Costante Pastori brought his family to the United States from Lombardy in the early 1900s. They settled in the Geyserville, California, area and opened the first Pastori Winery in 1914[9] but closed it during Prohibition.

In 1975 Costante's son, Frank Pastori, opened the new Pastori Winery, and added grapes to his farming of pears and prunes. The majority of wine produced at Pastori Winery is sold as generic red and white wine, though some is bottled as varietal wine. The Pastori family intends to move to vintage dating and estate labeling of their wines. Most of the wines produced are sold in the tasting room.

Grape varieties produced: Cabernet Sauvignon, Pinot Noir, Zinfandel, Pinot St. George, Johannisberg Riesling, Chenin Blanc, Sauternes

Proprietary blends and other labels: none
Pastori Winery, 23189 Geyserville Avenue, Cloverdale, California 95425 phone: 707-857-3418

PEDRIZZETTI WINERY
Morgan Hill, California

Camillo Colombano came from Italy in 1913 and planted Barbera vines near Morgan Hill. In 1923 he started the Camillo Colombano Winery. In 1945 John Pedrizzetti, whose family came to the U.S. from Piedmont, bought the Camillo Colombano Winery and took up Colombano's plan. Wines made at Pedrizzetti from 1945 until 1967 were sold in bulk. It was with the vintage of 1968 that the winery started producing varietal wines.

Since 1963 it has been owned and operated by John's son, Ed, and Ed's wife, Phyllis. They have maintained the winery as a family operation and, while their kids have grown up and left for other careers, Ed and Phyllis still carry on. They make a wide selection of white and red wines, all from purchased grapes.

John Pedrizzetti died in 1995, but his plan to produce good, affordable wines has been carried out. Even Phyllis Pedrizzetti, of Irish/Scottish descent, has adopted her husband's Italian ethic about wine: "We produce wine on the theory that good wine should never be a luxury. Everybody should be able to afford a good bottle of wine."

Grape varieties produced: Cabernet Sauvignon, Barbera, Zinfandel, Merlot, Chardonnay, Riesling, Chenin Blanc

Proprietary blends and other labels: none

Pedrizzetti Winery, 1645 San Pedro Avenue, Morgan Hill, California 95037 phone: 408-779-7389, fax: 408-779-9083

J. PEDRONCELLI WINERY
Geyserville, California

In 1904 John Canata built his winery, named, logically, the John Canata Winery. In 1927, John (Giovanni) Pedroncelli, Sr., bought Canata's winery and vineyards and changed the winery's name to Pedroncelli. Since Prohibition was still underway, the purchase was a risky one, but John, Sr., was planning to market his grapes to the home winemakers throughout the state, an industry that had grown considerably since 1919 when Prohibition went into effect.

Canata's vineyards had been mostly planted to Zinfandel between 1905 and 1915. This worked well for Pedroncelli, since Zinfandel was a hardy grape that stood up well to the rigors of shipment in bulk, therefore making Pedroncelli's plan to work the home-winemaking market a realistic possibility.

After Repeal, the Pedroncelli family improved and reconditioned the vineyards, purchased additional land to increase their yield, and by 1948, were ready to start producing varietal wines.

True to its origins, the Pedroncelli production has always had a strong commitment to Zinfandel. In 1948 their first varietal was a non-vintage Zinfandel and, in 1958, the winery produced a Zinfandel Rose, among the first of the so-called "blush" wines that swept the

Jim Pedroncelli inspects the grapes arriving at the crusher.

consumers off their feet in the 1970s.

Sons John, Jr., and Jim took over management of the wine program in 1963. They enlarged the family's commitment to varietal wines and started producing vintage-dated wines in 1966. Today, the wines are highly valued for their consistent quality and fair price.

Like most Italian Americans, the Pedroncellis are proud of their legacy on both sides of the Atlantic. As Julie Pedroncelli says, "We are very proud of our heritage—of both Italy and the United States, and how that heritage has worked to give us a wonderful way of life."

Grape varieties produced: Cabernet Sauvignon, Zinfandel, Pinot Noir, Merlot, Chardonnay, Sauvignon Blanc, Sangiovese

Proprietary blends and other labels: Primo Misto (Cabernet Sauvignon, Zinfandel), Primavera Misto (Chardonnay, Chenin Blanc, Sauvignon Blanc)

J. Pedroncelli Winery, 1220 Canyon Road, Geyserville, California 95441 phone: 800-836-3894 fax: 707-857-3812

PELANCONI WINERY
Los Angeles, California

This winery was near Los Angeles and operated during the mid-nineteenth century. One of its significant features was that it employed Native Americans to crush the grapes barefoot, a method by then abandoned by most of the wine world. This practice continued at Pelanconi Winery at least until 1876. The winery no longer exists.

PELLEGRINI BROTHERS WINE
Santa Rosa, California

The Pellegrini family emigrated from Tuscany around the turn of the century. Their first involvement with the American wine industry was as grape merchants, shipping fruit to home winemakers nationwide during Prohibition. The family wine business started when Prohibition ended, but Anthony Dias Blue indicates in his book that the Pelligrinis might have been making wine prior to Repeal, quoting Bob Pellegrini saying: "We were cooking long before [1933]!"[10] The winery was formally bonded in 1933.

The vineyards total 120 acres, all in Sonoma, but the family is also involved in the importation of wine and the distribution of it all over the world. Wine distribution appears to be still the principal Pellegrini business. The current owner is Bob Pellegrini, grandson of the founder.

Grape varieties produced: Barbera, Zinfandel, Merlot, Cabernet Sauvignon, Carignane, Chardonnay, Sauvignon Blanc

Proprietary blends and other labels: Deux Cepages, Olivet Lane, Cloverdale Ranch, Cotes de Sonoma

Pellegrini Brothers Wine, 4055 West Olivet Road, Santa Rosa, California 95401 phone: 415-761-2811

PELLEGRINI VINEYARDS
Cutchogue, New York

Bob Pellegrini started his professional career with the United States Army, traveling through Europe and becoming spoiled by regular encounters with the culinary and oenological treasures of the continent. When he returned to the United States, he worked as a graphic designer, and added to his résumé the design of *Foods of the World*, the Time-Life cookbook series.

Pellegrini enjoyed a brief partnership with Gristina Vineyards until 1988, then purchased a thirty-six-acre tract of land previously known as Island Vineyards. He produced his first vintage as Pellegrini Vineyards on that property in 1991, and adheres to a goal of combining Old World winemaking traditions with state-of-the-art technology, with minimal manipulation by the winemaking team. The winery's success has marked Pellegrini as one of the leaders in the up-and-coming Long Island viticultural district.

In addition to the table wines, Pellegrini Vineyards makes Commonage, a line of light, fruity wines in both red and white for easy drinking.

Grape varieties produced: Cabernet Sauvignon, Merlot, Cabernet Franc, Petite Verdot, Chardonnay, Sauvignon Blanc, Gewürztraminer

Proprietary blends and other labels: Encore (Cabernet Sauvignon, Cabernet Franc, Merlot), Finale (a dessert blend of Sauvignon Blanc and Gewürztraminer), Commonage

Pellegrini Vineyards, 23005 Main Road, Cutchogue, New York 11935 phone: 516-734-4111 fax: 516-734-4159

ROBERT PEPI WINERY
Oakville, California

The Pepi family came from Lucca, in Tuscany, around 1900, but didn't become involved in winemaking for quite some time. It was in 1966 that Robert Pepi and his wife, Aurora, left the fur business they owned in San Francisco and moved to the Napa Valley. They planned the move as a shift into retirement, but were lured by thoughts of their Italian farming roots and ended up planting a vineyard.

Planting grapes simply followed Robert's Italian heritage, but it helped that the property they purchased already had fifteen acres planted to Cabernet Sauvignon. The original plantings were Sauvignon Blanc and Chardonnay, though the Pepis later added Semillon and Cabernet Sauvignon. In time, they yielded to the temptation to produce Italian-style wines, and planted Sangiovese in 1983.

They originally sold their grapes to Christian Brothers winery, but began marketing Robert Pepi Wines in 1981. The Robert Pepi Winery is now owned by Artisans and Estates.

As Robert Pepi said: "Our intent is to make wines of Old World charm and drinkability, with elegance and balance."

Grape varieties produced: Cabernet Sauvignon, Sangiovese, Sauvignon Blanc, Semillon

Proprietary blends and other labels: Colline di Sassi (Sangiovese)

Robert Pepi Winery, 7585 St. Helena Highway, Oakville, Calif. 94562 phone: 707-944-2807, fax: 707-944-5628

MARIO PERELLI-MINETTI WINERY
St. Helena, California

Giuseppe Perelli-Minetti family, from Milan, fought on the side of Giuseppe Garibaldi when Garibaldi was leading the revolution to

unify Italy in the 1860s. After the war, Giuseppe settled in Barletta in southern Italy. His son, Antonio, went to the United States in 1902, and maintained his father's adventurous spirit.

Antonio Perelli-Minetti lived first in California, then left there to seek his fortune in Mexico, sticking with his love of viticulture throughout. Mexico fell on hard times during that era, and a few years before Prohibition, Perelli-Minetti returned to California and was hired as the winemaker of Beaulieu Vineyard by Georges de Latour. He lived to be ninety-five years old; when he died in 1976, he was the oldest pre-Prohibition winemaker still alive.

In 1988 a winery was built to handle the production of Cabernet and Chardonnay wines. Today, the family winery is a smaller rendition of the original, but is still going strong under the management of Mario Perelli-Minetti.

Grape varieties produced: Cabernet Sauvignon, Chardonnay
Proprietary blends and other labels: none
Mario Perelli-Minetti Winery, 1443 Silverado Trail, St. Helena, California 94574 phone: 707-963-8762 fax: 707-963-8762

PESENTI WINERY
Templeton, California

Frank Pesenti left Bergamo in 1914 with his sister, Maria, to join Maria's husband, Pietro, who had been working since 1910 in Willow Creek, California. Frank had no money and didn't understand English, but he knew how to work, so he joined Pietro in cutting trees and selling the lumber.

By 1922 Frank had earned enough money to bring his fiancée, Caterina, from Italy and buy some land. In 1923, he planted it to Zinfandel, on the advice of Adolf Siot, who had been growing Zinfandel since 1890. Since this was during Prohibition, the Pesenti family could only produce wine for home consumption, limited to two hundred gallons per year. Then, in 1934 the winery was bonded as the Pesenti Winery and has remained in operation since.

Aldo Nerelli joined the family in 1946 when he married Frank and Caterina's daughter, Silvia. Aldo was familiar with winery work since his parents, Lorenzo and Rena Nerelli, purchased a vineyard on York Mountain in 1917 and operated the Templeton Winery there until World War II. Today, Aldo Nerelli and Victor Pesenti, sons of the founders, along with Frank Nerelli, the grandson, pool their efforts to continue the tradition of the Pesenti winery.

Grape varieties produced: Cabernet Sauvignon, Zinfandel, Chardonnay, Sauvignon Blanc, Riesling, Johannisberg Riesling

Proprietary blends and other labels: none

Pesenti Winery, 2900 Vineyard Drive, Templeton, California 93465 phone: 805-434-1030 fax: 805-434-1030

PETRI WINES
California

Raffaello Petri had come from Tuscany and traveled to California to settle. In 1887, while running a hotel in the Italian North Beach section of San Francisco, he got involved in making wine. The Petri family, which also had a successful cigar business, established itself as a major bulk wine producer and, during World War I, Raffaello joined Dante Forresti in buying vineyards and a winery in Escalon. They named it Petri Winery.

During Prohibition Foresti maintained the business by selling grapes to home winemakers while the Petris concentrated on the cigar business. After Repeal, Raffaello's son, Angelo, returned to the wine business, but never gave up on the family cigar-making business either. His son, Louis Petri, quit school in 1933, married Flori Cella of the Cella wine family, and went to work in the Petri family business.

Never satisfied, and showing an enthusiasm and energy level that many admired, Louis Petri decided to enlarge the family wine dynasty. By 1944 he had become president of the business and within a few years had acquired the Italian Swiss Colony operation, the Shewan-Jones winery in Lodi, and the Gambarelli & Davitto cellars in New York. He founded the Allied Grape Growers Association, then United Vintners, and used each organization to further the interests of the Petri wine family. According to Adams, in the late 1950s, Petri's company was selling nearly 25 percent of all the wine consumed in the United States.[11]

In the 1960s Petri bought Inglenook, the famous property in Napa that has passed through many hands and is now owned by Francis Ford Coppola (see Niebaum-Coppola). Petri ultimately sold Inglenook to Heublein.

His empire competed with the Gallos for years, as Ernest and Julio Gallo were building theirs. In time, Petri Wines lost the position as the largest producer of American wine to the Gallo family.

Petri Wines no longer exists.

PETRONI VINEYARDS
Sonoma, California

Lorenzo Petroni came from Lucca, in Tuscany, in 1957. He spent years working in San Francisco restaurants learning the wine and food business, then finally opened his own restaurant in 1970, called North Beach Restaurant (1512 Stockton, San Francisco).

Lorenzo's passion in wine has always tended toward Sangiovese, and, around 1982, he started looking for property on which to plant and grow his own grapes. It took years to settle on the right property but, in 1990, he found a thirty-seven-acre parcel of land in Sonoma. Lorenzo was drawn to the slopes on the land, though they had to be terraced to support the vineyard, and he finally planted his Sangiovese in a vineyard he calls Poggio alla Pietra for all the rocks that were found—and had to be removed—from the property.

While this Tuscan grape took up most of his land, he found room for Cabernet Sauvignon and thirteen hundred olive trees, truly capturing the spirit of his native Tuscany. He has since bought additional property in Napa and Sonoma.

Grape varieties produced: Sangiovese, Cabernet Sauvignon, Syrah
Proprietary blends and other labels: none

PEZZI KING VINEYARDS AND WINERY
Healdsburg, California

Peter (Pietro) Pezzi came to the United States from northern Italy in the late 1800s. Pezzi settled in California, and quickly became involved in the Italian American community there. He worked for the Bank of Italy (later the Bank of America), primarily in the Central Valley, helping many Italian families get the financing they needed to start their agricultural businesses.

Prohibition was especially hard on Pezzi, since the troubled times included foreclosing on many of the businesses he had helped start. He quit the Bank of America and focused his efforts on his own agricultural business in the San Joaquin Valley.

Pezzi's grandson, James Rowe, grew up in this environment and seems to have had an eerily similar experience moving from financial affairs to wine. Although he also pursued a career in finance with the company he founded (Strategic Capital, Incorporated), he ultimately returned to the agricultural heritage his grandfather had passed on to him.

The rolling hills and lush landscape make up the scenic Pezzi King Vineyard.

In 1993 Rowe and his wife were visiting Sonoma County when they decided to buy a small vineyard in Dry Creek Valley. The Pezzi King Winery was founded on that property, specializing in Zinfandel, Cabernet Sauvignon, and Chardonnay. The Pezzi King Winery has recently added the vineyards formerly owned by Robert Stemmler.

Grape varieties produced: Zinfandel, Cabernet Sauvignon, Chardonnay, Petite Syrah, Sauvignon Blanc, Merlot

Proprietary blends and other labels: none

Pezzi King Vineyards and Winery, 3805 Lambert Bridge Road, Healdsburg, California 95448 phone: 707-433-3305 fax: 707-431-9389

PICONI WINERY
Temecula, California

The Piconi family had made wine at home in Pittsburgh, Pennsylvania, but John got into the commercial end of it when he formed a partnership with Vincent Cilurzo and established the Cilurzo-Piconi Winery. When that partnership dissolved, John established the Piconi Winery with his wife, Gloria, in 1981.

Grape varieties produced: none identified

Proprietary blends and other labels: none

Piconi Winery, 33410 Rancho California Road, Temecula, California 92390

PIETRA SANTA
Hollister, California

The Cienega Valley had been planted to vines since 1850, ever since Frenchman Theophile Vache planted the region's first vines. By 1880 Vache was producing fifteen thousand gallons of wine per year. In 1883 William Palmtag bought the property, added more vines, and expanded the winery.

All this was happening in what was to become known as the San Benito Vineyard. In 1906 John Dickenson bought the vineyard, added some more land, and built a home on the property. Another expansion in 1916 beat Prohibition by only a few years, but the winery went dormant during Prohibition.

Following Repeal, the Valliant family bought the property and reopened the winery, but couldn't bear the expenses involved in refurbishing the aging winery, so they sold it in 1943. In the next four decades, the winery saw a variety of owners, before the property was purchased in 1989 by Joseph Gimelli.

When Gimelli came along, the vineyards had not been farmed for three years and were overgrown with weeds and overrun with wild boar. Gimelli was not discouraged, however, and went on to plant Merlot, Sangiovese, Dolcetto, Zinfandel, and Cabernet Sauvignon. In 1992 he hired Alessio Carli whose experience at Badia a Coltibuono and Sonoma County's Viansa Winery made him an easy choice. The first vintage was harvested in 1992 and released in 1994.

Grape varieties produced: Sangiovese, Merlot, Dolcetto, Cabernet Sauvignon, Zinfandel

Proprietary blends and other labels: Sassolino

Pietra Santa, 10034 Cienega Road, Hollister, California 95023 phone: 408-636-1956

PLYMOUTH COLONY WINERY
Plymouth, Massachusetts

Charles Caranci bought an old cranberry-screening house in this prime cranberry-producing region, and opened the Plymouth Colony Winery. He has decided to keep the original crop incorporated into the modern business, though, and is now producing a variety of fruit wines to accompany his Cranberry Grandé. There is also a Bog Blush made from cranberries and white wine, Bog Blanc, and Whale Watch White from French hybrid grapes.

The winery grounds include picnic tables, and visitors can also visit nearby historic Plymouth, Massachusetts, when they are finished with their lunch.

Grape varieties produced: Nearly all of the Plymouth Colony wines are non-grape fruit wines, such as cranberry, blueberry, and peach.

Proprietary blends and other labels: none

Plymouth Colony Winery, Pinewood Road, Plymouth, Massachusetts 02360 phone: 508-747-3334

PONZI VINEYARDS
Beaverton, Oregon

The Ponzi family left Campotosto, Italy and settled in Michigan. Dick Ponzi grew up there, breathing the smells of his father's homemade wine in the basement. Dick decided to follow in his father's footsteps, at least in making his own homemade wine when he grew up.

Later, he moved to California where he met and married his wife, Nancy. Dick was an aerospace engineer for United Technologies and Lockheed, but he and Nancy both loved wine and Dick's earlier flirtations with home winemaking presaged the next decision: they would move to Oregon and buy vineyard land, and there make their dreams come true. That puts them among the pioneers of Oregon wine, with faith in the state's viticultural future years before anyone else thought it was possible.

Together, they founded the Ponzi Vineyards winery in 1970, harvesting their first vintage in 1974. Unfortunately, Dick knew more about winemaking than about farming so he had to rely on the wisdom of his farming neighbors and learn quickly. He did, and he has left a legacy for many Oregonians to follow. Among his contributions to the local wine industry, he was the founding member and first president of the Oregon Winegrowers Association, and served as founding director of the Oregon Wine Advisory Board in 1987.

Ponzi grows some grapes and buys some as well, but keeps the lots separate. He uses about one-third new oak on his Pinot Noirs, which are clearly the flagship of his winery and have been ranked among the best American Pinot Noirs produced.

Ponzi was also intrigued by beer, so he created the first microbrewery system in Oregon and opened BridgePort Brewing Company, Oregon's first microbrewery, in 1984. The November 1995 issue of Gambero Rosso magazine quotes him as saying "To make a good wine you need a lot of good beer." The beer business was sold in 1995, but the winery has stayed in the family and is now under second-generation management of the Ponzi children.

Dick Ponzi keeps his Italian heritage alive in Oregon, from his involvement with the Italian Businessman's Club in Portland, to his planting of Italian varietals, and his sponsorship of bocce ball tournaments at the winery in summertime. In 1996, Ponzi reentered the microbrewery market by opening a brewery, pub, and restaurant, called Red Hook, in Brooklyn, New York.

Grape varieties produced: Pinot Noir, Nebbiolo, Dolcetto, Pinot Gris, Chardonnay, Riesling, Arneis

Proprietary blends and other labels: none

Ponzi Vineyards, Route 1, Box 842, Beaverton, Oregon 97007
phone: 503-628-1227, fax: 503-628-0354

BATISTE PREVITALI
Amador County, California

In 1889 Batiste Previtali left Lombardy to come to the United States. He tried to get settled in the new country before bringing his family over, which he did eight years later in 1897.

In the early 1900s the Previtali family bought a four-hundred-acre plot of land in Amador County and opened a winery. In 1912, using proceeds from their successful venture, they built a new winery. The winery no longer exists.

PUCCI WINERY
Sandpoint, Idaho

In 1982 Eugene and Nancy Pucci founded the Pucci Winery, using Eugene's heritage as a sixth-generation winemaker from a family that had begun making wine in Italy. At first, the Puccis bought grapes from California for their own use, had them shipped to Idaho, and vinified and bottled the wine there. In time, the popularity of their wine caught on and Eugene and Nancy decided to go commercial.

In 1995, the Pucci Winery went out of business.

RAFANELLI WINERY
Healdsburg, California

Alberto Rafanelli came from Tuscany to Healdsburg in 1911. He and his wife were so proud to be in America that, when they found they were expecting a child, they were determined to name her America. As it turned out, the first child was a boy; so as not to waste a good idea, they named him Americo.

Alberto had started a small vineyard and winery in 1913 but, like many vintners, the squalls of Prohibition swept them out of business in 1919. Fortunately, Alberto's wife, Laticia, insisted on maintaining the vineyards, certain as she was that the foolishness the Americans called Prohibition could not last. She was right and when Repeal came about, the Rafanelli family already had vineyards planted.

Americo grew up in this environment of grapes and wine, but the family had resorted to more general farming for subsistence. So Americo considered himself a farmer first, and a winemaker second. Whenever winery visitors arrived during the noonday meal, they usually saw Americo enjoying a bountiful salad of local produce. Like most Italians, Americo was taught to be hospitable, and he often invited these visitors to join him in the meal.

In the 1950s Americo bought a ranch in Dry Creek Valley and replanted the orchards of pears and prunes with grapes. His son, David, had been an avid home winemaker and, with his father, established A. Rafanelli Winery in 1974 in the basement of Americo's house.

When Americo died in 1987, David became the winemaker and was joined by his wife, Patty, who takes care of marketing. James Laube says that "[I]f one were accepting nominations for California's most underrated winery, A. Rafanelli would have to be given serious consideration."[12]

Grape varieties produced: Cabernet Sauvignon, Zinfandel

Proprietary blends and other labels: none

Rafanelli Winery, 4685 W. Dry Creek Road, Healdsburg, California 95448 phone: 707-433-1385

RAPAZZINI WINERY
Gilroy, California

In 1929 Angelo Rapazzini came to the United States from Varese, Italy. By the 1950s, he was operating a bakery in San Jose, California. In 1961 his sons, Jon and Victor, founded the Rapazzini Winery.

In 1978 Jon Rapazzini decided to make a wine to commemorate the most famous product from Gilroy, California: Chateau de Garlic. It is, admittedly, a garish wine that would serve best as the base for a wine and garlic sauce, but it got loads of attention for the Rapazzini Winery in an area that prides itself on garlic.

Grape varieties produced: Cabernet Sauvignon, Zinfandel, Merlot, Chardonnay, French Colombard, Gewürztraminer, Johannisberg Riesling, sparkling wine, apricot wine

Proprietary blends and other labels: Chateau de Garlic (white wine infused with garlic)

Rapazzini Winery, 4350 Monterey Highway, Gilroy, California 95020 phone: 408-848-3646, 800-842-6262

ROCHIOLI VINEYARD AND WINERY
Healdsburg, California

Joe Rochioli, Sr., was only twelve when his family moved from Italy to California. In 1938 he leased some land and started growing grapes, building his business as one of selling fruit, not wine.

In 1959 Joe, Sr., and his son, Joe Jr., planted Sauvignon Blanc and Cabernet Sauvignon on their plot of land in the Russian River Valley. In 1968 they added Pinot Noir and Chardonnay. Planting of premium varietals was a risky step then, when Americans still hadn't accepted wine as an integral part of the culture and could easily tolerate nondescript bulk wines rather than pay the price for premium varietals. However, the varietals were perfect for their microclimate and the Rochiolis grew excellent grapes there.

Joe Jr.'s son, Tom, became the winemaker for the family vineyard in 1983. He convinced the family that it was time to start making wine from the family's vineyards rather than simply selling the grapes. Tom's foresight was repaid when the Rochioli Vineyards starting winning awards for nearly every wine they produced. It is now common for a Rochioli wine to win medals, but the sincerity and dedication has not ebbed from the family and the production is just as trustworthy as when the family affair with grapes started in 1938.

Grape varieties produced: Pinot Noir, Cabernet Sauvignon, Chardonnay, Sauvignon Blanc, Zinfandel

Proprietary blends and other labels: none

Rochioli Vineyard and Winery, 6192 Westside Road, Healdsburg, California 95448 phone: 707-433-2305 fax: 707-433-2358

To promote the biggest winery in the world, Roma hired the biggest man in the world, Jack Earle, who attended this New York dinner party in 1941.

ROMA WINERY
Sonoma, California

There are two Roma Wineries, historically, named as such in different contexts. The first was founded in 1889-90 in Sonoma by the

Scatena brothers who initially called it the Santa Lucia Winery before it was named Roma Winery. It was sold in the 1920s to the Domitilli and Massoni families, who sold it in 1944 to the Alta Vineyards Company. Finally, the Roma Winery ended up in the hands of the Seghesio wine family who purchased it in 1949 to add to their current winery buildings.

Another Roma Winery was founded after Prohibition by John Battista and Lorenzo Cella, who expanded their operation to become the biggest single producer of California wines in the days following Repeal. This winery was later taken over by the Cribari family, and the Cribari label was bought by the Wine Growers Guild in 1970, which later became the Guild Wineries.

ROTTANZI WINERY
San Francisco, California

The Rottanzi Winery in the Mission District of San Francisco was bought by Vittorio Sattui in 1899 when he got into a dispute with this landlord at the property on Columbus Avenue which Sattui called the St. Helena Wine Cellars. He renamed the Rottanzi Winery the V. Sattui Wine Company and renovated it to permit more wine to be produced and to provide apartments above for his family.

The Rottanzi Winery name ceased to exist upon that purchase.

SAN ANTONIO WINERY
Los Angeles, California

Santo Cambianica emigrated from Italy and founded the San Antonio Winery in 1917. It stands right in Los Angeles, complete with smog and traffic, and is even listed as Historical Landmark No. 42. It is now run by descendants of Cambianica, the Riboli family.

Grape varieties produced: Cabernet Sauvignon, Chardonnay, Chenin Blanc, Johannisberg Riesling, Muscat, sparkling wine

Proprietary blends and other labels: Maddalena (named after one of the owners, an inexpensive line of wines)
San Antonio Winery, 737 Lamar Street, Los Angeles, California 90031 phone: 213-223-2236

SANTINO WINES (now Renwood Winery, Inc.)
Plymouth, California

The Santino Winery was founded in 1979, but the Santino family owned only the winery and purchased grapes from the 125-year old Grandpere Vineyard. In 1994, Scott Harvey, of Renwood Winery, bought the property but continues to market some of the wines under the Santino label.

V. SATTUI WINERY
St. Helena, California

Vittorio Sattui was the son of a Frenchman raised by Italians, who traded his father's occupation as the village baker for one as the village winemaker. He heard the stories about California in the mid-1800s and left his poor country to travel there.

In 1882 Vittorio married Katerina Rossi. On their honeymoon, they went to California, arriving in San Francisco virtually broke. They settled in the North Beach district of the city, along with most of the Italian immigrants who landed in San Francisco, and Vittorio made bread by night and wine by day, from grapes he purchased from St. Helena. He served the wine to the boarders that Katerina took in to pay the bills, and what remained was sold on the side. By 1885 Vittorio's wine was selling well enough that he quit his job as a baker and devoted himself full time to making wine. He purchased a property on what is now Columbus Avenue and called it St. Helena Wine Cellars, named after the area from which he still bought his grapes.

In 1899 following a dispute with the landlord who wanted to raise the rent, the business was moved to a building in the Mission District formerly known as the Rottanzi Winery. It was at this time that the business got the name V. Sattui Wine Company. The building was renovated, allowing room for wine production in the cellar, retail space on

Employees and neighbors stand outside the old V. Sattui Winery at 23rd and Bryant St. in San Francisco circa 1910.

the main floor, and apartments for the family and boarders on the upper floors.

Everything seemed to be going well—until Prohibition struck. Then the prosperous life that Vittorio and Katerina had built for themselves and their children fell apart. By 1921, the winery had closed. Vittorio gave up commercial wine production, but he continued to make some for himself and his family, and they still lived in the apartments above the winery.

This interruption was a tremendous setback for the Sattui family and its wine business. By the end of Prohibition, Vittorio was too old to restart the winery. Even his children were by then middle-aged and not inclined to abandon their own careers to venture in the risky business of wine production.

Little was done for the extinct V. Sattui Winery for several decades. Then Daryl Sattui, who for years had dreamed of resurrecting the family winery, embarked on a mission to do just that. He spent most of his time pleading with investors to back him. He gradually got enough from investors and savings to get a lease option on a plot of land in 1974. The house that sat on the property was in such bad shape back then that Daryl and his wife slept in his old Volkswagen van for a month while making the house livable.

Daryl was still unable to get investors and faced the prospect of losing the property altogether. Finally, down to his last five hundred dollars, he leased the property for one more month, desperate to find someone to back his venture and save the land for him. He did find someone and secured a long-term lease that gave him the option to buy back the property in the future.

Construction of the winery began in July 1975 and they opened their doors on March 4, 1976. Daryl's travels through Europe had convinced him to build a deli and picnic grounds into the design, a combination that wins many fans each year.

In 1984 Daryl switched from buying grapes from local vineyards to growing his own on a thirty-four-acre plot of land he purchased adjacent to the four acres he already owned.

Now, a beautiful stone winery stands on the lovely, tree-shaded grounds dotted here and there with picnic tables. The deli that now occupies the original building still gets rave reviews and the wines continue to win medals throughout California and accolades throughout the wine media.

Grape varieties produced: Pinot Noir, Zinfandel, Cabernet Sauvignon, Gamay Beaujolais, Chardonnay, Sauvignon Blanc, Johannisberg Riesling, Muscat, Madeira, Champagne

Proprietary blends and other labels: none

V. Sattui Winery, 1111 White Lane, St. Helena, California 94574 phone: 707-963-7774 Fax: 707-963-4324

SEBASTIANI VINEYARDS
Sonoma, California

Samuele Sebastiani, the founder of Sebastiani Vineyards, learned to make wine in Tuscany, where he was born in 1874. He emigrated to the United States around 1895 and stayed in New York only long enough to earn the money needed to move to California. Although he had a working knowledge of winemaking, Samuele did not at first take up that occupation in the United States. He started looking for a job in the artichoke and cabbage fields and, when they told him there were no jobs, he worked for free to show them how hard he could work.

He worked in the Sonoma foothills, quarrying stone for the cable car tracks in San Francisco, and as a woodcutter in the Sonoma hills. One day playing bocce ball at the Lone Star Saloon, he met Ted Riboni, owner of the Burgess Winery, and when Riboni found out that Samuele had learned winemaking in Italy, he hired him to work at his winery. Burgess Winery was subsequently closed in 1903 after a great fire gutted the buildings.

In 1904 Samuele purchased a vineyard and winery in Sonoma Valley from another Italian immigrant, Milani, who had grown disaffected with the business. Samuele's first wine was Zinfandel. The same year, he married Elvira Eraldi, the daughter of the man who owned the Lone Star Saloon.

In 1908 he leased a ranch originally owned by M. G. Vallejo, the Mexican general who was in command of the Mexican government's forces in California in 1833 when the missions (and their wineries) were secularized. During Vallejo's ownership, and before the secularization, Franciscan missionaries had planted grapevines there in 1825. By 1909 Samuele owned the Vallejo vineyard outright.

Sam Sebastiani, Don Sebastiani, and August Sebastiani converse amidst the foliage of Sebastiani Vineyards.

Originally, Samuele Sebastiani produced wine and brandy, but the brandy distillery was significant because it provided some breathing room for Samuele during Prohibition. In 1924 Samuele got a permit to produce fortified medicinal wines, using the brandy he produced in the distillery. In 1926 he purchased Woodbridge Winery, partly because it had a great supply of the port and sherry Samuele was permitted to sell.

Samuele Sebastiani was among the first to conclude that the immigrant population in New York and New Jersey would be the wine industry's salvation during Prohibition. As soon as wine sales became illegal, Samuele began shipping grapes in refrigerated cars to the East Coast to supply the home-winemaking boom that was born in the days following the Volstead Act.

Samuele contributed heavily to the community of Sonoma. He built and operated a cannery for the undisguised purpose of putting as many people to work as possible. He paid for lighting in the streets of Sonoma, and later paid to have the streets paved.[13] He added a water-line, to be used in case of fire, to Sonoma's main street. His obituary in the *Index Tribune* hailed him as a fine and generous man, who had invested much of his earnings in community improvements.

When he died in March 1944, his son and daughter-in-law, August and Sylvia, took over the winery operation. In 1952 they purchased the remaining interest in the winery from Samuele's widow. August was adept as a wine producer, but his forte appears to have been market-ing and promotion. He had a keen sense for what the American peo-ple would buy. He concentrated on jug wines and raising the level of his wine so that an American public just awakening to the joys of wine would find it pleasant and error-free. When August died in 1980, his son Sam took over operation of the winery.

Sam quickly showed the experience he had gained growing up in the winery. While maintaining an interest in the Sebastiani mainstays, Sam shifted some of the emphasis to premium varietals. He estab-lished the Sebastiani name in that field, but in 1986, in a family feud that made headline news, Sam was fired by his mother and replaced by his brother Don. While at first it appeared that Don would return the Sebastiani Vineyards and winery to the market-conscious jug wines, he has surprised many by maintaining an interest in the premi-um-wine game and has even sharpened the focus of the operation in that arena.

The winery now produces many lines of Sebastiani wines, includ-ing those of the Sonoma series and the Dutton Ranch series, produc-ing fine examples of premium wine from Sonoma County.

Grape varieties produced: Cabernet Sauvignon, Cabernet Franc, Zinfandel, Sangiovese, Barbera, Merlot, Petite Syrah, Mourvedre, Chardonnay, Sauvignon Blanc

Proprietary blends and other labels: Dutton Ranch, Sonoma Series, Sonoma Cask, Oakbrook, Richard Cuneo

Sebastiani Vineyards, 389 Fourth Street East, Sonoma, California 95476 phone: 800-888-5532 fax: 707-935-1218

SEGHESIO VINEYARDS AND WINERY
Healdsburg, California

In 1886 Edoardo Seghesio accepted an invitation from his friend Pietro Rossi to emigrate to the United States. He left his hometown of Dogliani, in the Piedmont region of northern Italy, and arrived in California to become the superintendent and head winemaker of Italian Swiss Colony.

In the early years, Edoardo worked without pay and stayed at the Italian Swiss Colony cookhouse. By 1893, he was ready to start a family, but rather than returning to Italy to marry his childhood sweetheart, Edoardo was introduced to Angela Dionisia Vasconi. She was much younger than he, but they were married June 12, 1893.

On November 18, 1895, Edoardo and Angela bought their first grape ranch in an area near Geyserville, called, appropriately, Chianti. Originally, they sold the grapes they grew, mostly to Italian Swiss Colony, but they earnestly saved money to allow them to enter the winemaking business.

Rachel Ann Seghesio & Eugene "Pete" Seghesio of Seghesio Vineyards & Winery.

By 1902 they were ready to build their own winery. The production was primitive at first, and Edoardo crushed all the grapes with a hand-crank crusher. He made the wine in bulk and sold it to Italian Swiss Colony. Later, as his business grew, Edoardo started selling bulk wine to Petri Wine Company, Frei Brothers, and a couple of companies in New York.

Edoardo was also trying to improve and expand his business. In 1905 he bought an additional eighty-three acres of vineyard land to add to his first purchase. At this point Edoardo and Angela decided to divide the work: he oversaw the winery and she did the books and purchased grapes from other growers in the area.

In 1934, just after Prohibition was repealed, Edoardo died. He left the property and winery to Angela, who in turn gave it to their children in 1941. They continued the Seghesio tradition of making bulk wine and selling it to other wineries in the area.

Meanwhile, the Seghesio clan was looking for another land purchase. There was a winery that had been founded in 1890 by the Scatena brothers and called the Roma Winery, until they later gave it their own name. In the 1920s the Scatena brothers sold it to the Domitilli and Massoni families from Healdsburg who, in 1944, sold it to Alta Vineyards Company. In 1949 the Seghesio family bought the Alta Vineyards Company for seventy-five thousand dollars. Keeping with family tradition, this new facility only produced bulk wine.

In the early 1980s, the family that had made wine in the United States for ninety years finally started putting their name on the label. The Seghesio Winery now produces wines from a wide variety of grapes and the family recently started a program of cultivating traditional Italian varieties. Almost as if it were destiny, they discovered a vineyard planted by Edoardo to a field blend of the classic grapes in Chianti. Seghesio makes a wine from the blend and calls it Chianti Station. With all the recent interest in planting Italian varieties in the United States, this plot of land could be the oldest vineyard in the country planted to such varieties.

In 1995 Seghesio Winery celebrated its one-hundred-year anniversary with a classic Italian garden party attended by four hundred guests from the wine industry. The menu that described the meal served that day carried the following quote: "Wine is our history, our tradition, our way of life."

A fire in 1996 destroyed the old family winery but the Seghesios rebuilt it and dedicated the new facility in 1998.

Grape varieties produced: Zinfandel, Cabernet Sauvignon, Cabernet Franc, Pinot Noir, Sangiovese, Barbera, Petite Syrah, Nebbiolo, Chardonnay, Arneis, Pinot Grigio

Proprietary blends and other labels: none

Seghesio Vineyards and Winery, 14730 Grove Street, Healdsburg, California 95448 phone: 707-433-3579 fax: 707-433-0545

SIGNORELLO VINEYARDS
Napa, California

Ray Signorello owned a natural resources company in Canada, but fell in love with a plot of land in Napa Valley in 1977. He sealed his fate by buying it, a full one hundred acres, and farmed grapes for nearly a decade before deciding to make his own wine.

In 1980 he planted Chardonnay, and added Sauvignon Blanc and Semillon in 1982, all of which he sold to other wineries. Then, with the bumper crop in 1985, the grape market went flat just as it had for Andrea Sbarbaro's Italian Swiss Colony in 1886. Just like Sbarbaro before him, Signorello decided to keep the grapes he couldn't sell and turn them into wine. He teamed up with his son, Ray, Jr., and launched into a new business.

The Signorello Winery, built in 1984, is a fine example of Robert Keenan architectural design.

In 1986 the Signorellos started building a winery to house the crop they had formerly sold to other winemakers. In 1988 he added red wines to the list, growing Cabernet Sauvignon and Pinot Noir for the production. In 1990, they added Merlot, Cabernet Franc, and Syrah, then put in some Viognier vines.

Grape varieties produced: Cabernet Sauvignon, Pinot Noir, Cabernet Franc, Merlot, Syrah, Chardonnay, Sauvignon Blanc, Semillon, Viognier

Proprietary blends and other labels: Il Taglio, Founder's Reserve
Signorello Vineyards, 4500 Silverado Trail, Napa, California 94558 phone: 707-255-5990 fax: 707-255-5999

SIMI WINERY
Healdsburg, California

In 1848 Giuseppe Simi left Montepulciano to find gold in the fields and hills of California. Unfortunately, his dreams of gold didn't pan out, and he moved to San Francisco to join his brother, Pietro, who was making a living farming lettuce and cabbage.

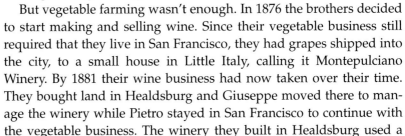

But vegetable farming wasn't enough. In 1876 the brothers decided to start making and selling wine. Since their vegetable business still required that they live in San Francisco, they had grapes shipped into the city, to a small house in Little Italy, calling it Montepulciano Winery. By 1881 their wine business had now taken over their time. They bought land in Healdsburg and Giuseppe moved there to manage the winery while Pietro stayed in San Francisco to continue with the vegetable business. The winery they built in Healdsburg used a gravity-flow design, one of the first of its kind and a signpost for future winery designs. They called it the Simi Winery.

Isabelle Simi attended the annual Santa Rosa festival in 1904 where she won the popular Rosé Queen pageant.

Suddenly, in August 1904, both brothers died. When the San Francisco earthquake followed two years later, the wine business struggled. Then Giuseppe's daughter, Isabelle, took over. She was only fourteen at the time, but her spirit and drive rescued the winery from economic trouble. When she was only eighteen, she undertook a nationwide tour to promote Simi wines, and later that year she married Fred Haigh, a bank teller with the financial knowledge to complement Isabelle's vision.

During Prohibition, Simi Winery struggled. Instead of switching to rugged grape varieties that could withstand shipment by railcar to home winemakers, Isabelle decided to continue to grow fine grape varieties. To survive, she and Fred had to sell off some of the vineyard land, but they retained the core. It was the same stubbornness that convinced them to keep the wine they produced legally—before the ban in 1919—until 1933 when Prohibition was repealed. The half million gallons of wine in their tanks provided a jump start in 1933 to get Simi Winery back into business before most other wineries could.

In 1970 an aging Isabelle Simi sold the winery. The dedication and stubbornness she had inherited from her father had ensured the Simi Winery's survival and prosperity for nearly ninety years before it was passed on to other capable hands. Today, it is owned by the Canandaigua Wine Company.

Grape varieties produced: Cabernet Sauvignon, Petit Verdot, Cabernet Franc, Merlot, Chardonnay, Sauvignon Blanc, Semillon, Pinot Noir

Proprietary blends and other labels: none

Simi Winery, 16275 Healdsburg Avenue, Healdsburg, California 95448 phone: 707-433-6981 fax: 707-433-6253

STAGLIN FAMILY VINEYARD
Rutherford, California

Pasquale Stagliano was born in 1912, in the small village of Bella, in Calabria. He was only two years old when his family decided to emigrate to America, where they ended up in Rochester, New York.

By then, Pasquale was known as Pat. His interest in wine started at an early age with home winemaking, but later he moved to New York City to pursue a career in music, changing his name to Ramon Staglin and becoming a naturalized citizen.

He and his wife, Darlene, moved to California in 1945. He worked in other trades for a while, but kept up with his home winemaking. When his son, Garen, was born, Ramon quickly indoctrinated him in the process of making wine. With that, Garen was bitten by the wine bug. He attended school at UCLA and the Stanford Business School, but kept traveling to Napa to explore his love of wine.

The breathtaking Staglin Vineyard lies in the Rutherford Bench of Napa Valley.

In 1985 Garen and Shari Staglin purchased a vineyard in the Rutherford Bench of Napa Valley that had belonged to Beaulieu Vineyard and was used in the BV's famous Georges de Latour Private Reserve line of wines. The vineyard had been planted by André Tchelistcheff in 1966, and Tchelistcheff showed his love of the vineyard by agreeing to advise Garen and Shari in their efforts to replant the acreage to their wishes. Budwood for Stagliano, the Staglin Vineyard Sangiovese, was purchased from the famous Brunello producer, Biondi-Santi, in Tuscany.

Grape varieties produced: Cabernet Sauvignon, Sangiovese, Chardonnay

Proprietary blends and other labels: none

Staglin Family Vineyard, 1570 Bella Oaks Lane, Rutherford, California 94573 phone: 707-963-1749 fax: 707-963-8784

Garen and Shari Staglin pose in the threshold of the Staglin Family Vineyard.

SUNNYHILL WINERY
(also known as the Riorda Winery or Sunny St. Helena Winery)
St. Helena, California

The Sunnyhill Winery was opened by Gioachino "Jack" Riorda and Charles Forni in 1933, and was sometimes called the Riorda Winery. In 1936 it was purchased by Cesare Mondavi. Renamed the Sunny St. Helena Winery, it formed the basis for the Mondavi wine empire that would later include Charles Krug and, by way of Cesare's son, Robert, the Robert Mondavi Winery in Napa.

The Sunnyhill Winery no longer exists.

SUTTER HOME WINERY
St. Helena, California

In 1890 the Sutter family established the Sutter Home Winery on Howell Mountain. In 1906 the winery operation was moved to St. Helena, but throughout most of its next four decades it made mostly bulk wine.

Mario and John Trinchero came from Asti, Italy, in the 1920s, descendants of a family that had been in the wine business for six generations. The Trincheros started out in the hotel business in New York, but Mario and John sold that and moved to California. They bought Sutter Home Winery in 1947 and produced a line of decent, moderately priced wines. By the 1960s they were buying other vineyard land and improving their sources of grapes. They bought the already renowned Deaver Ranch in 1968.

This exquisitely restored Victorian house, built by the original winery owners, is now used as the Sutter Home Hospitality Center

In time, Mario's son, Bob, got involved in the business. According to legend, the Trincheros produced their first White Zinfandel "blush" wine by accident. They tasted it and decided that the slightly sweet, fruity taste would appeal to Americans who were just discovering wine, so they marketed it. It was a huge success and formed the basis for the explosive expansion of Sutter Home Winery.

Bob also got the family involved in Amador County grapes. He started making wine from Amador fruit, especially Zinfandel, and liked it so much he bought Montevina Winery. That property is the source of the Trincheros' experiments with Italian grape varieties, but Sutter Home is still the source of the family's income.

Bob has been President of the Napa Valley Vintners Association and serves on the board of directors for the Wine Institute.

Grape varieties produced: Zinfandel, Chenin Blanc, Moscato, Chardonnay, Sauvignon Blanc, Gewürztraminer, Cabernet Sauvignon, Merlot

Proprietary blends and other labels: via Trinchero's Montevina Winery: Terra d'Oro, M. Trinchero, Soleo

Sutter Home Winery, 277 St. Helena Highway S., St. Helena, California 94574 phone: 707-963-3104 fax: 707-963-5397

F. TELDESCHI WINERY
Healdsburg, California

Michele Teldeschi left Casabasciana, near the town of Lucca in Tuscany, and came to America with his son, Lorenzo, around 1900. They settled in Healdsburg and worked for Sargenti brothers in the vineyard (Sargenti later became Frei Brothers Vineyard, and was bought out by the Gallo brothers).

In 1910 Michele and son established a winery, producing bulk wines for other wineries. In 1914 Lorenzo returned to Casabasciana, but was stuck there when World War I broke out. While in Italy, he got married and started a family. In 1922 Lorenzo returned to the United States but, like many Italians emigrating to the America, he had to come without his family. He worked hard to save money to bring his wife and three children over and, finally, in 1929 they joined Lorenzo in California.

Michele died in 1934. When Lorenzo died in 1935, his children were forced to quit school and go to work. The winery struggled for a few more years, but went out of business at the beginning of World War II. Following the war, Lorenzo's sons, Michele and Franco, bought a ranch in the Dry Creek Valley.

Michele and Franco sold most of their grapes in the 1950s to Italian winemakers in the San Francisco area, a practice that continued until about 1980. In time, the old Italian immigrants died off and the customer base dwindled, so less and less of the grapes were shipped into San Francisco. In the early 1950s the brothers bought another ranch but, in 1958, they parted ways, each taking one property with them. In 1962 Franco bought a second ranch which was already planted to grapes.

In 1966 Franco invested in a third ranch which

Frank Teldeschi was one of the "old timers" of the California wine industry. An Italian immigrant, he arrived in the United States in 1929 and began farming his ranch on the Dry Creek benchland in 1946. His family continues the tradition of growing fine zinfandel grapes in the Dry Creek Valley.

GOVERNMENT WARNING: (1) ACCORDING TO THE SURGEON GENERAL, WOMEN SHOULD NOT DRINK ALCOHOLIC BEVERAGES DURING PREGNANCY BECAUSE OF THE RISK OF BIRTH DEFECTS. (2) CONSUMPTION OF ALCOHOLIC BEVERAGES IMPAIRS YOUR ABILITY TO DRIVE A CAR OR OPERATE MACHINERY, AND MAY CAUSE HEALTH PROBLEMS.

1991
ZINFANDEL
DRY CREEK VALLEY
CELLARED & BOTTLED BY TELDESCHI WINE CELLARS, HEALDSBURG, CA. ALCOHOL 13.8% BY VOLUME * CONTAINS SULFITES

was planted to prunes but which he ripped out in favor of grapes. In the next twenty years, until his death, Franco Teldeschi bought another two ranches and planted sixty-five acres of grapes. He taught his son Dan to make wine and Dan started entering his wines in amateur competitions in the late 1970s.

Franco died in 1985 and John Teldeschi took over the vineyard operation. He has since developed a business selling grapes to such large wineries as E. & J. Gallo, Ravenswood, Rafanelli, and others. But Dan Teldeschi started buying grapes in 1985 from his brother and mother, Caterina Teldeschi, to make commercial wine from Teldeschi grapes. By 1993, Dan had a license for his new winery in Dry Creek Valley. He buys grapes from his mother.

Grape varieties produced: Cabernet Sauvignon, Zinfandel, Petite Syrah, Carignane, Napa Gamay, Malvasia, Moscato Frontignan

Proprietary blends and other labels: none

F. Teldeschi Winery, 3555 Dry Creek Road, Healdsburg, California 95448 phone: 707-433-6626 fax: 707-433-3077

TRENTADUE WINERY
Geyserville, California

Leo and Evelyn Trentadue lived in Santa Clara Valley until 1959, when they decided that the residential subdivisions were closing in on them. They needed more space, and they looked long and hard before purchasing the property that is now called Trentadue Winery.

It was actually two parcels of land, one belonging to another Italian American family. Together, the two parcels had forty-two acres planted to grapes. Leon and Evelyn originally sold the produce to Italian Swiss Colony, but later converted an old barn to a winery and started to produce the Trentadue wines.

They started with Carignane, but quickly added more grapes. In fact, the

Trentadue Winery produced a 1985 Sangiovese, ahead of the Cal-Ital wave that would later sweep California winemaking.

The Trentadue family prides itself on using environmentally sound practices, including the annual seasonal release of thousands of lacewings and ladybugs. These bugs are natural predators, feeding on vineyard pests and reducing the population sufficiently enough that pesticides are not necessary.

Grape varieties produced: Zinfandel, Sangiovese, Merlot, Carignane, Petite Syrah, Petite Syrah port, Merlot port, Cabernet Sauvignon, Chardonnay

Proprietary blends and other labels: Old Patch Red

Trentadue Winery, 19170 Redwood Highway, Geyserville, California 95441 phone: 707-433-3104 fax: 707-433-5825

VAL VERDE WINERY
Del Rio, Texas

Francesco Qualia was one of the millions of Italian immigrants who left his hometown in the waning years of the nineteenth century. He packed up his belongings and abandoned his farm in Castellanza, near Milan, in 1881, just as the Italian immigrant tide was beginning to build.

Traveling through Louisiana and Texas, he wound up in Mexico, and pursued farming outside of Mexico City. The conditions there were bad, and he decided to return to the fertile fields of Texas that he had seen on his way south. But by now (1882) he was nearly out of money and had to work as a railroad laborer until he could save up the finances to start his farm. He worked on the "Macaroni Line," so called because many of the laborers hired to work on The New York, Texas, and Mexico Railroad were Italian. The railroad ran into trouble and Qualia was once again without work, and without the funds to buy a farm.

Qualia heard about farming opportunities west of San Antonio, and found fertile land near the San Felipe creek. The family that owned the plot he was interested in refused to divide up the large farm, but agreed to sell it together. Qualia enlisted fellow Italian immigrants Franchi, Serafini, and Comolli, and purchased the entire farm.

In addition to farming, Qualia was encouraged to start growing grapes, relying on winemaking skills he had developed before leaving Italy. When he built a house for his family, he added an adobe winery behind it, but from 1883 to Prohibition, making wine remained a sideline for him. Prohibition struck most wineries hard, but Qualia hadn't gotten far enough into commercial production by 1919 for the new legislation to affect him very much.

In 1926 Francesco Qualia died and was succeeded by his son, Louis. Due to Louis's ambitious inclusion of such legal activities as the making of sacramental wine, amateur wine for home use, and the selling grapes for table use, he was able to jump right back into commercial production when Prohibition ended.

In the fall of 1935, Val Verde received its new license. In 1973 Louis retired and Tommy Qualia took over operation of Val Verde. Tommy is the first member of the Qualia family to make Val Verde his principal source of income, so he is approaching it more aggressively. Among other moves was his recent hiring of Enrique Ferro from Italy to serve as enologist and viticulural advisor for the winery.

Grape varieties produced: Cabernet Sauvignon, Shiraz, Sauvignon Blanc, Muscat Canelli, Lenoir, Herbemont

Proprietary blends and other labels: Don Luis (tawny port)
Val Verde Winery, Del Rio, Texas 78840 phone: 210-775-5394

VALLEY OF THE MOON
Glen Ellen, California

The Valley of the Moon vineyards were first planted in 1851 by Joseph Hooker, a soldier in the Union Army. A winery was added in 1857. In 1941, a man who had founded the Columbus Sausage and Salami Company purchased Hooker's vineyard, by then called Madrone Vineyards, and added a winery. The man was Enrico Parducci (no relation to the Parducci family of Parducci Wine Cellars).

The winery concentrates on generic table wines but also sells some of its better products from the tasting room. The winery was purchased by Kenwood Vineyards in 1997.

Grape varieties produced: none identified
Proprietary blends and other labels: none
Valley of the Moon, 777 Madrone Road, Glen Ellen, California 95442 phone: 707-996-6941

VENEZIA WINERY
Geyserville, California

Julius Nervo emigrated from Venice soon after the turn of the century and built a winery called Venezia in 1908. He changed the name to Nervo several years later and the name Venezia was lost to history for a while.

Nervo Winery stayed in the family for seventy-five years before being sold to the Schlitz Brewing Company. In time, Schlitz sold this property and Geyser Peak to the Trione family. It is now owned by Fortune Brands.

When the Triones transformed the Nervo production into the Canyon Road production, they resurrected the name Venezia and assigned it to another line of wines, and now bottle premium, vineyard-designated wines under the Venezia label.

Grape varieties produced: Cabernet Sauvignon, Sangiovese, Chardonnay

Proprietary blends and other labels: Bianco Nuovo Mundo White Meritage (Sauvignon Blanc, Semillon), Sangiovese Nuovo Mondo (Sangiovese, Shiraz), Stella Bianco (Chardonnay, Semillon)
Venezia Winery, P.O. Box 25, 22281 Chianti Road, Geyserville, California 95441 phone: 800-945-4447; fax: 707-857-3545

VIANO VINEYARDS
Martinez, California

The Viano family emigrated from Piedmont to the New World in the early part of the twentieth century. After three years in Alaska, Clement Viano brought the family to Martinez, California and in 1920 he purchased a vineyard that James Kelley had planted in the 1880s. In those days, the land was used mostly as a fruit ranch, so vines were not a big crop for a while. But in 1946, Clement's son, Conrad, started the Conrad Viano Winery.

Later, Conrad's son, Clement, and Clement's wife, Sharon, assumed responsibility for winery operations, and now Clement and Sharon's sons are running it, making it four generations in seventy-seven years to command the Viano Winery. John and David, the fourth generation, were trained at the University of California at Davis enology school.

Grape varieties produced: Cabernet Sauvignon, Sangiovese,

Zinfandel, Petite Sirah, Chardonnay, dessert wine

Proprietary blends and other labels: Private Stock, Reserve Selection

Viano Vineyards, 150 Morello Avenue, Martinez, California 94553 phone: 510-228-6465, fax: 510-228-5670

VIANSA WINERY
Sonoma, California

The Sebastiani family had already established a reputation for reliable wines when Sam took over the reins of the Sebastiani Vineyards following his father's death in 1980. Sam's vision took the family operation into the new age, slowly switching production from jug wines to premium labels and varietals. Then, in 1986, Sam was fired by his mother in a family feud that resembled the Mondavi split twenty years earlier.

The anguish suffered by the Sebastiani family in that breakup may pay great dividends for the consumer. While Sebastiani Vineyards survived some rocky times to regain its share of the market under the leadership of Don Sebastiani, Sam has started the Viansa Winery and Italian Marketplace, sticking to his dream of premium wines and bottling them behind ornate, Italian-style labels.

Viansa Winery and Italian Market Place is a popular tourist stop on Highway 21 on the way to Sonoma.

Viansa's operation is considerably smaller than the one Sam was used to when running the family wine business, but the size gives him time to concentrate on specialized wines. There are the usual Chardonnay, Cabernet Sauvignon, and Sauvignon Blanc, but Viansa has an ambitious program to cultivate and vinify traditional Italian varietals like Sangiovese, Nebbiolo, Trebbiano, Primitivo, Charbono, Vernaccia, Muscat Canelli, and Aleatico. This is a reflection of Sam's commitment to his roots: While his father and grandfather tried to assimilate and become more American, Sam is interested in strengthening his ties to Italy, not cutting them.

The Viansa label was created in 1988. The name is an amalgam of Sam's name and that of his wife, Vicki, and they emphasize food no less than wine. While Sam directs the vineyards and winemaking style, Vicki is left to pursue her interest in food, managing the visitor's center at Viansa that replicates the marketplace in Lucca, Italy, the Sebastiani clan's ancestral home. There is an abundance of fresh and prepared foods, sauces, condiments, cheeses, and olive oils.

The marketplace is surrounded by picnic tables on its perch atop a gentle hill, a perfect setting to sample the food and wine of Viansa. On each of the author's visits to this blissful setting, the picnic grounds have been populated by young couples, old couples, and families with kids small and large, all sharing the unique combination of fabulous climate, beautiful surroundings, and terrific wines to be paired with the mouth-watering food sold in the Viansa marketplace.

Grape varieties produced: Cabernet Sauvignon, Zinfandel, Barbera, Nebbiolo, Sangiovese, Primitivo, Charbono, Chardonnay, Sauvignon Blanc, Muscat Canelli, Aleatico, Pinot Grigio, Vernaccia, Trebbiano

Proprietary blends and other labels: none

Viansa Winery, 25200 Arnold Drive (Highway 121), Sonoma, California 95476 phone: 800-995-4740, fax: 707-935-7306

G. B. VICINI WINERY
Amador County, California

This winery was founded in Amador County in 1894, but is no longer in existence.

Notes for Part II

1. Anthony Dias Blue, *American Wine* (New York: Harper & Row, 1988), 473.

2. James Laube, *California Wine: A Comprehensive Guide to the Wineries, Wines, Vintages and Vineyards of America's Premier Winegrowing State* (New York: Wine Spectator Press, 1995), 184.

3. Ellen Hawkes, *Blood & Wine: The Unauthorized Story of the Gallo Wine Empire* (New York: Simon & Schuster, 1993), 25.

4. Leon D. Adams, *The Wines of America* (New York: McGraw-Hill Publishing Company, 1990), 384.

5. Ibid., 289.

6. Charles L. Sullivan, *Napa Wine: A History* (San Francisco: The Wine Appreciation Guild, 1994), 158.

7. James T. Lapsley, *Bottled Poetry: Napa Winemaking from Prohibition to the Modern Era* (Berkeley and Los Angeles: University of California Press, 1996), 59.

8. Adams, op. cit., 394.

9. Blue, op. cit., 175.

10. Ibid., 177.

11. Adams, op. cit., 381-83.

12. Laube, op. cit., 449.

13. Actually, as the story has it, he tried to convince the town leaders to pave the streets. When they didn't, he paved one half and left it up to them to pave the remainder. They did.

Epilogue

FROM AMERICA TO ITALY

The tide of Italian émigrés that broke onto American shores early in this century began a still-ongoing process of cultural infiltration. Pizza, pasta, espresso, and Italian-style wines are as familiar to Americans as are opera, Italian sports cars and fashion, bocce and soccer, and the dreamy scenes of *cinema Italiana* playing at local movie houses. An argument can be made that the Italian influence has been felt in every essential arena of American culture—as is argued for wine in this book.

The Italians who stayed behind are immensely proud of the achievements of their brethren who moved to the New World. The drama of visiting American cousins being drawn to the bosom of their ancestral villages is played out every day in Italy, from north to south, and on a personal level this *abbraccio* ("embrace") is symbolic of the deep affection Italians feel for Italo-Americani.

This kinship, this feeling of a shared destiny, is what binds Americans and Italians together as we enter the twenty-first century. As the Italians at the end of the last century left to seek their fortune in the New World, so Americans of Italian descent are going back to Italy at the end of this century, buying wineries and vineyards and completing the cycle.

Robert Mondavi is the most prominent of the Italian-Americans venturing back into the viticultural world of Italy. His success in America and his deep dedication to The Mission (discussed in Chapter 5) leave no doubt as to the historic importance of Mondavi to the world of wine. With a joint venture with the Frescobaldi family, which has been in the wine business itself for eight hundred years, Mondavi has added an Italian enterprise to his growing international family, now including businesses in four countries.

Daryl Sattui spent twenty years rebuilding the V. Sattui wine business, and he is now returning to Italy to broaden his success. Perched on a Tuscan hillside is the Monastero le Vallesi, an ancient monastery, and now the centerpiece for Sattui's new Italian winery. Four wines are currently produced there, using Italian and international varieties, and Sattui intends to expand the production line.

But perhaps the most impressive enterprise by Italian Americans in the Italian wine industry was started by the Mariani family in 1919. That year, John Mariani, Sr., started an importing company in New York called Banfi. Mariani was raised in Italy by his aunt, Teodolinda Banfi, who had been head of Pope Pius XI's household staff and who taught young "Giovanni" the secrets of fine wine and the importance of carefully choosing wines for a distinguished audience. In 1919 Mariani named his company to honor his aunt. Unfortunately, one year later Prohibition hit and Mariani was forced to shift his business to food products, such as Montecatini Salts, Ramazotti Medicinal Bitters, Florio Tonics, and others. Following Repeal in 1933, he went back to importing wine, bringing in classics like Brunello, Gattinara, Barolo, and Chianti, as well as a string of lesser-known Italian white wines.

In 1967 Banfi made a decision that would establish the company financially and propel it into a role as a major player in the wine world. That year, while expanding into other European markets, the Marianis decided to invest in a product that would appeal to a broad segment of the American population, so they arranged to import the wines of the Cantine Cooperative Riunite, known simply as Riunite in America. This wine had a grand history, having accompanied the Roman legions as they conquered the world in earlier days, but the Mariani family now had a twentieth-century audience in mind. The wine is denigrated by wine snobs as soda pop, a simple-minded wine that would only appeal to the misinformed, but the Mariani family wanted a light, appealing style of wine to provide a bridge for an American public that didn't have a tradition of wine with meals. The hunch proved be a good one, and from the first one hundred cases received in 1967, Riunite imports topped 125 million cases, including recent yearly averages above 2.5 million cases.

Sales of Riunite provided so much income for Banfi that the company was able to pursue another, some say more noble, goal: to buy a great Italian estate and produce world-class wines from it. In 1977 Banfi bought land in Tuscany that had never been planted to vines. But this property was carefully selected by renowned enologist Ezio Rivella, who researched the soil and climate, matched ideal clonal types with the environment, and built the winemaking business from the soil up. The land on the Banfi estate is rich with prehistoric fossils, the hillsides are angled for ideal exposure to the sun, and the scientific approach to vine selection and planting has ensured that the Mariani family will own one of the most prized vineyards in all of Italy.

Standing above the vineyards is a ninth-century castle that Banfi has restored, a towering symbol of the success of the Mariani family both in America and Italy. The inside of the castello now houses a museum of glass that would rival any in the world, and a restaurant that serves true Tuscan dishes accented with Banfi olive oil, aceto balsamico, and herbs, the food accompanied by a wide array of Banfi white and red wines.

While respect for local culture prevents the use of the American flag at the castello, the Marianis proudly fly the flag over the winery building, apt reminder of the country of origin of this transplanted Italian American family.

Today, Banfi is run by Harry and John Mariani, Jr., joined by their sons and daughters, the third generation of the Banfi wine family. The vineyards around Castello Banfi produce the premium wines for Banfi, including a Brunello di Montalcino that has received very high marks from wine critics, an ultra-premium wine called Summus (a blend of Brunello, Cabernet Sauvignon, and Syrah grapes), Santa Costanza (a novello wine similar in style to Beaujolais Nouveau), and a broad range of red and white varietal wines.

Banfi owns a nineteenth-century winery in Strevi, in the Piedmont region of northern Italy. It is now called Banfi Cellars and produces the company's sparkling wines. Banfi also owns Principessa Gavia, near the Strevi vineyard, which produces two more wines to add to the Mariani portfolio.

In spite of their heavy investment in properties in Italy, the Mariani family maintains strong ties to its New York heritage. A sixty-room mansion on a 127-acre estate in Brookville, New York, serves as the world headquarters for Banfi. And just like the Italians of the Old World, who can't resist planting grapevines just about anywhere there is an open patch of land, Banfi has planted vines around the Brookville estate. These vineyards were planted by Frederick Frank, the grandson of the wine legend Konstantin Frank. Currently, Banfi produces a Chardonnay and a sparkling wine from those acres.

There is no doubt about the significant contributions Italians have made to American culture. And now the Americans who have reaped the greatest share of that Old World influence are returning to share the blessings of American culture and finance with the Italians back home. It is a fitting, and complete, full circle.

TIMELINE FOR EVENTS
Related to Italians and Winemaking in America

1001 Leif Ericsson landed in America

1524 Giovanni da Verrazzano landed on Kitty Hawk and found vines

1565 French settlers in Florida made wine

1568 Vines (possibly *vinifera*) planted in what is now Parris Island, South Carolina

1584 Sir Walter Raleigh landed in North Carolina and found abundance of grapes

1609 Virginia Company predicted it could make wine in America

1611 Virginia criminal code made stealing from a vineyard a capital offense

1619 First attempts to grow *vinifera*, by Lord Delaware in Virginia

1622 Wine sent from Virginia to London was spoiled en route

1623 Virginia governor put price controls on other drinks to promote wine, and Virginia assembly required every householder to plant vines

1629 Massachusetts Bay Colony tried to recruit French vignerons

1645 Eusebio Chino was born

1658 Virginia Act of Assembly offered reward to whomever produced wine

1685 Virginia Assembly dropped offer of reward for production of wine (without ever giving award)

1711 Fra Eusebio Francesco Chino died

1716 Robert Beverley made seven hundred gallons of wine from Virginia native grapes

1720s William Byrd planted twenty varieties of Europeans vines in Virginia

1759 Group in Virginia offered reward for grape growing

1766 Dr. Andrew Turnbull brought Italian laborers from Italy to establish wine industry in Florida, but many were killed by malaria, scurvy, and other epidemics

1768 Virginia exported wine to Great Britain

1769 Junipero Serra brought vinifera cuttings to California

1773 Filippo Mazzei sailed from Italy with Italian vines and vignerons to help the American colonists

1779 First clear reference to planting wine grapes in California

(San Juan Capistrano)

1806	End of feudalism in Italy
1809	Antonio Lugo planted vineyard near Los Angeles
1817	San Francisco Mission established first settlement north of San Francisco in San Rafael
1821	Wine first made in San Rafael (first wine in northern California)
1823	Catawba vines planted in Washington, D.C., by John Adlum
1823	Sonoma Mission founded
1825	Missionaries planted grapes in a vineyard that would be bought by Samuele Sebastiani in 1908
1830s	Commercial viniculture began in California (around Los Angeles)
1833	Mexican missions in American Southwest were secularized
1833	Louis Vignes introduces French wine grape cuttings to California
1839	Thomas Winery built (see Filippi, 1967), part of first large vine planting in southern California
1841	Americans began to arrive in California steadily overland after this date
1844	Mariano Vallejo granted George Yount 4400 acres on Howell Mountain
1847	Charles Krug came to America
1848	Revolutions in Italy, *mezzadri* drifted to America
1848	Gold discovered near San Francisco
1848	Giuseppe Simi left Montepulciano to seek gold in California
1848	Agoston Haraszthy arrived in California
1850	Francesco Secchi di Casale started *L'Eco d'Italia* newspaper in New York
1850	Andrea Sbarbaro arrived in United States from Genoa at age twelve
1851	Domenico Ghirardelli opened chocolate factory in San Francisco
1852	Zinfandel vines planted in Oak Knoll by Osborne (later the vineyard became Eschol, owned by Trefethen)
1853	Splivalo Vineyard and Winery founded in San Jose
1853	Andrea Arata planted vineyard in Amador County
1854	Anthony Caminetti was born in Jackson Gate, California
1856	Agoston Haraszthy moved to Sonoma

1856	Adam Uhlinger founded winery that would later become D'Agostini Winery
1857	John Patchett made the first commercial shipment of wine from Napa
1857	Guiseppe Migliavacca came to America from Pavia
1857	Quirillo and Company formed in South Fork, California (Amador County), later called the Italian Garden and Winery
1858	Italian Mutual Aid Society founded in San Francisco
1859	California law exempted new vineyards from taxation until they were four years old
1860s	Much competition and legal battles to protect American wine from French imports
1860	Garibaldi liberated Mezzogiorno
1860	Edoardo Seghesio was born near Dogliano, Italy
1861	Italy is unified
1861	Charles Krug established his winery on land received in dowry for marrying M. G. Vallejo's grandniece
1862	Giovanni Foppiano left Genoa for America
1866	Guiseppe Migliavacca started wine business in Napa Valley
1868	Angelo Marre came to United States with his family
1868	Railroad reached Napa Valley in August
1869	National Prohibition Party formed
1870s	Bartolomeo Caramella opened his first winery in California
1870	A unified Italy given final approval by all provinces, including Rome
1870	General Erasmus Delano Keyes stone winery built (Edge Hill); later it became the Louis P. Martini home
1870	Guiseppe Migliavacca built a wine cellar in city of Napa
1871	Rome was declared the capital of newly united Italy (July 2)
1871	William W. Watson founded Inglenook on old Koenig farm
1871	Amador Wine Association was formed
1873	Phylloxera reached Sonoma Valley
1873	Napa Valley Wine Company was formed
1874	Samuele Sebastiani was born in Lucca, Italy
1874	Sutter Home Winery was built
1876	Wine market bust occurred, due to worldwide economic depression
1876	Pietro and Giuseppe Simi established the Montepulciano

	Winery in San Francisco, using grapes shipped in from Sonoma County
1877	Louis A. Foppiano was born
1877	Vincent Picchetti founded winery
1878	Secondo Guasti arrived from Piedmont, settled in Sonora, Mexico, and later went to Los Angeles
1879	Niebaum Estate founded by Gustave Niebaum, including Inglenook
1880s	Phylloxera killed vines in Europe
1880	Railroad came to southern Italy
1880	Joseph Vezzetti brought Nebbiolo cuttings from northern Italy to Colorado
1880	Winery founded by Augustus Quitzow (later named Geyser Peak)
1880	Frei Brothers built their winery (later to be bought by the Gallo brothers
1881	Simi brothers founded Simi Winery in Healdsburg
1881	Andrea Sbarbaro founded Italian Swiss Colony in Asti, California
1881	Twin Fir Winery founded, later bought by Rafael Martini and renamed R. Martini Winery
1881	Francesco Qualia left Milan for U.S.
1882	Giuseppe "Joe" Gallo was born in Fossano, Piedmont, Italy (father of Ernest and Julio)
1882	Vittorio and Katerina Sattui emigrated from Carsi, Italy to settle in San Francisco
1882	Oriental Exclusion Act
1882	Tosetti Winery founded by Baldisere Tosetti on Spring Street in St. Helena, California
1883	Bay View Vineyard planted by Felix Borreo (bought by Silverado Vineyards in 1992 and planted to Sangiovese and Zinfandel)
1883	Emilio Guglielmo was born in Piedmont, Italy
1884	B. Arata founded winery
1884	Martin Scatena bought ranch near Healdsburg and started winery in his cellar
1884-87	Cholera epidemic in southern Italy, killed 55,000
1884-91	Pierce's (or Anaheim) Disease devastated vineyards in southern California, closing all fifty wineries in Anaheim

1885	Michelo Gallo was born (brother of Joe Gallo)
1885	Vittorio Sattui's wine business was going well enough that he quit his job as a baker and devoted himself full-time to wine making
1885	*Padrone* system outlawed by Foran Act
1886	California grape market collapsed, causing Italian Swiss Colony to start making its own wine
1886	Edoardo Seghesio came to America from Dogliani, Italy
1886	Angelo Petri bought a vineyard in Central Valley
1887	Louis M. Martini was born in Pietra Ligure
1887	Severe economic depression in Italy
1887	First winery built for Italian Swiss Colony
1887	Rossini Winery built
1887	Guiseppe and Louisa Martinelli came to America
1887	Raffaello Petri got involved in the wine business
1888	Giovanni Demateis founded winery
1888	Bisceglia Brothers founded winery
1888	Felix Borreo opened the Bay View Ranch and Vineyard Winery
1889	Marco Fontana founded the California Fruit Packing Company; later started the Marca del Monte, later called Del Monte
1889	Giovanni Piuma founded winery in Los Angeles
1889	Batiste Previtale came to U.S. from Lombardy
1889	Bernardo Winery was started
1890s	By this time, wealthy families owned more than one hundred vineyards and were making very good wine in California
1890s	Luigi Banchero built his winery, but closed it at Prohibition
1890	Scatena Brothers founded the Santa Lucia Winery, later known as the Roma Winery, which later became the Alta Vineyards Winery, and was bought by Edoardo Seghesio in 1949
1890	Forces from northern Italy put down a rebellion in Sicily
1890	Phylloxera hit southern Italy and wiped out vineyards
1890	Trade war begins between France and Italy, raising tariffs and reducing exports of wine from southern Italy
1890	Anthony Caminetti was elected to Congress
1890	John Sutter established Sutter Home Winery

1891	Severe drought in southern Italy, reduced fruit production and cut total wine in half
1892	Ellis Island opened (January 1)
1892	Victor Sioli opened winery
1892	Pietro Biale was born in Santa Giustina
1893	Edoardo Seghesio married Angela Vasconi
1893	Guiseppe Franzia arrived in U.S. from Genoa
1893	Beginning of greatest industrial depression in American history
1893	California Wine Association formed
1893	Anti-Saloon League formed in Ohio
1894	California Wine Makers' Association founded
1894	G. B. Vicini built a winery in Amador County
1895	Samuele Sebastiani came to America from Lucca, Italy
1895	A. Piccardo opened a winery in Jackson, California
1895	Edoardo Seghesio bought grape ranch near Healdsburg, called the area Chianti, and founded Seghesio Vineyards
1895	Antonio Forni bought the Tychson property (later opened Lombarda Winery
1895	California State Board of Viticultural Commissioners disbanded
1895	Felix Salmina and John Battista bought Larkmead Winery (it later became Hanns Kornell)
1896	Giovanni "John" Foppiano bought Riverside Winery and founded the Foppiano family winery
1897	Severe crop failure led to riots in Sicily, Puglia, and Calabria
1897	Frasinetti Winery started in Sacramento, California
1898	Father Pietro Bandini resettled Italians in northwest Arkansas where they planted vines
1898	John Battista and Lorenzo Cella arrived in America from northern Italy
1898	Rossi Winery built
1899	Agostino Martini and his son, Louis M., left Petra, Liguria in Italy for America
1899	Vittorio Sattui bought the former Rottanzi Winery in the Mission District and moved his wine business there from North Beach and called it the V. Sattui Wine Company
1899	Anthony Cappello came to United States from Naples
1899	Caparone family came to United States

1900	Wine business started by Antonio Forni
1900	Secondo Guasti formed Italian Vineyard Company near Los Angeles
1900	Lombarda Winery founded by Antonio Forni in Napa Valley
1900	Antonio Nonini emigrated to U.S. from northern Italy
1900	(approximate date) Michele Teldeschi and son, Lorenzo, left Casabasciana in Tuscany for America
1901	Gino Speranza founded Society for Protection of Italian Immigrants
1901	Fire in Calistoga
1902	Antonio Perelli-Minetti came from Italy
1902	First Seghesio winery built
1902	U.S. Congress passed the Passenger Act, improving conditions for immigrants in transit
1902	Rafael Martini bought Twin Fir Winery and named it R. Martini Wine Company (later Martini & Prati Winery)
1902	Antonio Perelli-Minetti arrived in United States from Barletta
1903	Burgess Winery, where Samuele Sebastiani worked, burned down
1904	Samuele Sebastiani purchased a vineyard in Sonoma Valley from Milani and established the Sebastiani Winery
1904	Giovanni Filippi came to U.S. to work as a mason for Secondo Guasti
1904	Giuseppe and Pietro Simi died; family business is taken over by Isabelle Simi
1904	Secondo Guasti established a company town near Los Angeles and named the town Guasti
1904	Canata Winery built (see Pedroncelli, 1927)
1904	Conradi Winery built (now the Robert Keenan Winery)
1905	Kenwood Winery built by Louis Pagani
1906	Great San Francisco Earthquake; some Italians on Telegraph Hill saved their neighborhood from the fires by bringing up wine barrels and using blankets soaked in wine to protect their houses
1906	Cadenasso family left Genoa for America
1906	Antonio Forni completed his Lombarda Winery
1906	Agostino Martini and son, Louis M., made their first wine in a small shed behind their house in San Francisco

1906	Cesare Mondavi came to America
1906	Frank and Rose Leonetti left Calabria for America
1906	Sutter Home Winery moved from Howell Mountain to St. Helena
1907	Italian Swiss Colony built its famous church shaped like a wine barrel, the El Carmelo Chapel
1907	Year of single greatest influx of Italian immigrants into United States
1908	Andrea Sbarbaro formed the California Grape Protective Association to fight Prohibition
1908	Earthquake and tidal wave hit southern Italy; one hundred thousand died
1908	Samuele Sebastiani leased a ranch that originally belonged to M. G. Vallejo
1908	Emilio Guglielmo came from Piedmont to United States
1908	Severe depression in U.S.; many Italians returned home
1908	San Martin Winery built and operated by Bruno Filice from Cosenza
1908	Twenty-eight years after it was built, Geyser Peak Winery got its name
1908	Guiseppe Migliavacca retired
1908	Gustave Niebaum died
1908	Julius Nervo established the Nervo Winery
1909	Samuele Sebastiani took full possession of vineyard he leased in 1908 (formerly owned by M. G. Vallejo)
1909	Ernest Gallo was born
1910	Vincenzo Graziano bought a vineyard in Mendocino
1910	Antonio Nonini married Angiolina
1910	When his father, Giovanni, threatened to sell the family winery, Louis A. Foppiano secretly arranged to buy it
1910	Louis J. Foppiano was born
1910	Julio Gallo was born
1910	Ciocca Lombardi Winery Company bought Geyser Peak Winery
1910	Edoardo Seghesio planted a vineyard to Sangiovese cuttings from Italy; it was later discovered by his descendants and turned into Chianti Station bottling
1910	First time a refrigerated train car was used to ship grapes from California to Chicago

1910	Crescini family came from Asti
1910	Michele Teldeschi and son, Lorenzo, started winery
1910	Emilio Guglielmo arrived in San Francisco
1911	Agostino Martini and son, Louis M., bought vineyard in Pleasanton, California
1911	Emelio d'Agostini, Giuseppe Gualtieri, and Antonio Pieroni bought Uhlinger Vineyards in Amador County
1911	Alberto Rafanelli emigrated from Tuscany to U.S.
1911	Elmo Martini (of Martini & Prati) was born
1911	Guiseppe Magliavacca died
1912	Wylie Local Option law adopted in California, allowed each jurisdiction to chose whether to be wet or dry
1912	Demetrio Papagni emigrated from Bari
1912	Previtali Winery was built
1912	Libero Pocai established winery in California
1913	August Sebastiani was born
1913	Camillo Colombano planted Barbera vines in California that would later form the basis for the Camillo Colombano Winery
1914	Virginia passed state Prohibition
1914	Joe Cafaro's family emigrated from Adelfia-Canetto in southern Italy
1914	Giovanni Arciero came to United States
1914	Reno Nonini was born
1914	Enrico d'Agostini arrived from Italy
1914	Frank Pesenti left Bergamo with his sister, Maria, for America
1914	Pastori Winery founded
1915	Giuseppe Franzia started winery in 1915
1915	Gabrielli family came from Marches region to America
1917	Over President Wilson's veto, U.S. required that immigrants take a literacy test
1917	The Sheppard Amendment for national prohibition was passed by Congress and sent to states for approval
1917	In support of the war effort, Congress banned the use of food stuffs in the production of alcohol (wine and beer were exempted)
1917	Lorenzo and Rena Nerelli purchased vineyard on York Mountain and created Templeton Winery

1917	Santo Cambianica came to United States and founded San Antonio Winery in Los Angeles
1918	Agostino and Angelica Martini, parents of Louis M. Martini, returned to Italy
1918	Vines first planted at A. Nonini Winery
1918	Louis P. Martini was born in Livermore, California
1918	Guiseppe Martinelli died
1919	Prohibition was approved on January 16 and Volstead Act written to implement it on January 16
1919	Victor Sioli closed winery due to Prohibition
1919	Edoardo and Angela Seghesio bought Italian Swiss Colony for $127,500
1919	Rafanelli family winery went out of business due to Prohibition, but maintained their vineyards waiting for Repeal
1919	Cesare Mondavi started shipping grapes from Lodi to Minnesota
1920s	Scatena brothers sold Roma Winery to the Domitilli and Massoni families
1920	Prohibition went into effect on January 16
1920	Giovanni Filippi and his son, Joseph, left Schio, Italy for America (G. Filippi had originally come to America in 1904, but had returned to Italy)
1920	Demetrio Papagni planted Papagni vineyard
1921	New immigration policy for U.S. reduced immigration of Italians by 80 percent
1921	Adolph Parducci bought vineyard land in Mendocino County
1921	V. Sattui Winery closed due to Prohibition
1922	Louis M. Martini founded the L. M. Martini Grape Products Company
1923	Cesare Mondavi and family moved from Minnesota to Lodi, California
1923	Frank Pesenti planted vineyard
1923	Camillo Colombano founded winery that was later bought by John Pedrizzetti
1923	Mario and John Trinchero came to America from Asti
1923	U.S. National Origins Act set up immigration quotas restrict-

ing the number of Italian immigrants to U.S. to six thousand per year, while allowing proportionately more immigrants from England and northern European countries to enter the country

1924	Louis A. Foppiano died
1924	Samuele Sebastiani got a permit to produce fortified medicinal wines
1925	Gaspare Indelicato and his brother-in-law, Sebastiano Luppino, planted a vineyard on land they purchased the year before in the San Joaquin Valley to produce grapes for the home-winemaking market
1925	Emilio Guglielmo established family winery
1925	Bisceglia family bought Greystone Cellars
1926	Samuele Sebastiani bought Woodbridge Winery
1926	Operations ceased at Krug Winery when Bismark Bruck died
1926	Anselmo Conrotto built his gravity-flow winery in Santa Clara County
1926	Domenico Galleano bought Estaban Cantu's ranch
1926	Francesco Qualia died
1927	John Pedroncelli, Sr., bought winery and vineyards from John Canata
1927	Secondo Guasti died
1928	Bernardo Winery was bought by Rizzo family
1928	Angelo and Maria Sangiocomo moved to Sonoma County
1929	Angelo Rapazzini came from Milan to United States
1930	Olivetto Winery bought by Rachele Passalacqua and renamed Sonoma County Cellars
1931	Bisceglia family sold Greystone Cellars
1931	Adolph Parducci founded Parducci Wine Cellars
1932	Full-scale wine production started at Parducci Wine Cellars
1933	Repeal of Prohibition
1933	Bargetto Winery established (December 5)
1933	E. & J. Gallo Winery established
1933	Louis J. Foppiano took over Foppiano Winery
1933	Louis M. Martini built winery in St. Helena
1933	Charles Forni and Adam Bianchi reopened the Light Winery, renaming it the Napa Valley Cooperative Winery
1933	John Garetto built winery in Napa
1933	Bartolucci brothers built a winery in Napa

1933	Domenico Galleano converted his ranch into the Galleano Winery
1933	Louis, the son of Luigi Banchero, reopened his father's Banchero Winery
1933	Pellegrini Brothers Wine (California) founded
1934	Gemello Winery founded
1934	Grape Growers League formed to promote quality wine
1934	Bella Napoli winery founded by Anthony Cappello
1934	Joseph Filippi founded family winery
1934	Edoardo Seghesio died
1934	Joe Carrari was born
1934	Napa Cantina Winery bought the Lombarda Winery
1934	Giovanni and Maria Cambiaso start the Cambiaso Winery near Healdsburg
1934	Louis M. Martini family bought the Eccleston farm in St. Helena and moved his family to Napa
1935	Della Monica family from northern Italy formed Delmonico's in New York
1935	Delicato Vineyards was converted from grape production to wine production
1935	Val Verde Winery received new license, following Prohibition
1936	Cesare Mondavi family moved from Lodi to Napa Valley, and bought the Sunnyhill Winery, renaming it the Sunny St. Helena Winery
1936	Antonio Nonini founded Nonini Winery
1936	Bob Trinchero was born
1936	Louis Martini bought Mt. Pisgah Vineyard, called it Monte Rosso
1937	Mike Arciero joined his father, Giovanni, in U.S.
1937	Louis J. Foppiano tore down old winery and built another one; started bottling wines with Foppiano label
1937	Bagnani family bought Geyser Peak Winery
1937	Emil Bandiera came to United States and founded Bandiera Winery
1937	Pietro and Christina Biale purchased vineyard in Napa
1937	Ferrante Winery founded
1938	Joe Rochioli, Sr., leased land in California to grow grapes
1938	Andre Tchelistcheff arrived to take charge of

Beaulieu Vineyard

1938 Morello Cellar was built (would later be bought by the
      Bianchi family and turned into the Villa Bianchi Winery)

1938 Bartolucci Winery was closed

1939 Frank and Phil Arciero came to United States

1939 Mondavi rented DiMarco Winery in St. Helena

1940 Scatena bulk winery bought by Seghesio

1940 Lombarda Winery bought and renamed Freemark Abbey

1940 Louis Martini sold Kingsburg winery to Central California
      Wineries Corporation

1940 Cesare Mondavi assumed presidency of Acampo Winery

1941 Valley of the Moon Winery purchased by Enrico Parducci

1941 Angela Seghesio gave family winery and vineyard land to
      her children

1941 Cesare Mondavi leased the Gagetta Winery in Rutherford

1942 La Loma vineyard purchased by Louis M. Martini

1942 Stanley Ranch purchased by Louis M. Martini

1942 Pietro Biale died in accident in rock quarry

1942 Schenley Distributors bought the Roma Winery from
      Cella family

1942 Louis Bartolucci reopened winery, calling it
      the Oakville Winery

1942 Banchero Winery was closed

1943 Cesare Mondavi family bought Charles Krug Winery

1943 Ben and Mary Migliaccio bought Fagiani Winery

1943 National Distillers bought Italian Swiss Colony

1943 Bragno Wine Company bought Larkmead Winery, in
      partnership with Harry Blum

1943 Narciso Martini (of R. Martini Winery) sold family winery
      to Hiram Walker

1943 Napa Vintners Association formed

1943 Acampo Winery sold to Gibson Wine Company

1943 Oakville Winery entered into partnership

1944 Samuele Sebastiani died

1944 Domitilli and Massoni sold Roma Winery (once owned
      by the Scatena brothers) to Alta Vineyards Company

1944 Louis Petri became president of the Petri Wine Company

1944 John Battista Cella bought the Rusconi Vineyard and
      converted it to the Cella Vineyards

1945	John Pedrizzetti bought the Camillo Colombano Winery
1946	Mondavi family sold its remaining interest in the Sunny St. Helena Winery to concentrate on Charles Krug
1946	Cesare Mondavi made Krug's first Vintage Selection Cabernet
1946	Frank Teldeschi bought a farm in Dry Creek Valley
1946	Louis J. Foppiano bought the nearby Sotoyome Vineyard
1946	Louis J. Foppiano founded the Sonoma County Wine Growers Association
1946	Giumarra Winery founded
1946	Conrad Viano and family bought vineyard
1946	Harry Blum bought out Frank Bragno's interest in Larkmead Winery
1947	Mario and John Trinchero family bought Sutter Home Winery
1947	Gallo brothers formed a partnership with Frei Brothers in Dry Creek Valley
1947	Collapse of California market for wine
1948	Anthony Arciero and his mother, Cristina, join the rest of the Arciero family in U.S.
1948	Larkmead Winery bought by B. C. Solari from National Distillers
1949	Seghesio family bought the Alta Vineyards Company (formerly, the Roma winery, owned by the Scatena brothers until they sold it to the Domitilli and Massoni families)
1949	Michael R. Martini was born
1950	Elmo Martini and Enrico Prati bought winery (that had been R. Martini Winery) back from Hiram Walker and named it Martini & Prati
1950	Andrew Colaruotolo came from Gaeta, Italy; later founded Casa Larga Vineyards in New York
1952	August and Sylvia Sebastiani purchased remaining interest in Sebastiani Vineyards from Samuele Sebastiani's widow
1954	Louis P. Martini, son of Louis M., became winemaker for family winery
1956	First Vintage Select wines from Charles Krug Winery released by Mondavi family
1957	Lorenzo Petroni came from Lucca to U.S.
1958	Angela Seghesio (Edoardo's wife) died

1958	Louis M. Martini Winery installed a bottling line that injected carbon dioxide into the bottles before corking
1958	Charles Krug Winery adopted a system that pushed white wine to the bottler with nitrogen gas, rather than a pump
1959	Joe Rochioli, Sr., and his son planted Cabernet Sauvignon and Sauvignon Blanc
1959	Cesare Mondavi died
1959	Leo and Evelyn Trentadue bought forty-two acres in Alexander Valley and called it Trentadue Winery
1960s	Ernest Fortino left Calabria for America
1960	Adolph Parducci passed control of winery to his sons
1962	Louis P. Martini purchased first half of Las Amigas vineyard and the Los Vinedos del Rio vineyard
1963	Jim and John Pedroncelli, Jr., assumed management of Pedroncelli Winery from their father
1963	Ed and Phyllis Pedrizzetti took control of Pedrizzetti Winery
1963	Rapazzini family bought old Perelli-Minetti winery
1964	Frank Arciero started Arciero Ranches, an alfalfa business
1964	United Vintners bought Inglenook
1965	Mondavi family feuded over the operation at Krug Winery and Robert left
1966	Robert Mondavi Winery was founded
1966	Jim and John Pedroncelli, Jr., started producing vintage-dated wine
1967	Filippi family bought Thomas Winery (see 1839)
1968	Trinchero family (Sutter Home) started buying Zinfandel from Deaver Ranch
1968	First vineyard planted in Temecula by Vincenzo Cilurzo
1968	Joe Rochioli, Sr., and his son, Joe, Jr., added Pinot Noir and Chardonnay to their vineyard
1969	Mount Palomar vineyards planted
1970	Ponzi Vineyards winery founded
1970	Montevina Winery established
1970	Isabelle Simi retired and sold family winery to Russell Green
1970	Fortino Winery founded
1971	Bartolucci Brothers Winery was bought and turned into Oakville Vineyards
1972	Louis P. Martini purchased second half of Las Amigas vineyard

1972	Bob Trinchero of Sutter Home Winery made his first white Zinfandel
1972	Bagnani family sold Geyser Peak Winery to Schlitz Brewery
1972	Joseph Cagnasso moved to New York to work for Brotherhood Winery
1972	Cambiaso Winery was sold and renamed Domaine St. George Winery
1973	Franzia Winery was sold to Coca-Cola Company
1973	Dave Caparone imported Italian varietal clones from University of Turin
1973	Angelo Papagni built Papagni Winery
1973	Lou Facelli moved to Wilder, Idaho, and planted vines that would later become the Lou Facelli Winery
1974	Louis M. Martini died
1974	Tim Mondavi took over as winemaker at Robert Mondavi Winery
1974	Americo Rafanelli and his son, David, established A. Rafanelli Winery in the basement of his house
1974	Daryl Sattui leased land in Napa to reopen V. Sattui Winery, which had been closed in 1921
1974	Joe Carrari started the Vineyard Development Company (see 1984)
1975	Francis Ford Coppola bought the Niebaum estate
1975	Fred Bucci planted vines
1975	Frank Pastori reopened his father's Pastori Winery
1975	Mike and Rose Fiore opened Fiore's La Felicetta Vineyard and Wine Cellars
1975	Mount Palomar Winery opened
1976	Mack Sands of Virginia bought Bisceglia Winery in California
1976	Zonin family in Italy founded Barboursville Vineyards and Winery in Virginia
1976	Simi Winery was sold to Schieffelin and Company
1976	V. Sattui Winery was reopened
1976	Bartolucci brothers bought back their winery from Oakville Vineyards
1976	Gallo brothers bought remaining shares of Frei Brothers Winery in Sonoma
1976	Antonio Perelli-Minetti died

1977	Michael Martini took over as winemaker at Louis M. Martini
1977	Ray Signorello bought land in Napa Valley, on which the Signorello Vineyards and winery stand
1977	Joseph Cagnasso opened his own winery
1977	Greg Graziano started the Milano Winery
1977	Cliff Giacobine started the Estrella River Winery
1977	Greco Winery was founded
1978	Gallo brothers produce first vintage-dated Gallo wine, named "Vintage 1978"
1978	Fred Bucci started making wine at Buccia Winery
1978	Casa Larga started making commercial wine
1978	Cilurzo Winery started commercial production
1978	Paul DiGrazia planted vines in Connecticut
1979	Far Niente Winery reopened (see 1885, 1910)
1979	Robert Mondavi bought Woodbridge Winery
1979	Robert Mondavi joined with the French Rothschild family to produce Opus One
1979	Caparone Winery founded
1979	Baldinelli Winery founded
1979	Hank Donatoni started Donatoni Winery near Los Angeles
1979	Santino Winery founded
1979	Bob Frugoli bought a vineyard that was to become the source of the Armida Winery's grapes
1980	Schlitz Brewery sold Geyser Peak Winery to Stroh's Brewing Company
1980	August Sebastiani died. Sam Sebastiani took over the operation of the Sebastiani Vineyards
1980	Bandiera Winery bought by the California Wine Company
1980	Old Perelli-Minetti Winery, then used by Rapazzini family, was destroyed by fire
1981	Piconi Winery founded
1981	Ferrari-Carano founded
1981	Mitch Cosentino started Crystal Valley Cellars
1981	The Franzia Wine label was bought from Coca-Cola Company by The Wine Group
1981	J. H. Gentili Winery founded
1981	Lou Facelli Winery opened in Wilder, Idaho
1982	The winery that Secondo Guasti founded in California ceased operation

1982	Stroh's Brewing Company sold Geyser Peak Winery to Trione family
1982	Seghesio's started bottling its own wine under its own label
1982	Gustav Dalla Valle moved to Napa Valley and bought vineyard land
1982	Gemello Winery purchased and absorbed by Obester Winery
1982	Pucci Winery founded
1982	Rapazzini Winery opened
1983	Tom Rochioli became winemaker at family winery
1983	First vines were planted on Arciero Estate Vineyards
1983	Formerly named Napa Vintners Association (see 1943) became the Napa Valley Vintners Association
1983	Lou Fiore started West Park Vineyards in New York
1984	Arciero Winery was built
1984	Joe Carrari founded Carrari Vineyards
1984	Paul DiGrazia started selling wine from the forty-five acres planted in Connecticut
1985	Geyser Peak sold the Summit line of wines-in-a-box
1985	Signorello Vineyards started making wine under its own label
1985	Frank Teldeschi died; son Dan took over management of family's vineyards
1985	Robert Mondavi bought Vichon Winery
1985	Cecchetti Sebastiani Cellar was founded
1985	Staglin Family Vineyards founded
1986	Sam Sebastiani was fired by his mother and replaced with his brother Don
1986	Atlas Peak Vineyards founded by Piero Antinori, Bollinger, and Whitbread
1986	Basignani Winery opened
1986	Balagna Winery started
1986	Joe Cafaro opened his own winery
1986	Lou Facelli moved to Washington from Idaho, and later opened the Lou Facelli Winery
1987	Americo Rafanelli died; David Rafanelli became winemaker for A. Rafanelli Winery
1988	Trinchero family, owners of Sutter Home, bought Montevina
1988	Greg Graziano opened Domaine St. Gregory winery
1988	Estrella River Winery was sold to Wine World Estates

1988	New Perelli-Minetti Winery built
1989	Penfolds from Australia bought 50 percent of Geyser Peak Winery from Trione family
1989	Robert Frugoli bought a nonoperating winery in Dry Creek Valley, named it Armida Winery
1989	Mitch Cosentino opened Cosentino Winery in Yountville
1989	Sam Gabrielli started the Gabrielli Winery
1989	Joseph Gimelli bought San Benito Vineyard and renamed it Pietra Santa
1990	Viansa Winery opened
1990	Robert Mondavi passed control of the winery to his sons
1990	Petroni Vineyards founded
1991	Atlas Peak's first wine, the 1989 Sangiovese, released
1991	Elmo Martini (of Martini & Prati Winery) died
1991	First vintage of wines from Pellegrini Vineyards (New York)
1992	Trione family bought back 50 percent share of Geyser Peak Winery owned by Penfolds of Australia
1992	Dan Teldeschi founded F. Teldeschi, named after his father, Frank
1992	Silverado Vineyards bought Bay View vineyard planted by Felix Borreo in 1883
1993	Julio Gallo died
1993	Pezzi-King Winery founded
1994	Baldinelli Winery ceased winemaking
1994	Renwood Winery bought Santino Winery
1994	fire nearly destroyed Ferrante Winery
1995	Francis Ford Coppola bought Inglenook Estate
1996	Villa Fiore, Ferrari-Carano's hospitality center, opened
1997	Valley of the Moon sold to Kenwood Vineyards
1998	Geyser Peak, Canyon Road, and Venezia sold to Fortune Brands
1999	Simi sold to Canandaigua Wine Company

BIBLIOGRAPHY

Adams, Leon D., *The Wines of America*, McGraw-Hill Publishing Company (New York, New York, 1990).

Anderson, Burton, *Vino: The Wines and Winemakers of Italy*, Little, Brown, and Company (Boston, Massachusetts, 1980).

Blue, Anthony Dias, *American Wine*, Harper & Row (New York, New York, 1988).

Boyd, Gerald D., "The Return of Geyser Peak Winery," *Quarterly Review of Wines*, Summer, 1992.

Boyd, Gerald D., "California Goes 'Italian'," *Quarterly Review of Wines*, Summer, 1994.

Boyd, Gerald D., "Viansa Vivo!" *Quarterly Review of Wines*, Summer, 1995.

Bullard, Robyn, "Seghesio Goes Upscale with Old-Vine Reds," *Wine Spectator*, September 15, 1992.

Bullard, Robyn, "Silverado Plants Italian Varieties," *Wine Spectator*, November 30, 1992.

Bullard, Robyn, "Sutter Home's Bob Trinchero Honored by *Wine Spectator*," Wine Spectator, November 15, 1994.

Clarke, Oz, *Oz Clarke's Encyclopedia of Wine*, Simon and Schuster (New York, New York, 1993).

Cline, Harry, "Joe Carrari's `Dago Red' Wine: Central Coast Grower Custom Crushes to Minimize Losses," *California Grape Grower*, November 1985.

Conaway, James, *Napa: The Story of An American Eden*, Houghton Mifflin Company (Boston, Massachusetts, 1990).

Cordasco, Francesco [ed.], *Studies in Italian American Social History*, Rowman and Littlefield (Metuchen, New Jersey, 1975).

Costa, Eric, *Old Vines: A History of Winegrowing in Amador County*, Cenotto Publications (Jackson, California, 1994).

Darlington, David, *Angel's Visits: An Inquiry into the Mystery of Zinfandel*, Henry Holt and Company (New York, New York, 1991).

Elia, Richard L., "Ferrari-Carano's Winning Hand," *Quarterly Review of Wines*, Winter, 1995.

Elia, Richard L., "Major Barbera," *Quarterly Review of Wines*, Spring, 1997.

Elia, Richard L., "Banfi is Back," *Quarterly Review of Wines*, Summer, 1994.

Ensrud, Barbara, *American Vineyards*, Stewart, Tabori, and Chang (New York, New York, 1988).

Farrell, Josh, "Get Ready for Cal-Ital," *Wine Enthusiast*, April 1994.

Florence, Jack W., Sr., *A Noble Heritage: The Wines and Vineyards of Dry Creek Valley*, Wine Growers of Dry Creek Valley (Geyserville, California, 1993).

di Franco, J. Philip, *The Italian Americans*, in Chelsea House Publishers series called The People of North America (New York, New York, 1988).

Gigli, Gina, "Rendering Primavera Mista," *The Wine News*, August/ September, 1995.

Giuliano, Edward, "Lee Iacocca Shifts Gears," *Wine Enthusiast*, March 1994.

Goldberg, Howard G., "East End's '93 Wines: Uncorking the Best," *The New York Times*, May 21, 1995 (about Pellegrini Winery and Long Island wines).

Gray, Walter, "The Power House that Riunite Built," *Texas Beverage News*, July 1996.

Grossman, Harold J., *Grossman's Guide to Wines, Beers, and Spirits*, Seventh Edition, Charles Scribner's Sons (New York, New York, 1983).

Hare, Sara, "Sonoma's Italian Roots," *Wine & Spirits Magazine*, August 1997.

Hawkes, Ellen, *Blood & Wine: The Unauthorized Story of The Gallo Wine Empire*, Simon & Schuster (New York, New York, 1993).

Haynes, Irene W., *Ghost Wineries of Napa Valley*, Wine Appreciation Guild (So. San Francisco, California, 1995).

Heald, Eleanor and Ray, "Venezia Deliziosa!" *Quarterly Review of Wines*, Summer 1997.

Healdsburg Museum and Historical Society, *Historic Homes of Healdsburg*, Second Edition (Healdsburg, California, 1995).

Heimoff, Steve, "Sam Sebastiani Builds a Bit of Italy," *Wine Spectator*, March 31, 1990.

Hinkle, Richard Paul, "Atlas Peak Vineyards: Sangiovese and a Whole Lot More," *Quarterly Review of Wines*, Summer, 1992.

Hinkle, Richard Paul, "The Enduring Influence of Italy on Winemaking in California," Italian Wines and Spirits, September 1994.

Hinkle, Richard Paul, "Barbera: A New Era of Respect," *Italian Wines and Spirits*, December 1994.

Hinkle, Richard Paul, "Sutter Home: New World Gold," *Italian Wines and Spirits*, March 1995.

Horne, Yvonne Michie, "Rochioli," *Quarterly Review of Wines*, Spring, 1992.

Howie, Millie, "An Enjoyable Life," *The Healdsburg Tribune*, (Healdsburg, California), November 8, 1995, about David Coffaro Winery.

Iorizzo, Luciano J. and Mondello, Salvatore, *The Italian-Americans*, Twayne Publishers, Inc. (New York, New York, 1971).

Johnson, Hugh, *Vintage: The Story of Wine*, Simon & Schuster (New York, New York, 1989).

Julianelli, Jane, "Where Wine And Family Are No. 1," *The New York Times*, September 24, 1995.

King, Ralph T., "Parduccis' Spat Over Namesake Winery Is a Very Strange Case," *Wall Street Journal*, August 10, 1995.

Lapsley, James T., *Bottled Poetry: Napa Winemaking from Prohibition to the Modern Era*, University of California Press (Berkeley, California, 1996).

Laube, James, *California Wine: A Comprehensive Guide to the Wineries, Wines, Vintages and Vineyards of America's Premier Winegrowing State*, Wine Spectator Press (New York, New York, 1995).

Laube, James, "Sam Sebastiani Builds a Bit of Tuscany in Carneros," *Wine Spectator*, May 31, 1991.

Laube, James, "Like Father, Like Son, Don Sebastiani Turns Up the Volume," *Wine Spectator*, May 31, 1991.

Laube, James, "Tasting 25 years of Mondavi Cabernet Sauvignon," *Wine Spectator*, November 30, 1991.

Laube, James, "The Godfather of Wine," *Wine Spectator*, August 31, 1991.

Laube, James, "Robert Mondavi: Scenes from a Life in Wine," *Wine Spectator*, May 15, 1991.

Laube, James, "Simi Goes Back to Its Roots," *Wine Spectator*, February 29, 1996.

Laube, James, "David Coffaro: Rising Star in Sonoma's Dry Creek Valley," *Wine Spectator*, January 31, 1997.

Laube, James, a piece about Ponzi Vineyards in the Grapevine column, *Wine Spectator*, January 31, 1997.

Laube, James, "The Long, Long View of Antinori," *Wine Spectator*, January 31, 1997.

Lawrence, R. de Treville, III, [ed.], *Jefferson and Wine: Model of Moderation*, Vinifera Wine Growers Association (The Plains, Virginia, 1989).

Lee, Hilde Gabriel and Allan E., *Virginia Wine Country Revisited*, Hildesigns Press (Charlottesville, Virginia, 1993).

Mangione, Jerre and Morreale, Ben, *La Storia: Five Centuries of the Italian American Experience*, Harper-Collins (New York, New York, 1992).

Marcus, Kim, "Louis P. Martini's Bittersweet Success," *Wine Spectator*, November 15, 1990.

Marcus, Kim, "Mondavi Passes Control of Winery to His Sons," *Wine Spectator*, February 28, 1991.

Marcus, Kim, "Antinori Buys Vineyards at Atlas Peak from the Wine Alliance," *Wine Spectator*, October 31, 1993.

Matthews, T., et al., news note about Bandiera Winery, *Wine Spectator*, February 28, 1997.

Mayfield, Robert, "Ponzi's Pinot: Three's a Charm," *The Wine News*, August/September 1992.

McCarthy, Ed, "Searching for the Great American Pinot Noir," *Wine Enthusiast*, February 1996 (about Dick Ponzi).

McFarland, Stephen, "Forking Over Great Varietals," *Daily News*, January 26, 1996 (New York, about Pellegrini of Long Island).

McNutt, Joni G. [ed.], *In Praise of Wine*, Capra Press (Santa Barbara, California, 1993).

Meltzer, Peter, "Prohibition Pipeline: How Wine and Spirits Survived," *Wine Enthusiast*, May 1994.

Milioni, Stefano, *Columbus Menu – Italian Cuisine after the First Voyage of Christopher Columbus*, Italian Trade Commission (New York, New York, 1992).

Moquin, Wayne (ed.), *A Documentary History of the Italian Americans*, Praeger Publishers (New York, New York, 1974).

Morgan, Jeff, "California Vintners Struggle to Preserve Genetic Heritage of Historic Vineyards," *Wine Spectator*, October 31, 1995.

Morgan, Jeff, "The Director's New Script," *Wine Spectator*, December 15, 1995.

Morgan, Jeff, "Peter Mondavi Lets Sons Take Charge at Charles Krug," *Wine Spectator*, March 31, 1996.

Morton, Lucie T., *Winegrowing in Eastern America: An Illustrated Guide to Viniculture East of the Rockies*, Cornell University Press (Cornell, New York, 1985).

Musmanno, Michael A., *The Story of the Italians in America*, Doubleday & Co. (New York, New York, 1965).

Nelli, Humbert S., *From Immigrants to Ethnics: The Italian Americans*, Oxford University (Oxford, England, 1983).

Nicholas, Jonathan, "They Told Him He Was Crazy," *The Oregonian*, January 1995 (about Dick Ponzi).

Novitski, Joseph, *A Vineyard Year*, Chronicle Books (San Francisco, California, 1983).

Palmer, Jon, *Wineries of the Mid-Atlantic*, Rutgers University Press (New Brunswick, New Jersey, 1988).

Pescosolido, Carl A. and Gleason, Pamela, *The Proud Italians: Our Great Civilizers*, National Italian American Foundation (Washington, D.C., 1995).

Pinney, Thomas, *A History of Wine in America: From the Beginnings to Prohibition*, University of California Press (Berkeley, California, 1989).

Prial, Frank J., "Happy Days Again at Sebastiani," *New York Times*, November 22, 1995.

Roby, Norm, "From Tuscany to Temecula", *Wine Spectator*, November 15, 1990.

Roby, Norman S. and Olken, Charles E., *The New Connoisseurs' Handbook of California Wines*, Alfred A. Knopf (New York, New York, 1993).

Rolle, Andrew F., *The American Italians: Their History and Culture*, Wadsworth Publishing Co. (Belmont, California, 1972).

Rosano, Dick, "California's Italian Accent," *The Wine News*, August/ September, 1995.

Sawyer, Abby, "Arciero Digs Deep for Vine Planting Innovation," *Wine Business Monthly*, January 1997.

Schoener, Allon, *The Italian Americans*, Macmillan (New York, New York, 1987).

Schultz, Julian, "Mellea Wines Command Respect," *Worcester Magazine*, Worcester, Massachusetts, September 1996.

Scoblionkov, Deborah, "Ponzi: Pioneer Winemaker in Oregon," *The Philadelphia Inquirer*, May 7, 1995.

Street, Richard Steven, "Sonoma County's Italian Roots," *Wine Spectator*, August 31, 1991.

Stuller, Jay and Martin, Glen, *Through the Grapevine: The Business of Wine in America*, Wynwood Press (New York, New York, 1989).

Suckling, James, "Mondavi is Vintners' Vintner," *Wine Spectator*, February 28, 1991.

Sullivan, Charles L., *Napa Wine: A History*, The Wine Appreciation Guild (So. San Francisco, California, 1994).

Switzer, Jeff, "Life Has Never Been Better for the Facelli Winery," *Woodinville Weekly*, August 26, 1996.

Talese, Gay, *Unto the Sons*, Alfred A. Knopf (New York, New York, 1992).

Wine Spectator Press, *Wine Country Guide to California*, 1995 Edition (New York, New York, 1995).

Wood, Jim, "All in the Family: The Seghesio Wine Story is Over 100 Years Old," *San Francisco Examiner*, October 1, 1995.

INDEX

Note: Page numbers in italics indicate photographs.

Carrari, Joe, 87, 107, 145-46
Carrari, Miguel, 87, 145
Carrari Vineyards, 87, 107, 145-46
Casa Larga Vineyards, 93, 146
Cassa Brothers Winery, 105, 167
Castelletto, 198
Catawba grape, 20
Cecchetti, Roy, 113, 147
Cecchetti family, 147
Cecchetti Sebastiani Cellar, 113, 147
Cella, John Battista, 57, 67, 85, 147-148, 218
Cella, Lorenzo, 57, 147, 218
Cella family, 44, 91
Cella Vineyards, 147-48
Central California Wineries, 81
Ceres, California, 140
Chadwick family, 195
Chalone Group, 142
Chappellet Vineyard, 114, 142
Chateau de Garlic, 95, 217
Château Mouton-Rothschild, 194
Chianti Station, 44, 65, 111, 226
Chinese labor and Chinese immigrants, 35, 41, 50, 53
Chino, Eusebio Francesco, 23
Christian Brothers, 208
Cienega Valley, 213
Cilurzo, Vincenzo (Vincent), 104, 109, *148*, 148-49, 213
Cilurzo, Vinnie, 104, 213
Cilurzo Winery, 109, 148-49
Cilurzo-Piconi Winery, 213
Ciocca, Arthur, 104, 168
Ciocca Lombardi Winery Company, 40, 65, 174
Civil War, 35, 53
Cloverdale, California, 133, 204
Coca-Cola Company, 67, 168
Coffaro, David, 149
Coffaro, David Vineyard and Winery, 149-50
Coit, Lillie Hitchcock, 181
Colaruotolo, Andrew, 93, 146
Colombano, Camillo, 66, 80, 150, 204
Colombano, Camillo Winery, 80, 91, 150, 204
Colombo, Cristoforo, 14, 15, 145
Colombo (brand), 89

Colorado, viticulture in, 51
Columbus, Christopher. *See* Colombo, Cristoforo
Commonage, 207
Compagnone, Allie, 191
Compagnone, Joe, 191
Connecticut wineries, 157
Conradi Winery, 61
Conrotto, A. Winery, 81, 151
Conrotto, Anselmo, 81, 151
Coppola, Francis Ford, 64, 103, 107, *112*, 116, 199-200
corporations, entry into wine industry, 103
Corti, Darrell, 197
Cos d'Estournel, 152
Cosentino, Mitch, 111, 115, 151-52
Cosentino Winery, 111, 115, 151-52
Costa, Eric, 35
Coturri, H., & Sons, 109-10, 152-53
Coturri, Tony, 109, 152
Cousins, Bruce, 129
Cousins, Steve, 129
Covick Winery, 85
Crescini, Paule, 153
Crescini, Rich, 65, 153
Crescini family, 65, 153
Crescini Wines, 65, 153
Cribari family, 219
Criolla (Mission) grape, 23-24, 35, 44, 50
Crystal Valley Cellars, 111, 151
Cupertino, California, 38
CWMC (California Wine Makers Corporation), 56

D

da Nizza, Fra Marco, 22
D'Agostini, Emelio, 65
D'Agostini, Enrico, 77, 154
D'Agostini Winery, 32, 154
Dalla Valle, Gustav, 111, 154
Dalla Valle, Naoko, 154
Dalla Valle Vineyards, 111, 114, 142, 154-55
Daniel, John, Jr., 200
de Latour, Georges, 209

Prohibition, 74-78
grapes, native American, 14, 15, 16, 17, 20-21, 22
    See also Italian grape varieties; *Vitis*
    vinifera; specific varieties
gravity-flow winery design, 38, 81
Graziano, Greg, 109, 115, 158, 192, 196
Graziano, Vincenzo, 65, 196
Great Migration, 25, 28, 36-37, 41, 47, 57, 59
    See also Italian immigration
Greco, Anthony M., 177
Greco Winery, 177
Green, Russell, 103
Greystone Cellars, 81
Grignolino, 106
Gristina Vineyards, 207
Groom, Daryl, 111, 175
Gualtieri, Giuseppe, 65, 154
Guasti, California, 56, 79
Guasti, Secondo, 39, 56, 79, 112, 145, *163*, 163
    See also Italian Vineyard Company
Guasti Vineyards, 145
Guglielmo, Emilia, 80, 177
Guglielmo, Emilio, 63, 80, 177
Guglielmo, Emilio Winery, 63, 177-78
Guglielmo, Gary, *178*
Guglielmo, Gene, *178*
Guglielmo, George, Jr., *178*
Guglielmo, George, Sr., *178*, 178
Guild Wineries, 219
Gusmano, Andrea, 85, 136

H

Haigh, Fred, 228
Haigh, Isabelle Simi. *See* Simi, Isabelle
Harvey, Scott, 219
Hastings, Serranus Clinton, 199
Hat, Tony. *See* Cappello, Antonio
Haviland Winery, 114, 159
Hawkes, Ellen, 75
Hawkins, John, 15
Healdsburg, California, 128-29, 143, 161-62,
    165-66, 189, 190, 202, 212, 216-17, 217-18,
    225-26, 228-29, 232-33
Heitz, Joe, 103

Heublein, 91, 148, 200, 211
Hidden Cellars, 196
Hillside Vineyard Company, 145
hillside vineyards, 55
Hinchcliffe, Jeff, 169
Hiram Walker, 90, 93, 187
Hollister, California, 213
home winemaking
    after Repeal, 83
    as grape market before Prohibition, 64
    as grape market during Prohibition, 74-
      78, 80
    Volstead Act exception for, 56, 74, 142
Hooker, Joseph, 235
Hopland, California, 192
Howell Mountain, 29, 230

I

Idaho wineries, 159, 216
Il Santo Cellars, 131
immigrants
    Chinese, attitudes toward, 41, 53
    Italian. *See* Italian immigrants
immigration
    to the Far West, 35, 41, 50, 53
    See also Great Migration; Italian
      immigration
Immigration Act, 63
immigration policy, 59, 63, 78
    Foran Act, 45-46
    Oriental Exclusion Act, 41, 53
Indelicato, Anthony, *156*
Indelicato, Frank, *156*
Indelicato, Gaspare, 77, 87, 155
Indelicato, Vincent, *156*
Inglenook, 64, 91, 95-96, 116, 199-200, 211
Inglewood, California, 158
Island Vineyards, 115, 207
Italian Bureau, Ellis Island, 46
Italian Club of Minnesota, 62, 193
Italian Garden and Winery, 32
Italian grape varieties
    18th-century importation and planting of,
      18, 20

Milone, Jim, 109, 192
Mira Loma, California, 163, 170-71
Mission (Criolla) grape, 23-24, 35, 44, 50
Mission (of Robert Mondavi), 113, 195
Mission program and secularization, 22-24, 28
Missouri wineries, 162
Moceri, Frank, 192
Moceri Winery, 192
Modesto, California, 151, 171-73
Moffitt, James K., 85, 179
Monastero le Vallesi, 241
Mondavi, Cesare, 62, 75, 85-86, 86-87, 91, 94, 193
   Charles Krug purchase, 86, 179, 193
Mondavi, Marc, *180*
Mondavi, Michael, 194
Mondavi, Peter, Jr., *180*
Mondavi, Peter, Sr., 91, 94, 96, 101, *180*, 180, 193
Mondavi, Robert, 86, 91, 94, 193-195, 241
   leaves Charles Krug and founds Robert Mondavi, 96, 101-102, 180, 193
   Mission of, 113, 195
   relationship with Peter Mondavi, 94, 113
Mondavi, Robert Winery, 101-102, 103, 180, 193-195, *194*, 241
   Opus One, 109, 194-195
Mondavi, Tim, 194
Mondavi family, 90, 91, 179-80
Mont St. John Cellars, 136, 196
Monte Rosso vineyard, 84, 185
Monte Volpe Vineyards, 109, 115, 158, 192, 196-97
Montepulciano Winery, 38, 228
Montevina Winery, 61, 105, 114, 197-98, 231
Moramarco, Mario, 198
Morello Cellar, 89, 139
Morgan Hill, California, 150, 177-78, 204-5
Morreale, Ben, 30
Mount Palomar Winery, 102-3, 198
Mountain View, California, 173
Mouton-Rothschild, Château, 194
Mt. Pisgah Vineyard, 84, 185
Muscat Alexandria, 184

N

Nalle Winery, 149
Napa, California
   Italian settlement in, 64
   wineries in, 32-33, 35-36, 129-30, 138, 196, 227
Napa Cantina Winery, 44, 87, 170, 183
Napa Valley Grape Products, 89
Napa (Valley) Vintners Association, 84, 90, 112-13, 186, 231
Napa Wine Company, 85, 86, 179
National Distillers, 90, 181
National Distributors, 89, 140
National Origins Act, 78
National Prohibition Party, 35, 50
Native Americans, 22, 49, 50
   missionization, 22-23
   as winery employees, 38, 206
Nebbiolo, 51, 58, 106, 109, 131, 144
Nerelli, Aldo, Jr., 210
Nerelli, Aldo, Sr., 210
Nerelli, Frank, 210
Nerelli, Lorenzo, 67, 210
Nerelli, Rena, 67, 210
Nervo, Julius, 63, 143, 199, 236
Nervo Winery, 143, 199, 236
New Jersey, 20
New Mexico wineries, 131-132
New York, Italian immigration to, 25
New York wineries, 142-43, 146, 157, 207-8
Niebaum, Gustave, 64, 103, 199-200
Niebaum-Coppola Estate Winery, 107, 116, 199-200
A Noble Heritage: The Wines and Vineyards of Dry Creek Valley (Florence), 59
Nonini, A. Winery, 58-59, 66, 87-88, 201
Nonini, Antonio, 58-59, 87, 201
Nonini, James, 201
Nonini, Reno, 58, 66, 87, 201
Nonini, Tom, 201
North Beach Restaurant, 211
North Carolina, 16
Novitski, Joseph, 58

O

Oakville, California, 154-155, 193-195, 201-202, 208
Oakville Ranch Vineyards, 114, 142
Oakville Vineyards, 103, 136, 196
Oakville Winery, 85, 89, 201-2
    See also Bartolucci Brothers Winery
Obester Winery, 112, 173
Ohio wineries, 141, 160, 177
Olivetto Winery, 81, 202
Olson Vineyards, 196
Oneto winery, 86
Opus One, 109, 194-95
Oregon Wine Advisory Board, 215
Oregon Winegrowers Association, 105, 215
Oregon wineries, 105, 214-15
organic wines and viticulture, 109-10, 152-53, 197-98
Oriental Exclusion Act, 41, 53

P

Pacific Wine Company, 83
padrone system, 45-46
Pagani, Julius, 61
Palmtag, William, 213
Panteleo family, 75
Papagni, Angelo, 77, 105, 202
Papagni, Demetrio, 66, 77, 202
Papagni Vineyards, Papagni Winery, 66, 105, 202
Parducci, Adolph, 77, 94, 203
Parducci, Enrico, 89, 235
Parducci, John, 203
Parducci Wine Cellars, 94, 203-4
Paris tasting of 1976, 101
Paschina, Luca, 108, 134
Paso Robles, California, 127-128, 144, 159
Passalacqua, Frank, 81, 202
Passalacqua, Rachele, 81-82, 202
Passalacqua family, 61
passito method, 38, 176
Pastori, Costante, 67, 204
Pastori, Frank, 67, 107, 204

Pastori Winery, 67, 107, 204
Paterno, Tony, 83
Patrizi, Ettore, *31*
Paul Masson Vineyards, 87, 145
Pedrizzetti, Ed, 91, 94, 205
Pedrizzetti, John, 80, 91, 204-5
Pedrizzetti, Phyllis, 94, 205
Pedrizzetti family, 66, 150, 204-205
Pedrizzetti Winery, 66, 94, 204-205
Pedroncelli, J. Winery, 61, 86, 94, 102, 205-6
Pedroncelli, Jim, 94, 102, *206*, 206
Pedroncelli, John, Jr., 94, 102, 206
Pedroncelli, John (Giovanni), Sr., 75-76, 102, 205
Pedroncelli, Julie, 206
Pelanconi Winery, 38, 206
Pellegrini, Bob (California winemaker), 207
Pellegrini, Bob (New York winemaker), 115, 207
Pellegrini Brothers Wine, 206-7
Pellegrini family, 206-7
Pellegrini Vineyards, 207-8
Penfolds Wine Company, 111, 175
Pennsylvania wineries, 143
Pepi, Aurora, 208
Pepi, Robert, 208
Pepi, Robert Winery, 208
Pepperwood Grove, 113, 147
Perelli-Minetti, Antonio, 60, 77, 107, 209
Perelli-Minetti, Giuseppe, 208-9
Perelli-Minetti, Mario, 209
Perelli-Minetti, Mario Winery, 208-209, *209*
Pesenti, Caterina, 76, 210
Pesenti, Frank, 67, 76, 209, 209-210
Pesenti, Victor, 210
Pesenti family, 76, 209-210
Pesenti Winery, 209-210
Petri, Angelo, 76, 210
Petri, Louis, 90, 91, 96, 210-11
Petri, Raffaello, 43, 210
Petri family, 210
Petri Wines, Petri Wine Company, 43, 85, 90-91, 136, 201, 210-211, 225
    See also United Vintners
Petroni, Lorenzo, 211
Petroni Vineyards, 211

W

Y

Z